DATE DUE

	JAN 28 2020		

PRINTED IN U.S.A.

H M   SIDE OUT

R obin Le   Life Design, inte-
grating tradit   cient and modern
mysticism. Sh

Robin co   *art, Joy Playshops*, a
Life Design Su   faculty of the *Met-*
ropolitan Insti   *ng Program,* the first
accredited pr

Robin ha   appeared on radio
and televisio   her work.

Her comp   79, is a New York
City–based   e environments for
residential ar

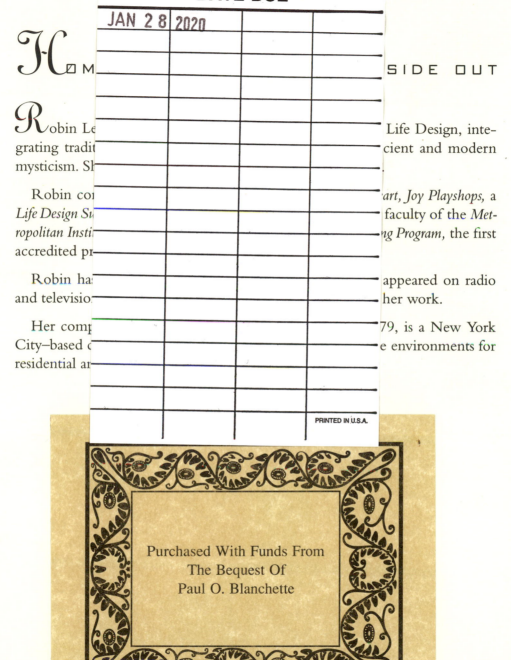

Purchased With Funds From
The Bequest Of
Paul O. Blanchette

Feng Shui,

Color Therapy,

And Self-Awareness

PENGUIN / ARKANA

HOME DESIGN

from the

INSIDE OUT

Robin Lennon

with Karen Plunkett-Powell

ARKANA

Published by the Penguin Group

Penguin Books USA Inc., 375 Hudson Street, New York, New York 10014, U.S.A.
Penguin Books Ltd, 27 Wrights Lane, London W8 5TZ, England
Penguin Books Australia Ltd, Ringwood, Victoria, Australia
Penguin Books Canada Ltd, 10 Alcorn Avenue, Toronto, Ontario, Canada M4V 3B2
Penguin Books (N.Z.) Ltd, 182-190 Wairau Road, Auckland 10, New Zealand

Penguin Books Ltd, Registered Offices:
Harmondsworth, Middlesex, England

First published in Arkana 1997

3 5 7 9 10 8 6 4

Grateful acknowledgment is made for permission to reprint an excerpt from
Living Color: Master Lin Yun's Guide to Feng Shui and the Art of Color by Sarah Rossbach and Lin Yun.
Copyright © 1994 by Sarah Rossbach and Lin Yun. All rights reserved. Published by Kodansha America, Inc.

LIBRARY OF CONGRESS CATALOGING IN PUBLICATION DATA
Lennon, Robin.
Home design from the inside out: feng shui, color therapy, and self-awareness /
Robin Lennon with Karen Plunkett-Powell.
p. cm.
ISBN 0 14 01.9539 4 (pbk.)
1. Feng-shui. 2. Interior decoration—Miscellanea. I. Plunkett-Powell, Karen. II. Title.
BF1779.F4L44 1997
133.3'337—dc21 96–43800

Printed in the United States of America
Set in Bembo, with display in Banque and Linoscript.
BOOK DESIGN AND ORNAMENTS BY JUDITH STAGNITTO ABBATE

ACKNOWLEDGMENTS

My soul's deep appetite and need for beauty and balance and grace.

My students and clients for the willingness to go where they have never gone before.

Maureen Walsh for pushing me beyond where I might normally go.

Marilyn Graman and Life Works.

Dawn Drzal for thoughtful, sensitive, and intelligent overview. Paul Morris for amazing endurance and tenacity.

The Pathwork for reorienting and basic training.

For Ling and Ed for persevering.

Special thanks to Jackie Fishell for the Home song, Charlotte Schwann for support in communication with the natural forces, Lawrene Groobert and Peter Donoso for unegotistically patient editing, Nancy Santo Pietro for my Feng Shui training and for friendship, Perelandra, Carole Foreman, Cheryl Birch for her Color Personalities chart, Patricia Sczerba for her Color Symbology chart, Joan Gilbert for going first, the New York Open Center for widening my audience, and especially Angel-Puff, my lifetime partner—so far.

All of the wonderful and difficult life circumstances that have been given to me so that I would bridge the gap between my wild inner life and the "real" outer world of home and our material world: the juxtaposition in my childhood home between beauty without love or love without beauty and then finally an ongoing integration.

CONTENTS

INTRODUCTION

Like a jigsaw puzzle, this book is made up of ideas and experiences that fell into place one piece at a time. The finished picture evolved as I evolved, both personally and professionally, over the past two decades. That journey began in my parents' opulent Beverly Hills' residence, where the ever present social pressure to "be a certain way" on the outside made it impossible for me to be myself . . . where I felt stifled and out of sync with my environment. After a great number of exhilarating (sometimes, frustrating) twists and turns of fate, and countless hours of study and inner searching,

I am three thousand miles removed from my starting point. I live and work in New York City, a place where I felt at home the moment I arrived. I truly understand the meaning of the adage, "there are houses and there are homes," and through the pages of this book, I am confident that you too can learn, and cherish, the difference.

My present surroundings support and nurture the self that had previously eluded me. I have made my inner dream into an external reality that I savor every time I walk through the entryway to my apartment; when I prepare a special meal for my friends; when I relax against the soft plush pillows that flank my living room sofa; or even when I watch my cat, Angel, curl up contentedly on my drafting table.

I have achieved my vision without benefit of an unlimited bank account or by conforming solely to an expert's sense of what denotes style and beauty, what is tasteful or in vogue. There is no doubt in my mind that you can achieve this as well. Yet I wouldn't be honest if I didn't admit that home decorating, like any other endeavor rooted in the material world, has its share of critics: "Interior design is as meaningful as a manicure, only more expensive," many people think—and, at this point, you may agree. However if you work from the inside out—if you tap into the dreams, wishes, and natural intuitions that lie nestled within your deeper self—decorating can become not only a method for changing your environment, but also a medium for personal and spiritual growth. And, designed mindfully, the reality you spawn will continue to grow with you for years to come.

Everyone is capable of envisioning, and then sculpting, a personal environment that both pleases the eye and nourishes the soul. You too can create your own *home for your heart*.

To make your journey both informative and inspirational, I have divided this book into two parts. In the first you will be guided through the basic interior design process from the inside out, and learn to recognize and trust your unique sense of style. You will begin to view your current surroundings objectively, with "new eyes," and you will identify (and break through) barriers that are preventing you from achieving harmony in your life. You will spot beliefs, habits, fears, and other aspects of your past history that exert powerful yet previously unrecognized influences on your present decorating decisions, and fully realize the all-important distinction between the things you think you must have and the things you really need.

In the second part of the book, I offer specific tools to allow you to take traditional and innovative design techniques and make them work for you personally. I offer tips on how to use objects, color, texture, fabrics, and scents to bring order and balance into your home; how to capture your family's preferences and needs into a unified design scheme; and how to plan for environmentally healthy spaces.

You will even discover the secret of decorating for a specific purpose—whether that be to attract love, strengthen a family relationship, encourage your child's creative talents, or become more productive in your home-based work.

These may seem like lofty goals, especially if, like many of my clients, you are not exactly sure how to choose from the vast array of furnishings available—never mind designing an entire room to attract your perfect soul mate. The thought of redecorating is daunting at times, but do be comforted by the knowledge that ninety-nine percent of my clients rarely know exactly how they want their homes to be, or where to begin. Some have never given much thought to their surroundings; others arrive with only preconceived notions of the perfect house gleaned from glossy magazines or talking with their neighbors.

In other cases, new clients express a longing for something different or new in their personal space, or a need to build a safe haven so they can have a respite from the pressures of the outside world. And there are those who want an environment that reflects their values and feelings, which may have recently altered because of a new marriage, a broken relationship, or an improved financial situation.

The point is that neither ambitious do-it-yourselfers or clients working with professional interior designers generally start their projects equipped with complete blueprints and color swatches for each room. The decorating process is not that clinical, nor should it be. The space we live in isn't just a place to hang a hat or prepare a microwave dinner. It is a place to dream, to recover from our sorrows, celebrate triumphs, and plot our futures. It is an environment that is intrinsically connected to the self. So important is this connection that I have developed a special, unique way of handling my private consultations, one that I have attempted to capture here in these pages.

My goal is to take you on a kind of archeological expedition into your own psyche, where you can uncover, interpret, and learn to express your personal sense of beauty. Drawing upon my metaphysical background, I will guide you toward translating what you know about yourself into material terms and then allow you to be guided by your own inner wisdom and spirituality. In the end, you can create beautiful, comfortable, personally sacred surroundings for yourself and your loved ones.

I know my home decorating system can work for you, regardless of any reservations, lack of experience, or uncertainty you may have because at one time I was the greatest skeptic of them all! I have developed this system based on *realities,* both positive and negative, that I experienced in my own life. Experiences that I feel are important to share with you now.

Early in the 1980s, I left Beverly Hills, California, turning my back on all the shallow materialism and traditional, approved artistic styles I believed my parents and their friends stood for. I enrolled in the New York School of Visual Arts and immersed myself in creating avant-garde art forms. The more shocking and inaccessible my work became, the more I liked it—convinced it was taking on great importance. If it repulsed or infuriated, I thought that was real power and impact. I was taking the art world by storm; I was making a statement. This ultra-revolutionary stage of my life continued until I met a perceptive and brilliant art teacher who suggested I wasn't changing much at all: I was merely using my inborn talent to express negativity and encourage abuse.

After that, it became clear to me I needed special guidance. I turned inward, soon becoming involved with the Pathworks Spiritual Community. This was a natural place for me, in part because I had studied metaphysics since age sixteen, and the principles the community focused on seemed to blend naturally with my own creative impulses.

There, I learned to listen to and trust my higher self, to reexamine my inner sense of beauty and become truly aware of my surroundings. I began to notice these surroundings more often. I looked at them differently, even seeing value in designs I once dismissed as examples of meaningless "Hallmark-style" cuteness. I would catch myself fondling fabric or watching light bounce off polished surfaces. Sometimes, I would impulsively purchase flowers or secondhand knickknacks for my apartment—but then feel strange or guilty about it, as if I had somehow sinned or betrayed a sacred promise to myself not to allow myself pleasure through the material world.

Still, there was a part of me that knew I wanted to use my art to contribute to society rather than totally reject it, to be part of the world, instead of constantly running away from or railing against it. I was now determined to affect people in a positive way.

Over the next few years I came in contact with fine artists like Claes Oldenburg, whose ability to make everyday objects whimsical fascinated me. I was inspired by the transformational productions of the Open Theatre and by the creative explorations of individuals like Joseph Chaikin. I learned about color therapy, healing, Eastern philosophy, bioenergetics, and the relationship between spirit and matter. I became sensitized to the powerful effect a person's environment had on his or her health, relationships, and overall emotional well-being. I would experiment with simple, everyday materials like wrapping paper and natural woods to make art and lend beauty to the surroundings of my friends. During this period I also worked in a decorating store where I began to truly enjoy sales and working with many different types of people.

In 1979, I started Robin Lennon Interior Design, and began to use this combination of new insights and professional design skills to implement my new system for interior design. While I helped people change their home and office environments, I also noticed a marked change in their lifestyles, physical appearance, even eating habits. As they thought about what they needed and wanted and began clearing things out of, bringing things into, and rearranging their living spaces, they went through a metamorphosis. It seemed as though they began to emerge from cocoons of obsolete beliefs and self-imposed limitations like they were butterflies, free to fly off in any direction they desired.

It was exciting and satisfying to watch this growth in others. Yet ironically, I had not applied my techniques to my own living space. I was still living in drab, Spartan surroundings, believing that for me to want beautiful objects and creature comforts would make me shallow. It wouldn't be spiritual or politically correct to totally succumb to my own desire for beautiful things.

But the outside pressures built up to the point where I was forced to do something to myself. "Let me see *your apartment;* let me see *your designs,*" clients and friends chimed. The pressure mounted, my excuses waned in strength, and I was finally plummeted into another major metamorphosis.

I sensed, more strongly than ever before, that my attempts to cut myself completely off from my need for material beauty had not freed me from the more troublesome aspects of my past, nor had it brought balance or peace into my life. I realized that my previous way of thinking had simply been an important early stage, part of another longer and more meaningful journey to find my calling and my true self.

It was time to redo my apartment to house my spirit and fulfill my needs. It was time to create a home for my own heart.

I did, and doing so had a wonderful effect on my life. I found myself becoming more autonomous, more emotionally self-sufficient. The constant friction between my deeper, true self and the person I had been told I should be decreased dramatically. I no longer felt any need to censor myself merely because someone might disagree with or disapprove of my point of view. I didn't have to behave in a shocking manner or vent my anger in the name of art, feminism, or anything else.

I too could become a butterfly.

I became a different version of myself—not just psychologically, but in every cell of my body, every aspect of my being. And this convinced me that interior design could be an extension of metaphysics, of spiritual awareness, and the search for a more alive, humanistic consciousness. It could be another way to acknowledge and manifest the deep longing that we all have to express the self.

I soon branched out from private consultations and began teaching this revolutionary/evolutionary approach to interior design at New York's Open Center and elsewhere. In the winter of 1992, I was asked to write this book in order to allow more people access to my knowledge. In that quest, I have tried to make certain that every idea, suggestion, personal narrative, meditation, and homework assignment in these chapters will help you to create a home and a lifestyle that are sources of pride and pleasure; reflect your true essence; and provide gateways to meaningful relationships as well as vehicles for fulfilling your fondest dreams.

But it is important to remember there are no "should's" in this book, no rules or strict formulas. Everything you learn here you must adapt to your own needs and desires. If you want to use the design process to accumulate more or better things, or to end up with rooms exquisite enough to be photographed for design magazines, you can. If you want to redecorate one room or ten, alter your spirit, or use interior design to attract love and money, you can. You may choose to redecorate your home in a new way with the material possessions you already have, use inexpensive objects purchased at yard sales and thrift shops, or spend a lot of money on top quality wallpaper or carpeting.

It is your home, after all.

What is most vital is that you choose respectfully and mindfully—with awareness and conscious consideration given to the potential physical, emotional, and spiritual impacts of your choice. It is vital that you allow the part of yourself that speaks softly to be heard, that you allow yourself access to yourself.

I offer you a road map but the journey is yours. To begin it, simply obtain a notebook to serve as your design journal, open your heart, and turn the page.

Part One

Designing a Home for Your Heart from the Inside Out

Chapter One

WHAT IS . . . WHERE IS . . . THE HOME FOR YOUR HEART?

"The stranger finds home within the reality of the core of his being."

—EVA PIERRAKOS (JANUARY 1961)

WHAT IS HOME?

What is the difference between a house and a home?

A home is more than a structure made of walls, windows, and a sturdy roof. It is more than carpets, furniture, top-of-the-line appliances, or shelves neatly displaying knickknacks. More than a three-and-one-half bedroom Colonial on a tree-lined street or a penthouse in Chicago.

Home is a feeling. A state of mind. A sense of being where we truly belong. We can find "home" almost anywhere—and we have. Do you remember sitting on a wooden stool in your grandmother's kitchen on bread-baking day? Or smiling as you stared at that whimsical wallpaper in your log cabin in the mountains? What about walking along that special stretch of deserted beach at sunset . . . or roaming through the odd but fascinating room at the history museum . . . or the experience of lying in a hammock in your backyard, listening to your children at play?

During moments like those, in those places, everything you said, did, saw, and knew was in perfect harmony with everything around you. You felt safe, relaxed, grounded. The aroma of spruce or cinnamon, of chocolate cookies baking in the oven—the lighting and colors and background music—made you feel fully alive and centered. Even the feel of the chair in which you were sitting or the ground on which you stood was totally comfortable. Every facet of your environment and every fiber of your being was in sync, balanced, singing the same song. It was a glorious sensation.

It was a feeling of at homeness.

For many, these special moments are all too fleeting and all too few. They are only wistfully remembered, quietly longed for, or left to chance. Yet we are capable of re-creating them and living with them every day. We can consciously orchestrate the connection between our inner selves and our outer worlds by designing what I call *a home for your heart*.

A home for your heart is a place that satisfies. It is an environment that celebrates the softer side of you, your thoughtful, contemplative side, along with your joyous, playful, sensual side. It is a setting that provides peace of mind, freedom, room to grow and change.

In its ultimate form, "home" is a sacred space, an artistic rendering of your psyche, that consciously pleases the eye and nourishes the unseen (but all-powerful and sensitive) parts of your being. Psychologist Carl Jung placed great emphasis on this important connection between our unconscious and conscious, noting that "cues" and "triggers" present in any work of art evoke subliminal responses in its audience that are often "beyond the scope of normal design intentions." To find these deeper meanings and symbols, in art and in his home, Jung used the dream state as a source. He treasured his insights, and the resulting, inspirational effect of his surroundings. In fact, he spent thirty years designing and building a country retreat—his dream home. In his case, the colloquial term "dream home" took on an added dimension. When speaking of his home, Jung called it "a kind of representation in stone of my innermost thoughts."

Yet simply because home can be considered an artistic rendering of your psyche, it does not automatically follow that it must also be elaborate, expensive, or the size of an English country mansion. Many artistic renderings of my clients' personalities and lifestyles have fit snugly into small city apartments or gardens in the backyard. Unlike Jung, the average person does not have the luxury, or the time, to spend three decades designing a dream retreat. Nor do they usually have the budget to fill their space with priceless antiques and artwork, or mirror a full-color spread in *House Beautiful* or *Architectural Digest*.

What home should be, whatever its size, is alive, lovely, energetic, and liberating. It should be an environment that functions well for its inhabitants, without necessarily conforming to the current preference of what is in vogue. The most beautiful home is one whose inhabitants enjoy looking at and being in. It totally supports the everyday habits, schedules and lifestyles of its owners, and evolves much more from the concept of "life design" (a topic you will hear more about throughout this book) as opposed to the more restricting techniques of traditional "interior design." Home is a balanced space that reflects your unique inner self and your lifestyle.

Like a supportive friend, a home for and from the heart embraces you the moment you walk through the door. You can practically hear the walls saying: "Welcome! Sit down and relax. Be yourself here." For many people, home also represents escape, a safe respite from external pressures and conditions over which we have little control. In the book, *A Philosophy of Interior Design,* Stanley Abercrombie wrote of the outside: "There are bears, snakes and runaway streetcars; there are uncharted paths with unpredictable turnings; there are strangers and no guarantee against their sudden appearance or irrational behavior. Outside, we are exposed."

Inside, we feel safe.

Throughout this book you will see the terms "decor," "decorate," and "design." People often use these words interchangeably, but I feel it is important to point out that they are quite different from one another—especially when it comes to creating a home for your heart!

Decor is really the decorative style or scheme you choose to use in a particular room or in your home in general. Decor is a broad term. It is used in many home magazines and books and is a rather impersonal general term.

Decorate refers to the way you actually choose to adorn, embellish, or otherwise ornament your home. In the strictest sense, it refers to the specific objects you choose to adorn your home—with fashionable or beautiful things or with whimsical objects. Decorate is an object related term.

But I feel it is the design aspect that is the most important! The design process comes before decor and decorate. It is an expansive, creative term. In designing you will plan, arrange, conceive, and invent. Design is also a multi-faceted term. When dealing with tangibles such as pen and graph paper in a room layout, for instance, the design is external, but the inner design aspect is where the heart is. It is through your natural sense of inner design that all else will come to fruition. Your sense of inner design, and the types of activities and exercises you do to make this sense of inner design come to life, is also what will make your home for your heart unique and special.

HOME THROUGH THE AGES

The notion of designing a home that functions as both an aesthetically pleasing haven and a mode of self-expression is not new. The primal need to belong to a place, to plant our personal mark on it and create precious memories, dates back to the days of cavemen recording their lives on the walls of their cave dwellings.

Traditions and rituals for creating that nurture and replenish people's bodies, minds, and souls have been a part of every world culture. Ancient Egyptians buried the dead with their household items so they could live comfortably in the spiritual world. There were Greek and Roman gods whose sole purpose was to protect and bring good fortune to people's homes. For centuries, the Chinese designed interiors (and entire cities) using Feng Shui—a technique of studying the *ch'i* (cosmic breath or life force) in a particular setting and then ensuring that all things in that space exist in harmony with one another. And both Eastern and Western designers have blended spiritual traditions into sacred structures and in constructing secular buildings and homes that reflect and support the needs of individuals and communities.

"The purpose of architecture is to raise men's spirits," John Ruskin wrote in the nineteenth century. In the twentieth, Frank Lloyd Wright said that space "should satisfy the fundamental, aesthetic, and spiritual needs of man." To this day, we see the remnants of American Indian totems . . . of Pennsylvania Amish symbols adorning new homes . . . of colorful symbols painted on the walls of children's secret forts. All such symbols and design techniques prove how very important it has been for people to brand their surroundings as their own—to make a visible connection between who they are, where they live, and where they've been.

I can't help but wonder, while viewing blocks and blocks of prepackaged houses, all alike, and constructed in record time: *When did we lose our consciousness of that connection?* Economic concerns certainly can account for part of the loss, a spiritually based approach to building shoved aside to save time and money for contractors. But this issue goes deeper. It is often the desire to want to be like others, to fit in, to avoid standing out in a crowd, that lures people to purchase condominiums or houses in developments where all the structures are basically the same. It is a throwback to the "gray flannel suit" syndrome of the 1950s, whereby people were encouraged (sometimes, required) to excise any signs of individuality. Even today, Americans seem to derive comfort in anonymity, in sameness, but unfortunately their stamp of uniqueness, certainly much of their cultural base, is too often lost in the shuffle. As you will learn in the chapter about color, to a large extent, people have repressed their need for self-expression, seeing it as a character trait that will leave them vulnerable or ostracized, rather than hailed for their uniqueness. All of these factors contribute to the loss of mindful, interconnected interior design, and they are certainly drawbacks to creating a sacred space, a true home for the heart. But they are not the only reasons why so many people are unhappy in their residences. It is not merely the unfinished walls and floors of a building, its structural sameness, or its material style, that prevents a house from being a home. Therefore, we must look deeper for the answer.

LEARNING TO TRUST YOUR OWN SENSE OF STYLE AND TASTE

Whether you rent a tiny carriage house, purchase a co-op apartment, or want to overhaul your suburban split-level, you are faced with the same basic challenge: to decorate.

Right at this starting point, many people begin to make costly mistakes, mistakes that eventually drain their bank accounts as well as their spirit, purely because they do not trust their own sense of style and taste. Rather than work from the inside out and call upon their psyches for answers, homeowners and renters (especially those with a lot of expendable income) rush out and hire professional decorators to tell them what is in or out of style, what should or shouldn't be in their homes. Homeowners too often allow a currently in vogue decorator to take total charge of the design of their interiors based on what is currently fashionable. They trust the "experts" to know what is best for them, regardless of whether this is true or not.

While there are some insightful decorators who make certain that every aspect of their client's decor reflects that client's lifestyle and needs, many professionals are more concerned with placing their own stamp—not their client's—on the home. Unfortunately, this is also a restrictive and impersonal stamp, with trusting, naive homeowners often pressured into choosing one of the standard decorating modes: traditional, modern, country, Italian, or southwestern.

To complicate matters, consumers are fed pages and pages (and hours of television specials) worth of information about decorating trends by self-appointed purveyors of "good taste" expounding upon fads, "in" or "hot" colors, and the dazzling allure of celebrity homes—all proclaiming: *This* is the way a home should look. We see this same tendency in the fashion world as well. Every day thousands of people dash to trendy hair salons, for example, and allow hairdressers to change their looks, sometimes drastically, without even questioning whether or not what works for professional models or movie stars really works for them, or whether the current fad makes logical sense based on their particular lifestyle. We are urged to be as fashionable about our bathroom as we are about the color of our hair, or the clothing we choose to adorn our bodies. In the fashion world, as with much of the interior design industry, form usually supercedes function. The result: *pressure and stress.*

Some trendy furnishing styles do happen to be comfortable, and virtually all are perfectly color coordinated, well arranged, and stimulating to look at. But can the average person live with someone else's sense of style every day of his/her life?

Not for long. If we allow ourselves to be divorced from our own needs and desires and marry ourselves to what is merely a trendy environment, we end up with living spaces that look right but feel wrong.

I'm reminded here of Elia, a Greek shipping magnate, who had great insight into this very concept, and I often cite Elia's story as an inspiration to others who are considering enacting changes in their homes, especially changes considered at total odds from the norm. Elia contacted me about one year after his wife had passed on. He was living in a huge estate in Connecticut, a home that had been decorated exclusively by his former wife with the assistance of the most famous architects and interior designers in the world. Although Elia had adored his wife, and missed her terribly, he had never felt comfortable with his wife's taste, which he thought was rather stuffy and subdued. Still, in his quest to make her happy, he'd allowed her free reign in the decorating aspects of their life together. Suddenly, he found himself alone in this large house, and he wanted it to reflect his own personal style. Before he called me, he had contacted several designers of renown, but added that, "he'd tossed them all out" after they'd scoffed at his eclectic ideas and tried to pressure him to conform to the latest trends. Elia had many ideas he wanted to bring to fruition and was brimming with enthusiasm. I was delighted with the sense of purpose he exhibited, and together we worked to create a unique, satisfying space. But it did take quite a bit of time and effort.

You see, Elia loved all things "British." He also liked funky, casual, and high-tech styles. He also enjoyed Oriental art, and he reveled in drama, in theatrics, and in the grand formality of seventeenth-century furniture. But another part of him preferred cozy spots for entertaining his important guests. Elia wanted a home that reflected all of these parts of his personality.

To meet his needs and desires, we made each room of his home a different style, at times a completely different period. For example, he enjoyed the luxury of rotating the bedrooms he used and insisted they be dramatic. Therefore, in one bedroom, which he called the "Travel Room," we did the walls in deep reddish/purples and similar dark colors, and then contrasted this with lighter-grained furniture. The result was a bed-and-breakfast look, reminiscent of a place he'd once stayed in during a trip to France. His other bedroom reflected the stark white colors and formal, "pillared" styles of ancient Greek culture, which fascinated him. Elia carefully named all of the rooms in his home: the Theatre Room, the Ballroom, the Forest Room, the Meeting Room, and so on. In essence, Elia reinvented himself through his home, and made certain that there was a room to match his every mood, his every need, his every fantasy, and most definitely his unusual and privileged lifestyle.

Elia trusted his own sense of taste, and he believed strongly that it was the homeowner (the one footing the bill), the person living day to day in an environment, who holds the key to what is truly right and best for his/her environment, and happiness.

I urge you, beginning right now, to learn to trust your own inner sense of style as well. You should make a pledge to yourself, and for yourself, to know that you are the true specialist when it comes to knowing how to make your home comfortable. If you choose to hire someone to assist you in carrying out your vision, then so be it. But always have confidence in your own ideas and dreams.

> "The house contains our dreams, but it is also contained by them, which is to say that our houses come to life in our imaginations, or, as an analyst might say, in our environment. That is why the places people have fashioned for themselves are more touching than those—no matter how splendid—that others have made for them."
>
> _____
>
> —WITOLD RYBCZYNSKI
> in *The Most Beautiful House in the World*

In this way you can create a home for your heart.

Sometimes your personal desires and tastes may agree with what is "in" or "trendy." Fine. But if they don't, you must challenge yourself to push onward and inward, because even the most astute professional decorators and magazine editors do not know precisely what your preferences are, what exact setting will make you happy. Neither do your parents, your neighbors, your friends, or the window dresser at your favorite furniture showroom. Nor do I, for that matter.

You are the only one who knows. You are the ultimate authority on your home: the wisest expert, the best decorator for the place intended to house your soul.

Right now you may find this hard to believe. Perhaps you think you couldn't possibly arrange a collection of paperweights in a pleasing manner much less redecorate your living room from the bottom up. Indeed, the idea of actually designing and then bringing to life a home for your heart may seem completely beyond you.

But the truth is *you already have that inner sense of home!* It exists within you. And it is time to search for, unearth, and voyage into your hidden vision.

$\mathcal{F}$INDING THE PLACE YOUR SOUL CALLS HOME: A MEDITATION

White coral bells upon a slender stalk,
Lillies of the Valley deck my garden walk.
Oh, don't you wish that you could hear them ring,
That will happen only when the fairies sing.

—AN OLD WELSH ROUND

If I had to choose the one special exercise that I felt was most important, among the many I use to guide my students and clients toward finding the home for their hearts, it would be what I call the Angel Meditation.

Imagine, for a moment, that you have no one to satisfy but yourself, and you don't have to worry about such material realities as time or money. Where would you live? If you were free of all fears, insecurities, and beliefs about what you can and cannot do, what would your home look like? Who would share it with you? How would it feel?

It you were angel—a pure, spiritual being, able to go anywhere, do anything, and experience life with no physical, emotional, or social limitations—where would you go at the end of day to feel at home?

Right now, you may not know all of the answers to these questions. But by following the guided meditation that follows, you can begin to find these answers . . . along with answers you never dreamed existed inside you!

So read through the Angel Meditation. You may even want to tape record it so that you can follow it more freely.

Then close your eyes, get comfortable, and begin.

THE ANGEL MEDITATION

Focus your full attention on your breathing and take several slow breaths . . . deep breaths.

Now, switch your focus to your body. Starting with your toes and moving upwards, you are going to relax every part of your body. Relax your toes. Imagine the tension melting away. First, tense the muscles in and around your toes. Hold them tight for two or three seconds, then release the tension and feel it being replaced by warmth and relaxation.

Move on to your feet . . . ankles . . . calves . . . knees . . . and thighs. Relax them too, taking as much or as little time as you need with each part of your body before moving upward. Then relax your buttocks . . . genital area . . . abdomen . . . lower back . . . upper back . . . chest . . . shoulders and neck. Relax your arms, hands, and fingers.

Slowly but steadily, continue to your scalp and facial muscles. Unlock your jaw. Relax your eyes.

Now, mentally scan your entire body. If you notice any areas of tension, actively ease and release the tension.

When your body is totally relaxed, take several more slow, deep breaths, and imagine a silver urn or pitcher suspended above your head. It is filled with light—you can picture it as white light or any other color you find soothing. Mentally tip over the pitcher and allow the light to wash over you. Imagine it forming a protective bubble around you.

Next, visualize a candle with a blue flame in front of you in the bubble. The flame represents the tension and problems in your life right now, or anything else that is worrying you.

Visualize the flame going out. Watch it slowly disappear, taking the last of your tension with it. Inside your bubble, you have no worries, no fears, no constraints. Only harmony, peace, relaxation. Take a moment to savor that feeling.

Now picture yourself standing up and calmly heading toward the door. Free of your troubles, feeling light, practically floating on air. Mentally walk out of the room you are in, out of your present home, and onto the street where you live. Start to walk down the street. With each each step you take, watch as the familiar scenery fades. Soon there is nothing but green grass and blue sky to either side of you, and, in front of you, a golden bridge crossing an expanse of calm, crystal clear water.

You walk across the bridge and find yourself in a new environment. It is a favorite landscape of yours—the desert, the beach, the forest, an open meadow— wherever you feel most peaceful and at ease. Now, visually explore the landscape and notice yourself in it. What are you wearing? How has your body changed? In this place you are not bound by the limits of physical reality. So allow yourself to see yourself any way you'd like to be.

At this point you can turn your attention back to the landscape. Up ahead you see a building. You can't make out the details yet, but even from this distance, you can tell that it is the type of building you love, possibly one that you've always wished you could live in. Begin to walk toward it. The closer to the building you get, the more excited you feel. You notice every nuance of its exterior and immediate surroundings. Both feel familiar, comforting. There is a special, magical quality to this place. You are drawn to it, and when you reach the front door, you understand why. There, on the door, is a sign with the homeowner's name on it.

It is your name.

This is your spiritual home, the place in which the most creative, fearless, compassionate, beautiful, and godly part of yourself resides.

You open the door and step inside. You look around the entrance area. Now picture it all . . . the floors and walls, the contour of the area. Drink in the details. What furniture and other objects can you see? How are they arranged? What colors are around you? How is the space lit?

When you are ready, move on to other rooms. You are walking through a hall, perhaps, or suddenly in the next room—whichever room you want to see next. Once you are inside, explore that space and get a sense of the activity that takes place there.

Now find the main living area . . .

The kitchen . . .

The room you do your most meaningful work in . . .

Your bedroom . . .

Perhaps you find a special room that holds your future, that contains all the things you've dreamed of but have not yet attained. Glory in that space. Feel good there.

Take your time in each and every space. Experience it with all your senses. Notice textures, colors, objects, sounds, scents. How do you feel in each space? What is beneath your feet as you walk? What do you hear?

What people, animals, spiritual entities, or guides, if any, share this space with you?

Continue to relax and allow your spiritual tour to unfold. Do not force anything. If you reach a door you cannot open, move on. You will see that space another time.

If you encounter resistance in the form of unsettling emotions, or have difficulty visualizing, then simply go back to the last spot you could visualize. Explore it further before moving on. If all you get are fleeting images, do not worry. You can come back. You can always come back. There is no hurry.

When you are ready to leave your spiritual angel home, return to the entrance area. Stop for a moment and savor, once again, the deep satisfaction being "at home" brings.

Experience the reassuring sense of belonging and unconditional acceptance that comes with knowing that the space exists for you and is available to you at any time.

Breathe in the peace, the power, and the beauty of this place. Let it fill you up.

Now, gently say good-bye for now, and walk out the door.

Take a good, long look around before heading back across the landscape toward the crystal clear water you can see shimmering in the distance. If you wish, pause at the bridge and glance back at your spiritual home. Then cross the bridge. Retrace your path to your neighborhood, to the entrance to your home. Go inside your home, the spot where your journey began.

Focus on the bubble of light surrounding you. Picture it dissolving. Focus on your breathing. Take three or four slow, deep breaths. Then focus on your body . . . the chair you are sitting in . . . the sounds in the room.

Finally, open your eyes and look around. Move your body slowly until you feel comfortably grounded in your physical environment.

If you have trouble visualizing specific scenes or objects the first time you perform the angel exercise, do not worry about it! Instead, focus on your senses, what you are feeling. Some people describe their first angel retreat as a visit to an empty or bare room, or as a sensation of being surrounded by emptiness. If this happens to you, simply allow yourself to go into this emptiness—to experience this emptiness.

You might even find that when you first enter your angel home you see negative things. One of my students visualized what she called an "ugly bathroom," and then realized it was similar to the one she had that time, a room she very much wanted to revitalize. She decided it was her unconscious bringing up her present sense of self and lifestyle for review. It was a call to re-examine and ended up being a very positive experience. Whatever your visions, positive or non-positive, it is all part of the natural cycle. In fact, it may take you three, even four times, before your ideal angel home completely shows itself.

REMEMBERING, ENJOYING, AND USING YOUR EXPERIENCES IN YOUR SPIRITUAL HOME

As you prepare to decorate your residence or workplace, you will want to pay regular visits to your spiritual home. Even after you have begun the work, check back to this inner home now and then.

After each trip, take time to make notes about your experience. Record the thoughts, feelings, or memories that popped in and out of your awareness, or any connections you see between your spiritual home and your home today, any images or sensations that stand out in your mind. You also might write down insights about yourself or your circumstances that are beginning to take shape in your consciousness. Feel free to draw pictures, even rough sketches in crayon or colored pencil, that capture some of the images that appear in your mind's eye. Some people like to leave a tape recorder running throughout the exercise, and actually record their responses by saying them out loud.

In your spiritual home, you envisioned what you truly want and need. Use that vision to bring you closer to your present reality—and to designing the home for your heart.

HEART HOMEWORK ASSIGNMENT: MAKING "I LOVE" LISTS

Now that you have experienced your first exploration into the home within, you can move one step further, beginning to crystalize what you have learned (and what you already know) about your tastes and design preferences. It is probably clear at this point that outside experts do not hold all of your answers. *You* do. Therefore, I'd like you to take a moment to ask yourself:

- What do you like in a home?
- What do you really need from your home?
- What do you sincerely wish to manifest in your home?

With some of the answers to these questions fresh in your mind, you should get out your journal or notebook, turn to a blank page, and at the top of it, write: "Things I Love to Do." Then, draw a line down the middle of the page. Above the left-hand column, write: "in general." Above the right-hand column: "at home." Now, start filling in each of the columns.

Congratulations! You have taken a major step. (If you so desire, you can also use the empty chart on the right as your "I love" list.)

Over the next few weeks, as new activities come to mind or into your life, add them to your list. Include things that you haven't done in ages along with things you are doing now. If you love them, they say something about you! Even though you may not know exactly what to do with this information yet, feel free to write it all down.

Now turn to another free page and title it "Things I Love About Myself." Draw a line down the middle of this page, too, only this time label the columns: "Past" and "Present." Then, list abilities, talents, traits, and interests that are now, or once were, highly valued qualities and elements of who you really are. They can be activities or aspects of yourself that bring (or brought) you recognition, that make (or made) you feel unique, that get you excited, or that fascinate and absorb you.

THINGS I LOVE TO DO . . .	
. . . in general	. . . at home

THINGS I LOVE ABOUT MYSELF	
Past	Present

ACTIVATE YOUR SENSES

This next assignment involves making sensory "I love" lists, an exercise which can bring you to an entirely new level of self-discovery. Done with thought and an open mind, this exercise can become an exhilarating sensory jump start.

You will need to devote at least one page of your journal or notebook to each of the six sensory categories below:

- THE SCENTS I LOVE: The types of incense, potpourri, cooking aromas, flowers, leather, you love to inhale and savor, that "wake up" your body.

- THE COLORS I LOVE: Your favorite hues, both those you find visually pleasing and those that seem to have a positive effect on you, whether that effect is to make you feel calm, exhilarated, powerful, or something else.

- THE SOUNDS I LOVE: Your favorite types of music or songs, sounds from nature, and human sounds, such as the laughter of your child or the purr of your cat.

- THE TEXTURES I LOVE: What fabrics and materials make you feel good? Do you like things that feel nubby? Silky? Soft? Go to your closets or dresser to help yourself remember the full range of textures you enjoy or miss.

- THE FOODS I LOVE: The foods you love to eat, home-prepared or out in a restaurant. The sensory aspects of foods, the silky feeling of ice cream or the crunchiness of nuts, for instance.

- THE ENVIRONMENTS I LOVE: List them all, indoor and outdoor; the atmospheres in which you enjoy eating, playing, or working.

Are your mind and senses beginning to awaken? This awakening is a vital step in designing a home for your heart.

Keep in mind that everything on your "I love" lists will not necessarily be represented in your home. By not rejecting anything, by allowing yourself freedom to write everything down, however, you give yourself the freedom to choose later.

You will probably start to see patterns in your lists. Perhaps the color green resurfaces in other sensory lists, such as your preferences for an environment like a meadow or a vegetable like celery. Look for this sort of pattern as you do these and other exercises.

Throughout the book, I will be asking you to go back to your "I love" lists as you make decisions about your home. But the primary purpose of these lists right now is to make you more aware of what you already experience as pleasurable, in your daily life, in your sensory experiences, and, to a degree, in your relationships with others in your home.

START CLIPPING AND PHOTO FILES

This is the final assignment for this chapter. I'd like you to begin immediately (and continue for at least a month) to look through magazines, catalogs, or department store advertising materials and cut out anything that appeals to you. What you clip out does not have to be something that would fit into your home. It doesn't even have to make sense. If you feel an affinity for it, clip it; maybe even jot down a margin note that says why it attracted you.

You can also begin looking around your living space and identifying things you like and want to keep and things you dislike and want to be rid of. (Don't throw anything away yet, though!) Take snapshots of each room in your home (or the rooms you want to redecorate) and paste them in a special notebook. These can act as your "before" pictures and will allow you to track and see your progress: your evolution, growth, and change. Make "like/dislike" lists around them. Try not to worry about making actual decisions about your possessions. Just strive to get a sense of what feels right and what doesn't.

After you have a healthy-sized cache of photos, clippings, and notes, you can stash it all away into a large file folder or manila envelope. Wait at least a week, then look through the file again. Chances are you'll find a few common denominators, just like you did in your "I love" lists.

What things keep showing up? What things keep drawing you in? You may be surprised by some of your choices. You may even discover that what you like is different from what you thought you liked—or that your tastes have changed a lot lately. That isn't surprising. As a matter of fact, it can be interesting and inspiring to learn how you've grown and developed over a relatively brief period of time. Your tastes—and you—may already have begun to change in very profound ways.

Change is the topic for the next chapter, as we begin to delve deeper into your inner self for clues to creating your ideal outer environment.

Chapter Two

EVERYTHING CHANGES

*"Our surroundings, like mirrors, reflect every value in our hearts.
As we change, so do they. And they change us in return."*

— YOGA JOURNAL [SEPTEMBER/OCTOBER 1986]

Have you ever really considered the vast number of emotional, spiritual, and physical changes you experience in just one twenty-four-hour period? The highways you travel on the way to work, the places where you shop, the people you meet, the scene beyond your living room: Each of these triggers unique sensations and reactions.

The effects of any one of these external forces may be great or small, but change is an integral part of every moment of our daily lives. Sometimes we welcome it, other times fight it, but our responses are always there.

Medical and psychological studies have proven that there is a very real connection between our surroundings and our inner sensations. If we find ourselves in a place we don't want to be, our bodies react—our pulse quickens, muscles tense, thoughts race through our mind, especially the thought: "I want to leave." And then there are those moments when we walk into a room, perhaps even one we've never entered before, and we're overcome by warmth. This time the thought is different: "I feel comfortable here. I want to stay." We feel alert, confident or safe in certain environments, and distracted, insecure, or anxious in others. Think about the way you respond to a hospital. Doesn't it make you feel and even act differently than would a jaunt through a busy airport or visit to your best friend's home?

The environment we sleep in makes a difference in how rested we feel when we awaken. The color scheme in our kitchens and dining rooms (or in a favorite restaurant) affects our digestion and appetite, even how quickly we eat. And at work, the slightest change in an office's lighting, arrangement of furniture, or noise level can affect our productivity.

Spending prolonged time in a setting that is uncomfortable to us can actually be physically harmful, increasing stress and negatively affecting brain waves and hormonal balance. On the other hand, the more pleasing our surroundings, the better we will feel in them. The exact nature of response varies from individual to individual and environment to environment, with your own personal preference being the most important. Beauty, it seems, really is in the eye of the beholder—and reverberates through the body.

Just as our environments influence us, we also influence them. A mood or ambiance is created by the activities that happen within a room's walls as well as by the decoration and design. A perfect example is a cathedral, where people pray, seek solace, and partake in ceremony. Just as the grandness of the architecture can alter the mindset of visitors, the behavior of the people inside a great cathedral lends itself to an aura of quiet, reverence, and order. We would never seek solace in a large department store, where hustle and bustle are the norm.

What is behind this phenomenon? Can we utilize an understanding of it to create balance and harmony in our lives and living spaces? By looking below the surface reality of life, you will see many different levels of reality in which much more is going on than meets the eye. Matter isn't the neutral, passive clay we imagine. The seemingly inert world of objects and spaces that make up our environment is actually an alive, active realm. To make certain that this realm is having the best possible effect, you need to learn what you react to in your own reality, and how you react to it, positively and negatively.

SPIRIT AND MATTER: UNDERSTANDING AND USING OUR LIVING REALITIES

The easiest level of reality to understand is our physical reality; what we experience with our five senses, seeing, hearing, tasting, smelling, or touching. You tune into your physical reality constantly and you will continue to do so very consciously when you choose the objects to adorn your home. As you browse through a furniture store, you may pause to touch a fabric on a sectional sofa that catches your eye, using your sight and touch sense how you feel about this piece. And what is it catches your eye—that makes you feel a texture is right or wrong for you?

The other realities are your perceptual and spiritual realities.

Perceptual reality is made up of thoughts, attitudes, beliefs, and expectations, mental states, and events that shape the way we interpret our experiences of physical reality. This perceptual reality is affected by our preconceived notions about ourselves, others, and the world around us.

The spiritual, or energetic, reality is a special realm where we gain access through our intuition or "sixth sense." At this level, every living being, every person, plant or animal, every inanimate object, even every spoken or unspoken thought, is made up of same force, and responds to the same energy. Although this energy is usually undetected by our five senses, it is nonetheless very real.

Let's return to the furniture store and that sectional sofa. It may be that, when you were a child, someone you cared about had a piece of furniture covered with the same fabric that has caught your eye now. It's that memory (a part of your perceptual reality), which has unconsciously led you to the present-day sofa. Or perhaps that particular sofa was one you just knew would give you hours of pleasure. In your spiritual reality its energy was exactly what you sensed you would need over the years to come. You don't know exactly why yet—*you just know.*

Whatever combination of realities you are perceiving at a given time, you should realize that everything in your universe—each solid, liquid, and gas, every attitude, emotion, personal characteristic, and dynamic, whether sensed or unnoticed, is a manifestation of spirit, a life force revealing itself in physical, mental, or emotional form. Each has its own energy, a specific vibration that can blend or clash with the vibrations emanating from the forms around it. To borrow a metaphor from Machaelle Small Wright, author of *Behaving as if the*

God in All Life Mattered, all the aspects of ourselves and our world are like instruments in an orchestra, each with its own sound and assigned notes to play. When the energy in all things is balanced and synchronized, the orchestra produces an exquisite, soothing, uplifting melody. But when this energy is out of sync, we get dissonant, random, nerve-jangling noise.

Because we live in the material world, we are not always aware of the hidden, quieter, life force in all things. Some don't believe it exists at all. Others lean toward the middle of the road. Through the science of physics we may accept that an inanimate object could give off some sort of vibration, but still doubt that something with no tangible form whatsoever—a thought or feeling, for example—could do so also. But it can!

To design a home for your heart mindfully and effectively, you need to be aware of and use all of the realities accessible to you. To attempt to understand what you need and desire in your home from only a physical perspective is restricting. There is so much more to experience and use as a guide for your fulfillment!

STRIVING FOR BALANCE IN YOUR ENVIRONMENT

Our energy field changes all the time, just as our consciousness ebbs and flows. When a new chair or plant is brought into the lobby you walk through each day; when you clear off your desk or allow papers to pile up on it, when the leaves fall from the trees outside your window in autumn, the energy field in your environment is altered. It's as if the very taste of life has been altered, just as perceptibly as when ingredients are added or taken away from a recipe. Even the slightest negative change on any level of reality can disrupt the energy balance, and leave us with a bad taste, feeling disoriented, dissatisfied for as long as it takes to restore that balance.

One key to achieving a comfortable, harmonious balance in your daily living space is to choose a blend of objects and other stimuli that feels right, that feels balanced. You won't find this blend by simply looking for balance from the outside in, either. Finding it involves an awareness that karmic balance is a two-way street. Simply stated, *when you and your emotions change, so does the energy field around you.*

You may have observed this the last time you arrived at work in a bad mood. Perhaps you'd spent the previous evening arguing with a loved one. You arrived at your office hurt, angry, but still determined to toil until you dropped (or worked off the anger). Well, that day, your usually friendly co-workers probably tiptoed around you, or blatantly ignored you, even though you hadn't verbally expressed your frustration or anger. Your aura, though, the spiritual reflection of your emotional state (which is rooted in your belief system), was negative enough to impact on others. Most people cannot see the aura, or circle of light surrounding another's body, but they do respond to it. That same day, you may recall that important papers seemed to disappear into thin air; your pen ran out of ink just as you were writing an emergency memo; a huge stack of papers crowded a cherished crystal paperweight right off your desk. Crash! At the time, it may have seemed a downright conspiracy was in the works. In actuality, *you* were causing a good deal of the dissonance and disturbing the balance in everything around you.

The same response can be seen when environments remain the same while you are changing: You may start to feel ill at ease in, stifled, or even disgusted by a physical reality that no longer suits you. As you will see later, things in your home that once brought you great joy and comfort, and helped you feel emotionally connected to the world, may suddenly become irritating or unsatisfying. You no longer identify with them, or they suddenly seem wrong for you.

What can you do to help put everything back in order? You can learn to work with this energy by, first of all, accepting that things do change, and second, becoming more in tune with the very existence of this unseen energy.

One of the most interesting examples of controlling unseen energy can be illustrated through a six-thousand-year-old discipline known as Feng Shui (pronounced FUNG SHWAY). I will be dealing with Feng Shui in more depth in chapter nine but I want to introduce the energy concept of this discipline here. Feng Shui is the art of proper placement to ensure that all things are in harmony with their surroundings. The feel of a place is called by the Chinese its Feng Shui. In the field of interior design or architecture, an experienced Feng Shui practitioner can effectively measure the type and flow of invisible energy in a site. The beneficial energy, called *ch'i,* meanders gently along irregular paths. The less beneficial *sha* strikes vigorously and in straight lines. Feng Shui practitioners, or geomancers, who are working in homes, analyze the present energy flow and then make suggestions to either enhance the positive currents, or disperse or redirect the negative currents. For example, it is considered bad Feng Shui to have an entryway to a home directly off the street. This is especially true if you have to leave the street, and then walk on a straight-lined path leading to the door. Geomancers feel that in this situation, the energy is too straight, too swift, and too powerful. (Imagine the strength of a gust of wind through a city side street to better visualize this concept.) A practitioner may suggest the homeowner add steps between the pathway and the front door, or perhaps that the pathway be redesigned in a curving design, in order to break the harsh flow of sha.

The growing popularity of Feng Shui in America is just one example of our culture's growing recognition of the existence and awareness of unseen energies. There is a great renewed interest in several different Eastern sciences, along with virtually all things metaphysical, from angels to astrology to color healing. It is finally being accepted that simply because we cannot see something, it does *not* follow that it doesn't exist. It is more accurate to say that, until recently, most people have not been looking (or sensing) in the right places. My point is that if you honor your instinctive, seemingly inexplicable urges and respond to them by modifying your surroundings to reflect them, the impact on your life can be profound. What starts out as a little decorating project can reverberate straight through to your soul, and lead to new insights, new spiritual awakenings, and a new round of changes in your outlook and lifestyle.

I will soon be asking you to probe deeper into how much you are conscious of the three levels of realities. After that, you can begin making specific decisions about what you need and want in your home. But first I want you to use what we've discussed so far.

Sensory-reality exercise

Read through the following list of adjectives. Then get into a relaxed state and focus for several minutes on each word. What meaning does it have for you? What environment, object, or visual image does the word conjure up in your mind? Think of at least one item or room in your home that comes immediately to mind when you say the word out loud. Also, notice the colors, smells, places, and memories that surface.

Simple	Exciting
Calm	Cozy
Joyful	Sensual
Inspirational	Warm
Fun	Safe
Playful	Relaxing

Notes: _____

_____

_____

_____

_____

Now, repeat the exercise using the next list of adjectives:

Claustrophobic   Cold
Distracting   Draining
Nerve-wracking   Sterile
Depressing   Overwhelming
Sad   Nauseating
Dangerous

Notes: _____
_____
_____
_____
_____

While your responses are still fresh in your mind, turn to your journal and write down your impressions, or use the free space on this page. You will use this information later, and see its connection to your decorating choices, as we move along in our journey.

𝓛IFESTYLE DESIGN VERSUS INTERIOR DESIGN: THE PLACE WHERE OUR INNER AND OUTER WORLDS MEET

External environmental changes, and the unseen energy currents in our environment, are only two kinds of variables in the vast field of existence. Life changes all the time, in both major and minor ways. Changes occur in your personal status—along with changes in your attitude: you fall in or out of love, get married or divorced, alter your financial base, have children, or see your eldest child leave the nest. You weather illness, lose loved ones, embark upon new spiritual practices, switch careers, or move from one place to another. Looking back, some of the changes you've experienced might not have appeared important at the time, while others forced you to face a completely new way of being—but no matter how you've changed, or whether that change was swift or slow, minor or major, it did have significance, and did affect you. Such changes affect what and who we are, but they also determine *what we respond to in our living spaces.*

Our homes are where our inner and outer worlds meet. The decisions we make at any given time about what objects to buy, how much to spend, or what to get rid of, are based on events happening in our lives. We need to acknowledge and control the effects of those changes.

It's not always easy to see the power of change in our living spaces and on our lives. Take Sarah, for example, a thirty-eight-year-old freelance writer, a self-proclaimed vagabond who had been suddenly overwhelmed with a need to find a permanent home, and decorate it with objects and styles that represented stability. In one of our first meetings, she looked at me, bewildered, and said, "I don't understand. I've always been a person who thrives on constant change. Why the sudden urge to put down roots?"

As Sarah shared her past experiences, we began to see why she was so confused. Her professional writing career, which had began at age thirty-two, was the latest and longest in a series of six careers. She'd enjoyed all her jobs, but always after a year or so she would become itchy to do something else—so she did. This behavior surfaced in her relationships with men as well. "I am still waiting to be with someone long enough to get a birthday present *and* a Christmas gift," she chuckled. "As for apartments, I would move out of a place before the dust even settled!"

Lately, though, Sarah had been coming home from business trips and really noticing her environment, something she'd scarcely done before. Now her apartment looked barren, unsatisfying. She started fantasizing about a different kind of homecoming—to a place that felt welcoming. She wondered what her living room would look like in the flashy colors she'd just seen in a magazine or what it would be like to sleep on the lavender satin sheets she'd spotted in a local store. She'd started to dream about walking into a home with a man who cared about her waiting in it . . . an apartment full of steady friends enjoying time together, and many other things she'd never thought overly important.

Sarah admitted that, at first, she'd thought these feelings and experiences were just a result of fatigue. She felt confused by these new urges for beautiful objects around her more of the time, but what she felt was "strange" didn't sound strange at all to me. Virtually all my clients come to me after life transitions or consciousness changing experience. Sarah was no exception.

Sarah realized her vagabond lifestyle had begun at nineteen, the year her parents divorced. That same year she'd been rejected by a man who wanted a less ambitious partner, and she was nearly raped by another man who had seemed ideal. Although she wouldn't be aware of it for years to come, Sarah had apparently concluded from these experiences that no matter how well things start off, if you stay around too long, even the best circumstances will come to a bad end.

So, from that year on, she'd danced away from anything and any place in her life as soon as she felt she'd stayed around too long.

But moving and running away didn't resolve her inner turmoil. Facing the reasons why she'd been moving and running did. Wisely, Sarah began seeing a therapist, which marked the beginning for her of a period of greater understanding and serenity. She began to accept that she wanted, and was ready for more permanent and pleasant surroundings. Sarah was not a totally new person, but rather a person who had uncovered her softer essense. Through self-exploration, she was able to dissolve barriers and fears that had once kept her from forming roots. She rented the roomier apartment adjoining her present one and signed a two year (instead of the usual one year) lease. Then we got to work. By the time we finished redecorating (she chose an airy, feminine, traditional style with a lot of light natural woods and soft-cushioned furniture) Sarah was more comfortable with her newly evolved self, and her surroundings reflected the person she had uncovered. I urged her to plant a garden on her terrace, as a living symbol that she was putting down roots. To make her feel totally comfortable, however, we repaired and refinished two large steamer trunks that had belonged to her parents, and then set aside a section of her closet for clothes and necessities appropriate for an overnight stay—just in case the vagabond urge resurfaced. Most importantly, the energy field around Sarah, and the energy inside her, had finally been blended into a more satisfying and more balanced whole.

I have always found it ironic that people sometimes put up much less resistance to changing their relationships with other human beings than they do to changes in their material world. When people don't change along with us or aren't able to adjust to our changes, our relationships with them become strained and unsatisfying, and we'll usually eventually accept that we've grown less suited to each other. People whom we wouldn't have given a second look to in the past can suddenly seem more interesting, and we change our behavior accordingly. When we fall into a new circle of friends, we usually enjoy ourselves without resisting the whole idea of having new friends. Yet, when it comes to our living environments, we don't so readily accept change—even though we could! *Change is a natural, evolving part of life.* So, if you feel you are outgrowing your environment or feel a need to alter it, you should trust yourself enough to do so. The relation between us and the energy in our environments ebbs and flows, just as our relationships with people change. When we begin responding to an old environment in a new way, the inner self is giving us clues to what we need now, today.

What changes have you experienced in your lifestyle lately? Are your tastes today different from those you had five or ten years ago? Are patterns in your life recurring, or have your lifestyle, values, and goals changed altogether?

You can benefit greatly from looking into your past to see exactly how you've changed, and then actively using this knowledge to direct change, rather than resisting.

EXERCISE: SEEING MYSELF: THEN AND NOW

One way to get in touch with yourself and the changes impacting upon you is to think of yourself as something else, such as an animal or plant, and think about it from a "then and now" perspective. Choose a time frame, whether one year, two, or five, and ask yourself:

(One year) ago, if I were an animal, I would have been a _____
Today, I am a _____

(One year) ago, if I were a plant, I would have been a _____
Today, I am a _____

(One year) ago, if I were an environment, I would have been a _____
Today, I am a _____

(One year) ago, if I were a building, I would have been a _____
Today, I am a _____

Notes: _____
_____
_____
_____
_____

You can continue this exercise with many different things, many different topics. Have fun, and when you are finished, look over your answers. Note connections between them, not only from then to now but between the different categories. Were you a red snapper fish five years ago and a tranquil trout today? A massive estate one year ago and an intimate carriage house today? Are you changing to become more sedate, or are you changing in ways that seem to show a wilder, sultrier, or more creative side? These are the

clues to what you need in your energy field today. Take the answers and connections you feel are most important and write them down here or in your
journal.

LEARNING TO TAKE A CHANCE ON YOURSELF

In my work as an interior designer, and teacher, the topics of change, self-trust,
self-confidence, and the past almost always creep into the conversation. As my
clients and I move deeper, attempting to relate these feelings and past experiences to today, the moment inevitably arrives when the client begins to understand his or her perceptual, spiritual, and physical realities as a unity. This is
the moment when they see what they must do to break through their barriers
and move into the next stage of their lives. These breakthroughs are as exciting
for me as they are for them . . .

At about the same time I was working with Sarah, the vagabond writer, I also
began working with Emily. We first met in the large, airy, two-bedroom con-
dominium Emily had just purchased. In some ways, Emily and Sarah were experiencing similar life changes. Emily was also in her thirties, and had recently
settled down after a gypsy-like life. She was not dating at the time I met her, and
her friends were few and far between—in part because of the fact that she had
become more and more reclusive through the years, and also because she moved
around so much it was hard to develop a steady relationship. Virtually all of
Emily's mental energies were directed toward her budding technical career, and
her physical energies toward frequent trips out and away from her home. Emily
was always going somewhere, and she was somewhat obsessive in this behavior.

Unlike Sarah, who had come to realize her need for stability naturally, and in
her own time, Emily was pressured into this need. She had just accepted a new
job (the highest-paying and most satisfying of her life), but the job required her
to work at home, in a freelance capacity, as a computer software developer.
Emily was already at war with herself when it came to making a total commitment—to reexamining, redecorating, and maintaining her new space—and this
anxiety was deepened by the turn of events in her lifestyle. Not only did she
need a more permanent, fixed environment, but she would now be expected to
spend the majority of her time in that space.

"I knew this place had potential from the moment I bought it," she said.
"But I can't seem to make any important decisions. I can't sit still. I am always
doing errands, even errands that could wait another week. I haven't yet replaced

my old furniture. I don't keep it any neater than my other places. I haven't un-packed all the boxes or built the huge closet I dreamed of having in my bed-room. And I am working on an old desk in the darkest room in the house. What is wrong with me?"

Emily had hit an impasse in her metamorphosis. When she took the first big step, actually buying a permanent home, she'd been fine, but when she moved into the space, she froze. This change in her physical reality started to disrupt her spiritual and emotional realities. This required Emily to sit down and really analyze her fears. When she delved into her inner self, she realized that it wasn't the fact of settling into a new home that she feared, but the fact that she felt trapped. As a child, her father had been imprisoned, and she'd always felt that one day she, too, would suffer this fate—deserved or not. To her, remaining in one place too long, or worse, being forced to stay in one place (as with her new job) represented a type of emotional prison. Eventually, this period of soul-searching would be a source of spiritual and emotional cleansing for Emily, but at the time it felt like anything but.

I suggested that Emily begin to ground herself, and learn to feel secure (but free) in her environment, by making small, positive changes in her daily habits. I suggested that every four hours or so, after she had completed a good portion of her day's freelance work, that she go outside and jog a few miles, then come right home. I also suggested she avoid making more than one trip per day out on errands, even to try going two days without running amok. After a few weeks, Emily walked through her front door one day ready to deal with, and not block out, the reality of her living space. "I realized it was time to do some-thing," she told me with a smile. "I wanted to make my home and workplace a safe, beautiful world, and I no longer viewed it as a prison, but simply a place to live in, to feel comfortable in. I was ready."

I suggested Emily work on redecorating her space much the same way she'd worked on the rest of her life, by making one small change in her environment each day, or each week. Over the course of the next month, Emily rearranged her living room furniture, sorted through old papers, and organized a home of-fice area. We made certain that her home office overlooked the gardens and street outside, and that the walls were painted in bright, cheerful colors. As Emily made her environment warmer and more inviting, her personality started to change too. She became friendlier, more open to visiting and exploring new places, and even to seeing new kinds of movies. Other people responded to the "new" Emily. "I've become closer to my old friends," she said. "I've also made new ones, and I've started seeing a guy I really *really* like." Once she'd finished making the smaller changes in her home, Emily announced that she was ready for the next big step. Not surprisingly, it was to create her dream bedroom: "Lately, all these wild ideas for designing it keep popping into my head!"

Both Sarah and Emily's experiences demonstrate that decorating, just like any other major activity, does not always run at a non-stop pace. Adapting to change takes time. It's not a straight line, and this period of transition is often necessary to work through. When it comes to changing your living space, you can proceed at any pace you want to, and you mustn't allow anyone to tell you differently! Some projects will move slowly, others in great spurts of energy, and you may need to make several adjustments before you feel satisfied. Like dancers whose fluid movements are so well synchronized that it is practically impossible to tell who's leading and who's following, our internal and external worlds subtly and gracefully influence one another—and the pace at which you dance through this world is up to you.

A PATH FOR INNER CHANGE: LIVING ART AND THE ART OF LIVING

What can you expect to happen after you start making changes in your space? Outer change creates an impetus for inner change. If you consciously and conscientiously use your living space as a focal point and a learning laboratory for growth, you can start to picture and move toward what you really want. The new energy in your environment will spread into your life, prompting you to adopt new attitudes, try out new behaviors, and move beyond old fears.

Our homes and what we do with them are metaphors for our lives and how we live them. They are windows to the spirit and soul, revealing our unconscious, fundamental beliefs, our personal histories, and hidden strengths. They replicate, in wood, cloth, and plaster, the various aspects of our personalities. As we start to make conscious choices, this replication takes on more clarity, and more meaning.

Although your experiences while creating a home for your heart will not be identical to Sarah's or Emily's, or anyone else you know for that matter, it is almost certain that you will experience a catharsis of some kind. By thoughtfully examining the energy, symbols, and patterns in the environment you've consciously or unconsciously created for yourself, you will gain valuable insights about who you are and how you live. In turn, by tuning into your inner world and drawing upon your internal resources at your own pace, you'll begin to clear away the rubble, identify your real needs, and make more choices that will truly enhance your environment and your life. Don't be surprised as you work through the exercises and meditations in this book, if you find emotional issues moving toward resolution, or find yourself letting go of burdensome beliefs. You are going to clean house emotionally and spiritually, and all sorts of life changes can occur!

In retrospect, these changes will seem miraculous. But the process of coming to them isn't always so dramatic or even visible. It's more than likely that each shift, each subtle alteration, will lead to another and yet another, creating the momentum to carry you closer to the living space—and the life—that supports, celebrates, and feeds the best parts of you.

Having a beautiful home filled with lovely things will not automatically make you happy. If you are unhappy with your life, career, or mate, you will feel that way anywhere. By focusing on the spirit and energy in all things though, by reaching to the highest and deepest parts of yourself and designing from your soul, it will become possible and probable for you to find true satisfaction. In the same vein, changing a color scheme or a floor plan won't calm down your family, or resolve their problems, but it can help their frame of mind, and the design process will help you recognize where and how you need to adjust your own life. Doing something to change your life will break up energy jams and start you in a new direction. The effort requires an emotional investment on your part, but it will pay off a hundredfold if you take the time to try.

To close this chapter, I've included several more exercises and activities that should help you in your quest for your dream home. After you have completed them, you will be ready to move on to the next stage: determine what is stopping you from being and creating all you are capable of.

QUEST EXERCISE, PART ONE:
TUNING INTO THE ENERGY AROUND YOU

Although the relationship between spirit and matter exists in any setting, it is most apparent in the home, the place which houses our dreams, fears, doubts, and desires, the place where we eat, celebrate, sleep, contemplate, raise children, entertain friends, fret over bills, get angry, and make love and war. Without conscious awareness of how energy and spirit emanate from and into our homes, we run the risk of designing spaces that create turmoil. With more awareness we can draw to ourselves what we need in order to ease our woes and open ourselves to more of what we really want.

To set this process into motion, begin by answering the following questions. Take your time, do what you can for now. If you don't know how to respond to a question, or have only part of an answer, come back to it later when new information enables you to form more complete answers.

WHO ARE YOU?

I am . . .
I would like to be more . . .
I would like to be less . . .

The things in my life that I most value and would most like to honor are . . .

Quest Exercise, Part Two:

LOOKING AT ME THEN, NOW, AND TOMORROW

[1] WHAT DO YOU NEED TO SUPPORT THE PERSON YOU ARE AND THE PERSON YOU HOPE TO BECOME?

Rank in order, from 1 to 5, the degree of importance for each of the following as you think about what you want in a home. (A rank of 1 being most important to you, 5 the least important).

VALUE		RATING
Comfort:	The ability to feel relaxed and at ease.	_____
Expression:	Of myself and my own unique sense of style.	_____
Function:	A space to comfortably accommodate all my activities and the planning involved with those activities.	_____
Atmosphere:	Rooms that create a particular mood.	_____
Entertainment:	A space where I can entertain and socialize with others.	_____

Now that you've rated the level of importance each of these values has for you, try to focus on what each means to you. Ask yourself:

What types of furnishings would make me feel comfortable? _____

What types of colors would make me feel comfortable? _____
_____

Is my personal style of expression tailored, warm, soft, feminine, masculine, eclectic? _____
___ _____

Do I have specific artworks or pieces I simply must have in my new space? What functions do I want to make space for? (work, cooking, lovemaking, watching TV, a special hobby)_____
_____

What sort of atmosphere do I desire: friendly, cool, serene, austere, sultry, impressive? _____
_____

While entertaining, how many people do I want to accommodate? How often? In what ways? _____
_____

Do I plan to have large or small gatherings? Formal or informal? _____
_____
_____

[2] WHO SHARES YOUR SPACE RIGHT NOW?

For each person who is living in your home, complete the following sentences.

_____ (name) is . . .

_____ wants to be more _____

_____ wants to be less _____

_____ most values _____

_____ needs most is _____

The ways I disagree with (name) are _____

The ways I agree with (name) are _____

[3] HOW DO YOU USE YOUR LIVING SPACE NOW?

Approximately how many hours per week do you spend at home? _____ Now, divide the circle below to create a pie chart reflecting the percentage of time you spend on each listed activity.

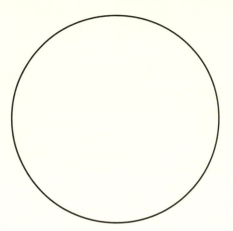

- sleep
- work
- child care
- time alone
- being with an intimate other
- entertaining
- coming and going
- preparing your body (bathing, makeup, dressing)
- cleaning
- cooking
- eating

[4] HOW DO YOU PREFER TO USE YOUR LIVING SPACE?

Now make your ideal pie chart, reflecting the percentage of time you'd *like* to spend on each of these activities.

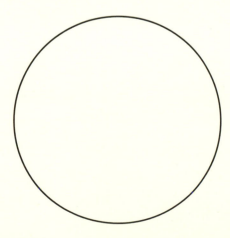

- sleep
- work
- child care
- time alone
- being with an intimate other
- entertaining
- coming and going
- preparing your body (bathing, makeup, dressing)
- cleaning
- cooking
- eating

[5] THE ROOMS IN MY HOME

a. Bedrooms:

How many people typically sleep in your home? _____

How many people would you like to accommodate?

What kind of mood do you want in your bedroom? _____

b. Workspaces:

What work do you need to accomplish in your home-office area? _____

What are your basic requirements for lighting? _____

For storage? _____

For furnishings? _____

For privacy? _____

c. Relaxation rooms:

When you are relaxing what do you do? _____

Watch TV, play board games, garden, meditate? _____

Do you need more space for these activities? _____

In which rooms do you relax most? _____

What furnishings would enhance your relaxation time? _____

a. Coming and going:

What sort of energy do you now use in your various comings and goings in your home? Harried? Reluctant? Relaxed? Efficient? _____

_____

How would you like to change this, if at all? _____

b. Cleaning:

How do you feel about it? _____

What problems do you now face? Clutter? Lack of storage? Using up too much time on the same activities? _____

c. Cooking:

How might you improve upon your present kitchen or dining room? _____

_____

What is most important to you while eating? (Enjoying the taste, developing a calm, happy mood for your family, etc.) _____

_____

How could your kitchen be more functional and make your life easier? _____

_____

[7] THE BIG PICTURE

a. What are you trying to build in your life as a whole or what is starting to un-fold? _____

b. What natural progression is already happening right now? _____

_____

c. What do you see as the biggest obstacle, right now, in achieving your dream home? _____

_____

d. What negative energies do you know you must address and deal with to help this become a reality? _____

e. What positive energies are already in place to help you overcome the drawbacks and find the big picture? _____

f. What resources do you already have to help you achieve your big picture?
_____

[8] FEELING LIKE A GROWN-UP

There is one more question I'd like you to answer before moving on to chapter three: *When you think about the term "grown-up," what does this mean to you in terms of your surroundings?*

For example, one of my students told me that she would feel truly grown-up when she had perfectly matched and monogrammed towels in her bathroom, just like her aunt had in *her* bathroom. Another told me that grown-up meant having a complete set of matching silverware and glasses to entertain with on special holidays. Another said that grown-up meant not feeling pressured to perfectly match her neutral-colored drapes with her neutral-colored living room carpet—and instead, to choose the bold colors she really wanted in that space.

Throughout our lives, we visit many places, many homes, that evoke such responses in us.

I believe that when I *(decorate a certain way, have certain things in my home, etc.)* ____
_____

that I will really feel grown-up.

Chapter Three

USING YOUR ENERGY
AND STRENGTH TO OVERCOME
BELIEF BARRIERS

"The outer condition of a person's life will always be found to reflect their inner beliefs."

—JAMES ALLEN

We humans are wonderfully resourceful. Our natural instincts and skills are geared toward building, arranging, inventing, shaping, and otherwise bringing visions and desires to fruition. Every day, that innate inner power is available to us to create beauty in the world around us—if we'd just get out of our own way and allow it.

A small percentage of my clients and students do allow themselves free reign, but many more come up against internal barriers as they start their life design projects. I'd like to help you go through any such barriers you might have so you can achieve your vision!

GAINING POWER FROM THE POSITIVE

Our homes can be forbidding fortresses that keep out people, or inviting, hospitable places where guests feel welcomed. A space can stifle us from reaching our true potential, or replenish our energies and encourage us to do our best. It can harbor discontent and smother our spirits, or spark ingenuity and allow our spirits to soar.

When you say the phrase, "my home," does it conjure up feelings of contentment and pleasure, a vision of a place you love coming back to? Or does it conjure up words like "crowded," "unsettled," or "ugly"? In the Sensory-Reality exercise you completed in chapter two, did you automatically relate any of the adjectives to specific locations in your house? For example, if you related your living room to the word "joyful," this this is extremely important and good for you. There is something in that room that you have already done . . . some way that you have already used your natural talents . . . that is now triggering this response in you. Then again, if you immediately related the word "sterile" to your bedroom, this tells you that your bedroom needs more life, that it needs to be more of a reflection of your present lifestyle, as opposed to a symbol or memory of a belief barrier from your past.

Most people view their living space with mixed emotions. Rare is the man or woman who says, "My home is perfect." There is always something to improve, something to repair, something else to change. I've heard clients lament this fact, whether they were about to reorganize their closets or had just completed a full-scale redecorating project.

The need for continual improvement is a natural part of the design process and of life. As we noted in chapter two, it is a natural extension of the types of changes happening in our lives, and of our character growth and development.

Unfortunately, I have found that the same dissonance or disharmony that prompts people to change their environments will also too often prompt them to dwell on all the things they don't like. They waste energy complaining about what they can't afford to change, and comparing their home (unfavorably) to other people's homes, to those in magazines, or to their own dream home.

They waste time on aspects of their life that are unproductive (a.k.a. procrastination) rather than take the chance on the new, the different, the unknown.

I urge you to think positively about your space, even if it's far from ideal. When you're pondering over what to change, think too, about what you already have to help you to make that change. What you already have may not be an unlimited bank account or a truckload of beautiful new furniture, but something as simple as extra paint in the basement that can now be used to spruce up a hallway. You may have simply your enthusiasm about seeing things in a new light and the physical and emotional energy to get to work, but that is a lot.

Take time to appreciate the little things in your home you already feel are right and look at them in a new light, with renewed appreciation. Think about the beliefs you have about your home that are positive: What do you like about your space? What do you like about you that you have already incorporated into your space? Such thoughts are building blocks, and positive starting points. You can always come up with something positive to focus on. Dwelling on imperfections only makes them loom larger in your mind. Such thinking saps your energy and enthusiasm.

Do not talk yourself out of your dreams! Allow yourself to have dreams!

It isn't always easy to create a home for your heart, but once you begin the process, it automatically becomes easier. Once you become conscious of your preconceptions and the challenges you face, you can transform what you don't like, you can change or alter what think you can or cannot have, you can redefine what you must or mustn't do, and you can reconceive what you think you do or don't deserve.

You long for, and deserve, a place where you truly belong and can be at peace with yourself and everything around you, and I promise, you can have this, if you begin to think positively and allow yourself to tap into your natural creative abilities.

The Land of Doubt

Sometimes, as people refashion their living spaces, the barriers they face are deeper than a simple tendency to focus on material imperfections or drawbacks. Psychological barriers, emotional upheaval, cultural stereotypes, and the effects of long-standing belief systems (many of them no longer needed) also arise to block productivity and positive energy. The fact is, between the homes and lives we see in our inner vision, and the reality of our homes and lives today, lies a land of doubt, fear, and self-limiting beliefs. That's a territory we can have difficulty crossing—just when our needs and desires start to move us closer to realizing our dreams, it's almost as though our own negative forces start pulling us back.

One of my students, Margaret, a forty-five-year-old book translator and artist, found herself caught up in just this type of tug-of-war. A self-proclaimed procrastinator, she'd lived in the same home for twenty-five years and had had well-meaning plans to redecorate it for the past ten. "On the rare occasions," she told me, "when I'd be ready to get down to business and actually start buying paint, for instance, there was always an unexpected work deadline or family problem that came up, and decorating would dive to the bottom of my priority list." When I asked her why she didn't simply begin with small projects in between her crisis times, she replied firmly, "If you are going to decorate a home, *you should do it properly.* You should give it your undivided attention, never cut corners, and never settle for second best," in other words, never make mistakes.

So, for a long time Margaret was torn between a strong desire to improve her surroundings on the one hand, and her own preconceived ideas about the "right" way to do it on the other. As a result, she did nothing.

She was hardly alone. For instance, Steven, a thirty-eight-year-old attorney, also wanted to decorate perfectly, only he believed that learning was the key to getting it right. He took design courses, filled his shelves with how-to books, and interviewed every carpenter and contractor he could pin down. Even all this wasn't enough, though. "I'm not quite ready," said Steven, three years after taking his first design seminar. "I still need to know a little bit more about decorating before I feel comfortable taking on such a big responsibility. It's a big job."

We all have our reasons for procrastination and we all have frozen notions from past experiences and relationships. These reasons vary in their impact and seriousness, yet they are very real to us. We need to acknowledge and respect them as important experiences that have led us through our lives, but we also need to recognize which ones are holding us back from creating a sacred space for ourselves.

Like Margaret, Steven, and many of my clients and students, you may realize that the home you have doesn't satisfy you or reflect who you really are, but still can't seem to muster the time, resources, energy, or motivation to do something about it.

What are our reasons for holding back? Why aren't you further along in your design project? You should write all of these these reasons down, so you can view them in black and white. It's time for you to see them for what they really are, and to decide whether each reason is real, imagined, or exaggerated.

Take out your decorating journal or a fresh piece of paper and finish the following statements.

I don't have a beautiful home now because . . .

I'll be able to create a home for my heart when . . .

Even though everyone will complete these statements in their own way, a way that reflects a unique self and frame of mind at a certain point in their lives, I do see many of the same reasons and excuses surfacing among people I meet. These include:

- I don't have enough money
- I don't have time or I don't have enough time
- I rent and my landlord might not approve
- My roommate might not agree
- Decorating is "a woman's thing"
- I'm not good at it; I'm not creative or artistic
- I don't know where to begin
- I don't know what good style or taste is
- I don't have the materials
- I am not organized
- I'm afraid I'll hate it; It will be a mistake
- I shouldn't spend my money on decorating when the family needs other things or my family needs me more as their emotional supporter than their designer
- I like too many styles, I can't decide between them
- I want to move (to the country, to the city, etc.)
- When I'm in a relationship, then I'll do it
- I am intimidated by professional designers or showrooms
- I don't deserve to pamper myself
- I am afraid to let go of my old things

That's quite a varied set of reasons, isn't it? Some are external, having to do with matters of economics or time; others reflect our psychological fears. What they all have in common, however, is that in the end, these barriers manifest themselves in resistance, and keep us from having the home that we say we want to have.

In chapter two, I discussed the importance of energy in your personal life, your environment, and the world surrounding you. Now I am going to illustrate how to take this energy phenomenon to yet another, deeper level.

Energy follows the path of least resistance, traveling where it's easiest for it to go, usually along a previously established route. Water will follow the same riverbed for centuries. Commuters travel on superhighways and rail lines that began as footpaths, trails that were first blazed one step at a time and then retraced repeatedly, because doing so was easier, safer, more comfortable, more expedient than blazing new trails.

The same principle applies to our lives. We tend to act and react in the ways most familiar to us, ways that are based on the underlying structures of our lives: our personalities, previous experiences and preexisting attitudes, beliefs, and behavior patterns. When we attempt to blaze a new trail, a part of us remains committed to maintaining the status quo and protecting us from foolhardy, presumably dangerous ventures.

You need to identify and address your barriers in order to help you better understand how they affect your life, and how you can start to overcome them. Sometimes, the barriers that we create in our own paths can be ingenious, strange, and varied.

Take Jan, an elementary school teacher I met early in my consulting work, who found that her barriers manifested themselves physically. Whenever she tried to buy new furniture, she would become "too tired to think clearly." She'd arrive at a showroom wide awake, then start yawning as she walked through the door. In minutes, she was exhausted.

As we tried to work through her unusual block, Jan told me that she was the daughter of a theatrical stage manager. As a child, she'd always lived in temporary quarters: nondescript mobile homes, rooming houses, and hotels. Between trips, home was a sterile bedroom at her grandparents' house. Later on, she lived in college dormitories, rented rooms, and sublet furnished apartments. When she married, her husband made all the decorating decisions. It was soon obvious to me that Jan lacked confidence in her ability to purchase furniture because she'd never seen her parents do it, and, in all her forty-two years, had never done it herself. Now, divorced and on her own, she found herself with an apartment, a few leftover furnishings, and a lot of empty space.

Lack of experience was certainly part of Jan's dilemma, but on a deeper level, her new determination to make her own choices (and to choose things that reflected her true self) was conflicting with a lifelong habit of fitting herself into other people's spaces. Even in her present job as a teacher, she was working within strict curriculum guidelines and classroom space assigned to her. Her discomfort with the notion that she had difficulty making her own choices was what undermined her confidence in her abilities. "I'll mess it up for sure," she would sigh.

I encouraged Jan to begin by selecting paint colors and accessories for her apartment instead of starting off with a major step, like selecting furniture.

Slowly, steadily, Jan brought her unique, fun personality and taste into play, and just as steadily, she began to forge her own new path to her goals. Since she experienced difficulty when she actually entered paint or furniture stores, I brought paint and fabric swatches to her. After a while, she became excited about her choices, and this naturally led to shopping sprees where she could see and touch her choices, and be a part of the experience. I also tried to pinpoint the areas of Jan's life where she did feel confident, or at least enthusiastic, and use these areas as stepping stones. For example, because of her childhood experiences, she knew a lot about the theater, and she loved memorabilia. Therefore, the first big project we undertook was her den, for which she chose whimsical art objects and sheet music framed in dramatic shapes and colors that reminded her of her favorite big state theaters. Jan made great strides after she accepted her insecurities and began to capitalize on her strengths.

There are many such hidden influences that can undermine your efforts to create a home for your heart: habits; fears; unresolved issues associated with places you've lived in the past, or with the people whose taste they reflected; perfectionism; low self-esteem; the negative implications of spending money on yourself or on something that you consider frivolous. Cultural attitudes about owning things can get in your way. Particularly debilitating are self-limiting beliefs about who we are and what someone like us is supposed to have or what we are capable of doing. "I am not creative," you may think. "I can't get involved in any activity that requires creativity." Or, "I am a spiritual person and should not be interested in material things." These assumptions stop us from achieving our visions much more effectively than any financial or material obstacles. If we assume we can't succeed, too often we won't: It's a self-fulfilling prophesy.

Equally important, if we are automatically expected to be able to achieve our goals, in life or in home design, we feel even more pressure. In some cases, our barriers are not rooted in the unrealistic expectations we set for ourselves, but in unrealistic expectations set by the outside world.

I work with a lot of women in my business, and I have noticed that, even though we live in this allegedly enlightened age, there is a great pressure that women most feel when it comes to decorating. There is a preconceived cultural notion that women should instinctively know how to cook, entertain, and arrange furniture; how to choose and hang curtains; how to design the perfect kitchen. They should know how to set a table, choose coordinating wallpaper and flooring colors, arrange flowers, and plant a garden. Now, it is true that all women have the potential to create, design, and learn these things, but it does not follow that they automatically know. This expectation causes shame and

USING YOUR
ENERGY AND
STRENGTH TO
OVERCOME
BELIEF
BARRIERS

45

anxiety. Some women respond by avoiding any kind of design at all and leaving it to outside experts. Others just avoid making any changes in their homes until they are absolutely forced to, or pretend that they don't care about it.

One of my students, Diane, was so intimidated by this gender expectation that when she was planning her wedding and had to register her choice of dinnerware patterns with the area department store, she panicked. She was afraid to even enter the store because she felt so intimidated by the process. She didn't know what to choose, or even how to choose, and was convinced that she would make the wrong choice. She didn't know brand names, or what her executive husband's colleagues would deem acceptable. Eventually, she took along a friend who had already been through the process, and together they chose a pattern, but it was a frightening experience to realize she was expected to know.

On the other side of the coin, I work with plenty of men who keep their design projects a secret, especially when it comes to joining me on shopping sprees, because they do not see design or decorating as a "men's thing" and are afraid to exhibit their aesthetic needs and desires.

The reality is that we all have these barriers to one degree or another. Some of us deny that we have them. Others among us don't even realize how much they are affecting us—personally or in terms of our aesthetic choices. In this case, such barriers have evolved past pure reaction and have become ingrained into our psyches as a result of cultural conditioning. The problem is that what has been ingrained in us by the masses is not always what is natural for us personally—and certainly not what is best for us aesthetically.

I cannot stress enough that it is important for you to actively uncover these influences and barriers. You need to know what is truly authentic and aesthetic in you and what is not. You need to acknowledge, accept, and understand these influences and how they are affecting you now at this stage of your life.

I know that delving into this "stuff" can be a deep, even heady, process. But if you take it one step at a time, you can better assimilate what you are learning about yourself, and more easily move beyond these barriers . . . to unleash your sense of inner design.

STARTER-EXERCISE: THE AREA OF MY HOME I FIND THE MOST DIFFICULT TO CHANGE AND WHY

At this point, I'd like you to take another small, but important step in overcoming your path of resistance. Write down the name of the room or area of your home that you perceive as the most difficult to change or improve upon. Now, beside the name, write down your perception of why you feel that room

USING YOUR
ENERGY AND
STRENGTH TO
OVERCOME
BELIEF
BARRIERS

——

47

or area will be so difficult to tackle. Do this in two ways: first, the material or physical reasons, and second, the psychological or emotional reasons. For example, you might perceive your kitchen as most difficult because you know you need all new cabinetry to make it even remotely acceptable. That's the physical challenge. The emotional or psychological challenge is that you know you'll have to work with a professional carpenter to achieve your goal, and this idea totally intimidates you.

Next, and this is very important, write down one simple task that you can do to begin tackling that job. For example, you can go out and purchase a few magazines on cabinets and choose your ideal cabinet. You don't have to order it, simply choose your ideal, whatever its cost. Then, you can talk to your neighbors who have recently worked with carpenters, and ask them about their experiences.

Step by step, you see? It is no doubt obvious to you by now that designing from the heart isn't the same as decorating to purely aesthetic and functional standards. With every design project, there are both aesthetic and emotional issues at play. And please don't assume that there is a certain schedule according to which you need to achieve your vision. Decorating isn't a test, and you don't need to finish before the buzzer rings.

*T*HE QUEST FOR PERFECTION

I want it done yesterday! I want it perfect! I want an exact, step-by-step plan to construct my ideal home!

I hear these phrases a lot in my work, especially from people accustomed to following rigid schedules, to being the best, or to getting things done efficiently.

Ultra-perfectionism, along with its companions, impatience and control, are common belief barriers. They are also unproductive, simply because wanting it all, especially all at once, just means you want the impossible. Worse, since you can't usually get everything you want immediately, you can easily overlook the steps you could take and sacrifice the things you could have.

Perfectionism also leads to procrastination, another form of resistance: determined to redecorate flawlessly, terrified that we won't, we put off projects indefinitely rather than risk making a simple mistake. Many people are afraid of settling for less than perfection, as if nothing is better than something that falls the tiniest bit short of our lofty standards. But *perfectionism* is not possible! It is not even a natural state; certainly not an earthly state. In a way, perfectionism is a form of self-rejection; and perfectionism based on comparison with other people is really a fear of our inner selves. All in all, perfectionism is a self-defeating process.

Once you realize your tendencies toward perfectionism in your personality, then, believe it or not, the best way to overcome it is to first accept it, and then to ignore it as much as possible. Not entirely, of course; such transformations take time, especially since you probably want to maintain these traits at some level. A touch of high expectations never hurt anyone! But when you find that your tendency toward perfectionism begins to block your ability to make any strides at all, then you must ease up and allow positive action to replace negative thoughts so you can get back on track. You may feel uncomfortable or frustrated at first, especially if you've been a perfectionist for a long time, but this frustration will ease as you start to see how your efforts bring results.

This is a good time to mention a reality about the design process that is directly related to perfectionism and impatience. Many of my clients, especially those accustomed to schedules and strict routines, are unaware that the actual process of interior design is routinely imperfect in its time schedule. This realization can save you a lot of trouble and anxiety. From stage one, acknowledge the fact that your project will vary from your original time schedule. The time frame will not be perfect, some of the material tasks will not be in your control, but this will not be your fault.

During remodeling or redecorating, for example, if custom furniture is ordered, it takes time to produce it. Then to approve it. Then to arrange for shipment. Also, in large-scale redecorating, painters are often hired, and often they run over budget; plumbers are notorious for arriving late or taking longer than expected on the job; and delivery of large pieces of furniture sometimes arrive either too fast (the space is not prepared to accept it) or too late (you missed the chance to throw your anniversary party with your new dining room set in place). These days, I always let my clients know about this factor before they begin designing, and it does help to ease their anxiety, as well as tone down their unrealistic expectations.

Several years ago, I worked with a couple who lived in an upscale, waterfront community on Long Island. Sandy and Mike had recently married, and were ready to redesign Mike's home. Mike had lived there for fifteen years with his former wife and two children, and although the house had many interesting architectural details, virtually the entire space was done in beiges, or variations of ivory tones. Both Mike and Sandy agreed it was too bland and they wanted a new, livelier look. When I first met this couple, I was excited about working with them. They got along so well, they even looked alike, and they had a great deal of enthusiasm. Unfortunately, Sandy, a vivacious telecommunications executive, was also a perfectionist. An impatient perfectionist. Sandy enjoyed making decorating choices, but she resented the delays in ordering, the delays in renovations, the process itself. Mike was much more relaxed about this process, and attempted to help her work through this, but it wasn't easy.

This perfectionistic tendency began to impact on other areas of their relationship, and on the design project as a whole. For example, when the newly upholstered sofa finally arrived, after a substantial, but unavoidable delay, Sandy looked at it (a roomy, multi-striped design in sea greens and deep blues) and decided she hated it. The color wasn't what she had expected; the sofa looked too big in the room; the upholsterer had left a tiny seam, etc. Naturally, I felt confused because we had gone through hundreds of fabric swatches to make this decision. I left that day, somewhat discouraged, trying to decide on the best next step. When I returned two days later, Sandy announced that she now loved the sofa. After she had lived with it a few days, she realized that it was indeed exactly what she wanted. This scenario happened several more times, first with the new gold-tinted faucets in the master bathroom; again with wool carpeting in the den, until everyone involved was on edge. Finally, I asked Sandy and Mike to join me for lunch one day, outside of the home, a place where we could just talk. In our discussion, Sandy said that she'd always seen herself as a leader and tomboy type. She'd always been the neighborhood leader as a child, and continued this role as leader in her career as an adult. She added: "This design business is so unpredictable, and it takes so long to create. I am frustrated, I like everything to run on schedule, to be perfect, and now I feel totally out of control."

This story does have a happy ending, by the way. Once we identified Sandy's problem of feeling the compulsive need to be perfect, and her obsession with control, we were all able to cope better. Mike and I urged Sandy to ignore her initial negative responses and allow herself a waiting period. I also took the time to explain why delays often occur, and I urged her to try to experience some level of joy during the metamorphosis period. Sandy came through, because her love for Mike, and her need to do what was right, finally overpowered her perfectionism, at least enough to complete the project. Finally, one year later, their home was done. And both Sandy and Mike were back to their enthusiastic selves, planning a large dinner party to share their new creation.

In dealing with perfectionism tendencies in your own life, I feel strongly that it is best to first *accept* this trait, and then use this trait as a stepping stone toward achieving balance and harmony, rather than living to achieve all the time, and on time.

Also, remember that when it comes to inner design, nothing is permanent, or perfect, and if you don't feel totally comfortable with the end result, you can change it again. Before you envision thousands of dollars being wasted on an experiment, however, be comforted by the fact that it has been my personal, professional experience that even perfectionists are rarely unsatisfied with the end result—if they allow themselves the time to be an active part of the decision-making process and allow the project to progress at its own pace.

Another tip when dealing with perfectionism, or virtually any other type of barrier or resistance, is to actively, consciously keep yourself from blowing things out of proportion. Try hard not to obsess about imperfections, either those in your space or those in yourself. They are simply manifestations of certain aspects of yourself, *not all that you are.* They're definitely not proof that you can't have, do, or be different things. Every limitation or problem can provide material for the creative process, and act as a stepping stone for achieving balance and harmony. Realize this, and you will begin to appreciate your present circumstances in their entirety, in all of their minute aspects, including the parts that are not always on schedule.

We are all works in progress, still evolving, and that's exactly as it should be.

FINDING CLUES AND MESSAGES BELOW THE SURFACE

Belief barriers are not always easy to detect, and not all external behavior is obvious. Ideas and attitudes that linger below the surface of our consciousness sometimes set up barriers and sabotage us without our knowing it. We may not even be aware of the messages we are constantly sending to our inner selves. As long as they are undetected, those forces will continue to draw you back to the path of least resistance—even when it is no longer the path you want to be on.

I recall my first New York apartment. It was full of interesting artistic and found objects, but there was no place to sit comfortably, no desk large enough to work on, no place to hang all my clothes or to access important papers. I used a giant trunk as a dresser where my socks, leotards, and sweaters were forever intermingled. It all looked great, but I could never find anything.

I had been resisting changing my wild, unconventional, "artsy" home. My apartment was like a child's playground and reflected my refusal to grow up. The environment I created was communicating that "to be a grown-up is to be boring, a conformist, bourgeoise, and (in my deepest fear) a Stepford person."

The chaos finally got to me. I had not known how to integrate my eccentricities into a functional home lifestyle. My identity as an avante-garde artist had kept me from experiencing grace and ease in my daily life. I thought I could only be either an interesting artist or a boring grown-up.

Eventually I did renovate my apartment. It took me a long time, but I finally had a beautiful, functional home. I was more organized and less frustrated each day. I found myself enjoying strolling around, choosing my clothes, standing in front of a full-length mirror, dressing up in this lovely, newly evolved space looking at this "grown-up" version of myself. What particularly surprised me was how having such a home truly supported me when I was not at home. It was as if I were a trapeze artist flying through life who suddenly had a net underneath to catch me if I fell.

I was able to achieve a balance that reflected my multifaceted personality, to begin to discern what really mattered to me and what was extraneous. I kept what best reflected the childlike and playful parts of myself while adding useful furnishings and objects that truly enriched my life.

I had identified my barriers and moved through them. *I learned I could tell the difference between my real needs and what I thought I had to have.*

USING YOUR
ENERGY AND
STRENGTH TO
OVERCOME
BELIEF
BARRIERS
———
54

Moving Belief Barriers Out of Your Way

"When we change our commitment to ourselves, we change our cellular vibration and therefore our magnetism and what we attract. We can then attract something different."

—MARILYN GRAMAN, PSYCHOLOGIST

Soon after my clients and students begin to identify their paths of resistance, their belief barriers, they ask me, "How do I get rid of them?"

At this point, I urge them to maintain a positive attitude, but also to realize that it is not easy to completely get rid of such barriers. There is no quick cure-all or emotional Band-Aid that I can give them to make it all go away. The answers and solutions lie inside them and *you,* and sometimes these take months, even years, to find.

But once you acknowledge your barriers (a major step in and of itself), you immediately *diminish* the power these barriers have upon you and your life by shedding light on them.

To achieve this, the first step is to focus on the positive. The second step is to find productive actions or thinking patterns to replace the less productive patterns, which often involves making important choices about how you will respond in given situations. The third step is to plunge in and begin to actively, physically change a portion of your living space, based on your uncensored vision of what it could eventually become.

Let's begin with step one, the positive thinking process. Remember like attracts like, positive attracts positive, negative attracts negative. When our thoughts are chaotic or unfocused, so are our lives. When our belief systems are built around "I can't," "I don't deserve," or "I must cling to what I already have," the unconscious, unfulfilling paths we take repel the positive influences that could be part of our daily lives.

Therefore, at any moment (right now is a good time), you can start attracting the positive by thinking positive.

Begin by viewing your current circumstances, not as a mine field, but as a starting place. View your environment as a schoolroom of sorts, full of information about the past and present that can help you make your dreams come true, now and in your future. View your inner self as the teacher and actively seek out that wise teacher who is on your side and knows what's best and most authentic for you versus the obsessive, pained, scared, disappointed part of you.

Sometimes, the difference between feeling excitement instead of anxiety is a matter of where you are coming from. It is impossible to be creative from an outside place. It is all a matter of location. In this case, the location is the teacher within you—the harmonious, positive, productive part of you that needs to be released and relied upon.

The positive thinking process can be part of your daily life and I suggest you make a habit of it. Perhaps, every morning, you can begin your day by meditating and repeating the following affirmation, which was delivered during a guide lecture at the Pathworks Community.

My DAILY AFFIRMATION

*"I am strong. My possibilities are manifold,
and if outer difficulties come to me,
I can overcome them,
first by facing them fully,
then by my willingness to cope with them truthfully,
not superficially nor for the sake of appearances.*

Using your
energy and
strength to
overcome
belief
barriers

———

53

I do not have to be great.
I do not have to be glorious or special.
I am a simple human being, like many others,
but as such, I am endowed with great powers
that I have yet to realize."

Exercise: my gratitude list

Now, to continue our path toward the fulfilling and positive, I want you once again to reflect upon the areas of your life, your self, your family, and your environment, for which you feel grateful. To make this concept a material, living reality, you can complete the following exercise.

The things in my present living space I value most are _____

_____

I am grateful for them because _____

_____

The way I would like to use these things more is _____

_____

The way I feel I can enhance these things is to _____

_____

I am grateful because at this point in my life I already have _____

_____

The people in my life I am most grateful for are _____

_____

I feel these people can work with me to achieve my outer vision, by helping me

_____

The skill or talent I already have that I am most grateful for is _____

_____

One thing I learned today, that I feel excited about, is _____
because _____
I deserve a beautiful home because _____

_____

The most loving thing that I can, and will, do for myself today _____

_____

What is the most loving thing that I can do for myself tomorrow? _____

_____

Now that you've triggered your positive thought process, you can move on to the next step and find actions or thinking patterns to replace your less productive patterns. On page 43, you identified your reason for not having a beautiful home right now. Look back at your journal and see what you answered in order to refresh your memory. You may have also realized that one or more of the belief barriers mentioned in this chapter also related to you. You can now move further in your request to move past these barriers by making important decisions and choices about how you will respond to them.

In Robert Fritz's book, *The Path of Least Resistance,* he mentions several choice-making strategies. Some may be already familiar to you. I have listed them below, along with my own feelings and ideas about each one. Take a moment to consider the pros and cons of each strategy, and decide which one, or which combination, is right and best for you at this point in your life:

1. CHOICE BY REACTION: If something in your life is causing you pain, guilt, or anxiety, you can choose a course of action that you hope will reduce your discomfort.

    This is fine, as long as the course of action you take is a positive one. All too often, people go from the proverbial frying pan into the fire, the result being that what they manifest simply brings them to a different kind of discomfort.

    For example, if you are feeling anxiety because the garage is so packed with clutter that you can't get inside to find the boxes of summer clothes you put away last season, and you react to this by closing and locking the garage and simply buying new clothes, you have not achieved anything at all. If, however, you at least muster enough strength and enthusiasm clear one path through to your summer clothes boxes (organizing that path along the way) then you have reached a middle point.

2. CHOICE BY CONSENSUS: In this form of choice, you base a decision on expert advice, or resolve a problem totally on the advice of others.

    The alleged logic to this approach is that you don't have to take full responsibility if it doesn't work out. Still, even if there is the chance you will end up doing what you secretly wanted to do all along, the odds are that you won't. You risk getting nothing of what you want, and it's not really yours anyway.

    A typical example of this choice is the home decorator who listens only to what the "Jones's" feel is best their lifestyle. But, as you have already learned, only you know what will work best in your home, with your family. So, you can gather opinions and ideas, but you should always combine this technique with other techniques.

Using your
energy and
strength to
overcome
belief
barriers

55

3. CHOICES BASED ON ANTICIPATING NEGATIVE CONSE-
QUENCES: By thinking about the adverse effects of not following
through with the plans you might have (illness, depression, guilt, etc.),
this technique leads you to go ahead because you don't want to invite
these negative, future consequences.

The positive side of this choice is that possible negative consequences can be positive motivators! But, on the negative side, remember that simply avoiding what you don't want is not the same as
choosing what you do want. If negatives are all that drive your decision, the results will almost never be as satisfying as they could be.

4. CHOICE BY DEFAULT: You don't make a clear-cut decision. You
wait to see what happens.

This choice is perhaps the most tempting of all, but it's also the least
productive. Choice by default translates into no action, until outside
forces are thrust upon your path. The something you're waiting for may
never happen, and then you will never see any results. Or, what you
do get may bear little or no resemblance to what your heart desires.

5. CHOOSING A PROCESS RATHER THAN A RESULT: Focusing on
the "how" instead of the "what," you might decide to take design
courses, hire a decorator, or purchase a bedroom set. You then assume
that by doing so, you'll eventually end up with a home for your heart.

This is not necessarily the case. You can go to college without becoming educated, eat health foods and still feel unhealthy, decorate
your home and still, in the end, not have a home for your heart. A
process that looks as if it will bring about positive design results can
only do so if you've already identified and chosen the result that will
work for you.

Therefore, you can opt to use the actual steps of the design process
to further develop your vision, but don't entirely rely on them to
bring about what you need and desire.

6. CHOICE BY ELIMINATION: You procrastinate, letting things go un-
attended until they become intolerable, and then you have no re-
course other than the one you could have chosen months earlier!

This approach only brings about frustration, and it begins to crip-
ple your creativity. Rather than calmly and clearly manifesting your
true desires, you finally act hastily, doing something, anything—to
change your surroundings. The end result reflects this, and is rarely

balanced or harmonious. But if you are aware of any tendencies you might have to rely on this choice-making option, you can avoid its negative effects.

7. **CONDITIONAL CHOICES:** You decide that before you can totally commit yourself to your inner vision, you must meet some arbitrarily chosen condition. You tell yourself that you'll create a home for your heart after you've saved up enough money, or completed your education, or worked out your marital problems.

In this case, you are setting up false cause/effect relationships, and endowing external circumstances with the power to bring you happiness, or keep you from it. It's usually the latter that tends to happen.

8. **CHOOSING ONLY WHAT SEEMS REASONABLE AND POSSIBLE:** You allow your self-limiting beliefs, fear of failure, and the like, to compromise your vision. You convince yourself to settle for what you think you can have, instead of going after what you want.

You see the end results of this sort of choice daily. It is one of the reasons you may not yet have a home for your heart!

As you can see, each of these decision-making methods can produce some level of results. They can even get you moving in the general direction of your heart's desires. But they, alone, will never take you all the way to your destination. They're strategies to use along the way. You can only get there by identifying outcomes that are clearly desirable for their own sake, and then consciously deciding to bring them about.

I felt it important to mention them, however, because one or more of these strategies is often exhibited by my clients and students, especially at the beginning phases of creating a home for their heart.

I would like to add several of my own choice-making options to the list, to provide you with even more alternatives, and concrete ways, to move past belief barriers or unproductive behavior.

- **BEGIN TO REPLACE NEGATIVE OR UNFULFILLING PATTERNS WITH DIFFERENT, MORE PRODUCTIVE ONES:** One way to achieve this, on a very basic level, is to do things you wouldn't ordinarily do, or change a small habit of your daily lifestyle. By making such changes, especially at times when you are feeling the urge to respond negatively about something, you can prove to yourself you can change or replace unproductive patterns.

For example, if you travel road A every morning at seven o'clock on your way to work, then for an entire week try an alternative route. If every morning you drink coffee and eat a bran muffin, then for a few days try tea and scones. If every Friday you tend to wear your blue suit, then wear your green one. Allow yourself to see that you can change, that you can break patterns in your life!

Changing behavior, even in small ways, challenges you to experiment and take a chance on yourself. When making changes in your home, take a chance on the new, the different, the unusual. If you don't have a green thumb then go out and buy a geranium, give it a prominent place in your home or office, and make a daily ritual out of tending to it. Make a frivolous purchase. Waste a half hour taking a bubble bath. If you're a creature of habit, alter your routine—and if that makes you nervous, then set a time limit and tell yourself that, if you want to, you can go back to your old behavior when the time is up.

But take the time to revel and play around in the new.

- CONSIDER THE POSSIBILITY THAT WHAT YOU BELIEVE MAY NOT BE TRUE: Look for evidence that refutes your self-limiting beliefs; search for examples from your own life which demonstrate, for instance, that you have acted spontaneously, or engaged in a new activity, without dangerous results.

- CALL UPON SUCCESSFUL TOOLS AND STRATEGIES YOU USED IN YOUR PAST: Make up a list of tools and resources material, emotional, spiritual, and physical that you have used in your past to overcome difficult turning points in your life. Then, determine if any of these can be used now to help you overcome present challenges.

- ACCEPT YOUR BELIEF BARRIERS AS A LEARNING EXPERIENCE, AND ACCEPT THEM FOR WHAT THEY HAVE MEANT TO YOU IN THE PAST: Before you move past, or rid yourself of barriers, you should also make lists of the ways they served you well in the past. Were they defenses? Did they help you get through a period of turmoil? There are positive aspects with even the seemingly most nonproductive patterns. Identify them so you can help yourself see them for what they are, before moving on. Replacing unfulfilling patterns or habits with new, more productive ones, often requires you to start thinking in different ways: to *courageously bring your self-limiting beliefs into conscious light and examine them.*

- MONITOR AND EDIT YOUR SPOKEN AND UNSPOKEN WORDS: You can actively catch yourself when you make self-deprecating statements and negative predictions about yourself and your home. Make a conscious effort to cut down on such comments and devote more time and attention to your good traits and to visualizing the good you want to bring into your life.

For example, let's say that every time you walk into the living room, you tend to focus only on the worn, outdated sofa and how much you despise it. Further, let's say that this response usually leads to an argument with your spouse, who you feel is not making enough money to help you pay for a new piece of furniture. You are obviously feeling frustration, and although it may be understandable, you may also realize that your spouse isn't entirely responsible. Just once, try to stop yourself from venting. Go into the kitchen and make two cups of herbal tea, then join your spouse on that old sofa and open the discussion with something nice that happened to you today. This is not easy, but it can be done. Eventually, you will automatically find yourself replacing negative outbursts with positive behavior, and this might tide you over until something really can be done about the problem at hand.

We will be exploring even more strategies for "cleaning house," both materially and mentally in chapter seven, but in the meantime, review all of the above alternatives and select at least one or two to help you move past the parts of your mind, body, and soul that are stopping you from becoming all you can be, or from creating all that you are capable of.

As you answer the questions and perform the self-exploration activities in this and other chapters of part one, you may not always like what you see—you may even be startled at what you see—*but the actual process of answering and thinking is as important as the finished product,* your dream home. At times, it is necessary to startle ourselves into reality. Inviting surprises can be a stimulating process. It expands our boundaries, exercises our minds, and helps us to grow.

It's worth the effort to delve into our inner feelings, because by being disconnected from them we miss out on the entire point of life. The process of learning life, and what we really appreciate, gives us power and can remain a continuing part of our lives. And what we don't appreciate, or no longer use mindfully, need not be part of our lives, or our daily environments.

We do have control over our living spaces. We should welcome the chance to make the changes we can, and to open up to the world inside us. Interior design, your process of life design, can be stimulating, and this stimulation often grows out of the element of surprise. We must get away from thoughts of what life should be, from what it was, from giving in to the yearning for more, and experience the wonder that arises when we see our yearnings become realities. You are not merely carving out a new living space for yourself, you are carving an environment which reflects a new lifestyle—a life different from the one you had before.

That does not mean that all your past beliefs, and all your old possessions, should be discarded. With life design, design of your sacred space, the secret is to hold onto only those things that still have meaning and purpose for you at this point in your life. You need not cast away everything from your past; your past is important, and you may have things that keep it alive for you. But there are probably other things that you can clear away to create space that will allow the new to live side by side with the old.

It would be best if you didn't wait, like I did, until you find it hard to function in your living space. Looking around, if you see clues that you are resisting changes, then try to begin taking action as soon as possible in whatever way you can. There's no need to wait for a trauma or an experiential "kick in the pants" to get you moving forward.

LEARNING TO SOAR

Back in March 1979, I came across a fascinating article in *The Wisdom Child,* which highlighted this connection between our inner attitudes and our external living spaces. In "Castle or Cavern," journalist Mary A. Huff quoted Jerome Kerner, a Manhattan-based architect and design consultant: "Our homes are more likely to reflect our limiting inner attitudes than our budgets . . . in order to change or improve the quality of our lives, which is in part, our homes, we must be able to identify the negative attitudes and begin to break old patterns of avoidance."

Eventually I took a class with Kerner, and realized that he (as did I) felt that if certain negative attitudes are brought to light, one can begin to design space more effectively from the inside out. Although this wasn't an entirely new concept it was through Kerner that I was able to learn several strategies to guide clients toward seeing their living spaces more objectively. Using his basic ideas as a foundation, I expanded upon them, and urged my own students to take a more objective look at themselves. I'd like to share one with you now. It is called the irrational floor plan.

This exercise is the third step toward overcoming belief barriers, and allows you to create a picture of your living space based on your uncensored vision of what it will eventually be. For many of my clients and students this is the most enjoyable exercise of all during the early stages of design.

In preparing you for this exercise, I want to stress that an irrational floor plan (pictured on page 62) is a sketch of your living space which is drawn from the way you *feel* about your space rather than from the way you *want it to look*. One purpose of the exercise is to allow you to view your space from the perspective of the child in you—that part of your psyche that has been suppressed, that part of you that is rarely given free reign. In doing so, you can view your space more objectively—unhindered by the subjective (often limiting) blocks of formal adulthood.

Irrational floor plans also enable you to view your surroundings in a fresh way, similar to the way you see them after you've been away from your home for a while. After a business trip or vacation, when we've been exposed to other environments, we often enter our home to find it looks different. For that brief moment, we are totally objective.

It is that type of objectivity, along with a feeling of pure creative and emotional freedom, that I'd like you to strive toward experiencing now.

To further enhance this feeling, I urge you to do the exercise with your non-dominant hand. I have found that when using the non-dominant hand, we can call on an entirely different level of unconscious creativity.

EXERCISE: DRAWING UP AN IRRATIONAL FLOOR PLAN

1. Take out a large sheet of paper (one that is sturdy) so that you can feel like a child again while you are drawing and not be concerned about things like running out of space, the paper tearing, or paint leaking through the paper onto your table.

2. Gather together pens, crayons, big or small markers, colorful paints, charcoal, or whatever other tools you feel will allow your creativity free reign.

3. Take a few minutes to sense your current living environment. Close your eyes and feel it: feel the constraints, the dullness, the emptiness. Think about the places where your spend a lot of your time: whether that is standing in front of your refrigerator; eating in bed by yourself; standing near or in the closet trying to find a belt or shoe; or sitting at your desk riffling through papers.

   Sense where the strongest focal points lie; where energy draws you in most (like a magnet). Notice the exact spots that seem to push you away, or those that tempt you to look away, or shy away from.

USING YOUR
ENERGY AND
STRENGTH TO
OVERCOME
BELIEF
BARRIERS

———

61

At this point these feelings are still in your head. You want to think hard, and be honest with your present feelings about your lifestyle and living space.

4. Now, I'd like you to choose one particular point in your space. Concentrate on that area and what it means to you. (If others are living with you and share your space, do not concern yourself with their points of view yet. Focus only on your feelings.)

5. You are ready to put pen to paper. Use your non-dominant hand and begin drawing. Keep in mind that your drawing does not have to be perfect. This is an experiment to allow yourself to feel like a kid again. You are unconcerned about what anyone else thinks about you or your drawing. You can portray your bed as a magic carpet or a narrow cot in a barren cell; your kitchen as the foyer of a fast-food restaurant if that is how you perceive it. Allow your imagination to run wild and create a portrait of your attitude toward your living space and of the subconscious forces that may be preventing you from changing it.

Sometimes it helps to begin by expressing the most emotional, focal points of your home; the space you identified in step four of this exercise. But wherever you begin, do so using a pen or pencil.

If you start out tentatively, don't be afraid to go over your drawing again to make it darker, more visible, more detailed. And do not fuss about scale and form here! The actual physical layout of your home need not have any relationship to your drawing. Continue drawing until all the areas of your home are represented on the paper. (If you leave things out, that is also meaningful.)

6. With your pen or pencil sketch in place, move on to your other tools (such as crayons) and choose colors that express how you feel about each room, or each area you've drawn. Fill in and accentuate places where a certain color helps you express how you feel about that area.

7. As you continue developing your irrational floor plan, also make sketches (on the side or in any other free space on the paper) of your family members, pets, garden, even the piles of clutter that are filling your living space. Simply let all of your feelings loose, and put them down on the paper. Allow them to spill out until there is nothing left in your unconscious concerning your feelings about your home.

8. When you have gotten it all out, look at your drawing carefully and allow your reactions to what you have created come to the surface. Allow your-

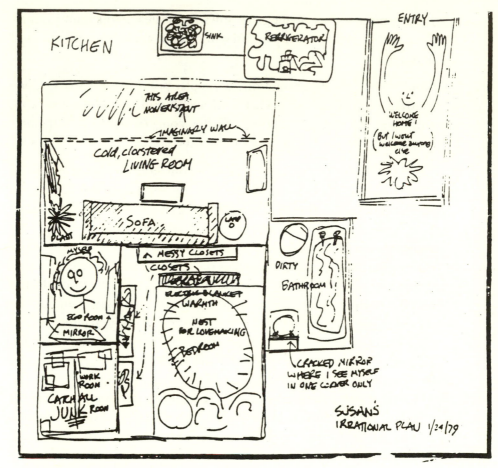

Example of a completed, irrational floor plan.

self to feel surprised, disenchanted, amused, disturbed, or saddened. Pay special attention to cherished images of yourself, or to familiar habits that you stand to lose, to self-deprecating perceptions of yourself, and to victim allusions (symbols of prisons, slavery, being held hostage).

What did you find that surprised you most?

9. Write all of these responses down in your journal (or on the back of the paper) so you do not forget them. Do not let these responses slip by, and do not allow them to slip back into your unconscious!

USING YOUR
ENERGY AND
STRENGTH TO
OVERCOME
BELIEF
BARRIERS

63

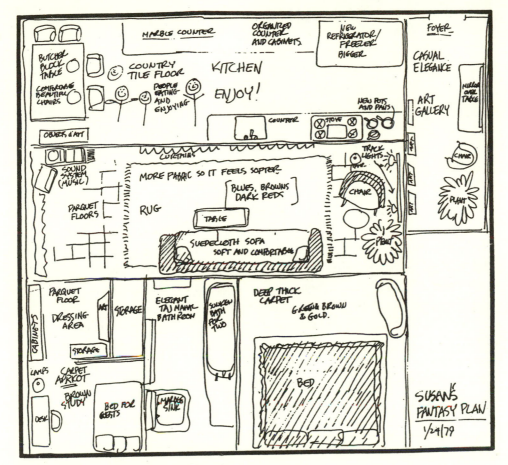

Example of a completed fantasy floor plan.

Exercise: DRAWING THE FANTASY/IDEAL FLOORPLAN

Now it is time to focus on your ideal, or fantasy, floor plan, which is quite different from the concept of the irrational floor plan.

In creating a fantasy plan, think about how your living space would look if you had no limitations. What if you had all the money, time, and space you could ever dream of? How would you use these resources?

What does your dream bedroom look like? Your dream bathroom? Dream kitchen? Using the same steps as before, draw a fantasy floor plan. (Before you do, you may want to look back at the notes you made while visiting your angel home.)

When you are finished sketching your fantasy plan don't forget to make notes about your responses to what you have created!

CONCLUSION

*"I will be likened to the rain drop which washes away the
mountains; the ant who devours a tiger; the star which
brightens the earth; the slave who builds a pyramid. I will
build my castle one brick at a time for I know that small
attempts, repeated, will complete any undertaking. I will
persist until I succeed."*

—OG MANDINO, *THE GREATEST SALESMAN IN THE WORLD*

With a renewed awareness and a visual floor plan of "me as I see me and my
surroundings," you will have begun to see how thoughts, beliefs, and attitudes
are as real as the ground beneath your feet, the food that nourishes your body,
the warmth of a campfire, or the sound of children laughing. Your thoughts
have form and substance. They are vehicles for energy, with the power to shape
our lives and to affect everyone and everything around us.

I've talked about barriers and drawbacks in this chapter, but I hope I've also
shown you the keys you need to realize your ideal home already lies inside you.
The barriers are internal, but so is a bounty of natural skills, knowledge, ingenuity, and resources for you to draw on, lying just beyond those barriers.

Someone once told me that due to the unique circumstances of my upbringing, I can now (in a metaphysical sense) "breathe under water and lead ex-
peditions to magical caves."

So, in guiding you toward reaching your treasure, your "magical cave," I urge
you to *bring positive energy and thought to yourself and your environment, as often and as
much as possible*. To bring in positive energies is like strengthening a new muscle!

And never forget all you already have, so that you can use both new and old
to create your future home for your heart, your personal sacred space.

The beauty surrounding us can remind us of who we are on the days we
forget.

Chapter Four

REDISCOVERING YOUR PERSONAL TASTE THROUGH THE THREE PHASES OF CREATION

"Every child is an artist. The problem is how to remain an artist after he grows up."

—PABLO PICASSO

What is taste? Where does it come from? How does someone know if he or she has it? Who decides if one's taste is good or not?

Generally speaking, "taste" should be defined as your ability to perceive certain things as pleasing to your senses and compatible with your own essence. The most important word in the previous sentence is "your," because when discussing taste, we are discussing an extremely personal matter: your fancies . . . your responses . . . your feelings . . . your unique sense of style. It is your innate preferences for particular colors, forms, textures, and objects in your home, and how you feel they should be combined, that adds up to form your unique, special sense of personal taste.

And "good taste" is already inside you.

It lies in the natural, creative, and artistic talents that you had as a child, and can recapture again!

In the Beginning

If you think back on your early years, you no doubt recall a preference for certain things: crisp apples rather than strained peas; cocoon-like corners of the living room over an open, airy porch; a soft cotton quilt over a scratchy wool blanket; or vice versa. By age four, you had a favorite color, whether that was purple or green or lemon yellow . . . and you had a favorite art medium, such as crayons, paint, or clay.

These preferences represented the first concrete decisions you were making about what was "tasteful." You already had a good sense of what pleased you, and instinctively knew when the vibrations of something outside yourself harmonized with your inside self. Even though our childhood homes were largely created for us, we usually found a special niche for ourselves and personalized it with things we loved to look at, be with, and touch. Unfortunately, as time went on, too many of us lost that natural preference. Or, worse, we began to call on others to determine what was right for us and our homes; to decide what constituted good taste; to make decisions for us about how best to personalize our space.

Virtually everyone can name a particular person who influenced their early aesthetic. As I already mentioned, my mother's aesthetics and tastes heavily influenced me. For you, it might have been your father, or a close relative, a neighbor, a high-school friend—even television. This influence certainly had its place in your development, but now, as an adult, you should feel free to define and experience your own aesthetic.

Another secret to creating a home for your heart is to forget, to a large extent, about what others have taught you, and begin to review your own early history . . . to reach deep inside your memory banks, in order to get back in touch with the creator you were (and still are). In doing so, you can rediscover the beauty within you, and in everything around you.

OUTSIDE INFLUENCES THAT SABOTAGE THE ARTIST WITHIN

With most of us, our early attempts to carve out a niche for ourselves in our homes and in our lives didn't attract much attention. "They're just kids, after all," laughed the powers that be. "Let them have their fun." In the earliest pre-kindergarten and elementary years, our childlike and natural creative talents were encouraged, and art was integrated into the daily curriculum. In kinder-garten, especially, we were urged to explore colors, to design our own versions of modern art, to finger paint, to express ourselves.

But then, as you got older, *something changed.* Suddenly, art was no longer a part of your daily curriculum but a special Friday event. You were urged to use pre-cut stencils and copy the art of others. Art was almost entirely cast aside in lieu of grammar and science. Art was extra. Your natural artistic flair was sud-denly being judged by "professional" standards. The talented children drew pic-tures that authority figures considered good—good representing the right way—the right way representing best.

Consider this scenario. One day you are drawing a lovely, expansive tree be-decked with giant purple and blue leaves, and being *praised* for your imagina-tion. The next day, it seems you get a great idea for another tree, and eagerly draw it. But you are told that your tree looks like purple broccoli. The child be-side you, who copies the shape and color of the brown and green elm from the teacher's board, is told that he/she is a good artist. You are not. You are acting contrary. At this point, you not only feel rejected and ashamed, but the pleasure you once derived from your art is suddenly shattered into a million pieces. *You are now simply the weird kid who draws those purple broccoli trees.*

This case scenario happens every day in America. Unlike most European and Eastern countries, which never let go of their art appreciation aspects of character-building, American children are forced into this transition in the second and third grades. Although I feel that we have much to learn from a country like Bali, where there isn't even a word for "art" because it is so indi-vidualized and special, it does not seem that the educational system will be changing anytime soon. In some school systems, in fact, the gifted and talented *art* programs are only open to those children who score high on standardized reading and math tests.

As a result, a mere one or two percent of our children are encouraged to ex-plore art, to continue doing art, to take art courses, or allowed entry into inno-vative art programs. When the remainder of the culture (the majority) reach adulthood, they are no longer comfortable with art, with their own aesthetic sense, or trust their own aesthetic. Further, the relatively small artistic community that survives the cut in the early years is later given all the aesthetic power in our culture. To a large degree, we are bulldozed into believing that their idea of what art is and isn't is the last word. The entire process is like fitting people into a constrained, framed, aesthetic square box, when in reality, a person may prefer a triangle or a rectangle, a circle or oval. And when, in reality, they *do* have deeply ingrained artistic senses and talents to contribute to society at large and to enrich their own daily lives.

By the time we reached our pre-teen years, we felt that we were being judged by everyone—our parents, our teachers, the neighbor down the street. We were told there were right and wrong (or nice and not-so-nice) ways to dress, eat, and play. We heard phrases such as "good" and "bad" taste, and learned that the deciding factor between the two was most often a societal decision—a decision being made by a society far removed from our own way of living. Still, it seemed logical that if "they" said it (and they knew more than us), "they" must be right.

Slowly but surely, many of us let go of the unconventional and chose to conform, while others among us completely bucked the system in an attempt to rebel. This period of rebellion often surfaces during adolescence.

But you can reclaim that wonderful, intrinsically motivated creativity of early childhood and use it to recover a balanced, harmonious relationship between your inner and outer self.

To return to one's childhood is not always an easy or comfortable task. Some of my clients relish their early memories, while others resist them and must be gently led back in time. Still others are surprised by what they remember, or to learn that many suppressed memories are now affecting their present tastes.

I recall one client in particular who used her rediscovered knowledge of her past to solve a present-day dilemma. Carol, a twenty-eight-year-old, recently married physical therapist, called me in a panic one week before she was scheduled to move into her newly purchased Victorian house. She felt totally overwhelmed at the thought of painting, carpeting, and furnishing this new, empty space. Carol was usually so in control of her life, especially her career decisions, that she was especially confused by her reaction. In looking back into her childhood and young adulthood, we found out why.

Carol was the daughter of a career military officer and had lived in ten different naval bases by age fifteen. The rooms her family occupied had been basically the same from state to state; even when her father was stationed on a particular base for a long time, her mother didn't make much of an effort to personalize or decorate the apartment. When Carol left for college she lived in already furnished dorms. Afterward, following a path blazed by her mother, she found a sense of "belonging" not in her home, but by becoming active in several organizations and with other, out of the home projects. When she became engaged to Ron, she moved into his fully decorated apartment. "Co-habitating was no big deal," Carol told me. "I simply transferred my stuff from one place that wasn't mine, to another place that wasn't mine."

When she and Ron married and purchased their own home, Carol realized that this time, she was moving into a place that was, in part, *hers*. "Now," said Carol, "I want this house to be a real home, a place to entertain and have kids and grow old in. I want my personal stamp on the home, along with my husband's. But I have no experience at all!"

Like Carol, you may have had few opportunities to explore or express your design preferences. Outside influences and pressures—everything from peer pressure to the belief barriers discussed in chapter three, could also contribute to your worries about decorating. Regardless of these past experiences, you still have the right and ability to live a creative life, to be your own designer. You arrived on this earth with needs, and a powerful desire to fulfill those needs. You arrived with your own personal essence and spirit, and can find ways to manifest it.

But how can you find that part of you again? You can begin right away by setting aside a few quiet moments of your day and allowing your mind to wander back to your early childhood.

Exercise: RECALLING MY EARLY CHILDHOOD HOMES

- What was the very first childhood home you remember living in?
- What were some of the sensory experiences you found pleasurable? For example, do you recall walking barefoot in the grass or watching fireflies light up in the evening? Do you remember watching a summer storm from your porch or the sensation of snow on your face while building a snowman?
- What types of make-believe environments did you create for yourself? How did you decorate these spaces?
- How did you feel in these places, especially as opposed to other areas of your home?
- What types of things did you carry around with you? (Security blankets, dolls, etc.) Did you carry these objects from home to home? Do you still have any of these objects?

- Which type of sensory experiences do you remember most and best? For example, do you recall your childhood in terms of things you touched? Saw? Heard? What were some of the smells? Colors?
- When you were relaxing on your childhood bed, what do you remember about the ceiling? The walls? Was there a particular wallpaper or piece of art you remember? Did it please you?
- What was the most important event that happened in your childhood home?
- Did you feel proud to have friends over?

You should record your answers to the above questions in your journal so you can use them later in personalizing your space. Whether your memories are vivid, vague, happy, or painful memory allows you to catch a glimpse of your lost internal aesthetic.

When Carol allowed herself to go back in time, she found it an exciting experience: "I'd forgotten about so many things," she chuckled. "Even though I thought I had no meaningful memories, I did! I began to visualize a certain wallpaper style I used to like looking at as a toddler, that I now want to find again. And I realized I already had a nostalgic collection of things: my old seashell collection, mementos from the various naval bases, and a tiny Christmas angel. Even though I moved around a lot, I had always placed them in a special spot in the apartment, *my own spot,* and arranged them the exact same way. Now, I can place them in my new home. I guess the key is to surround yourself with things you love and not worry about whether you're doing it right or not."

Carol realized she was a natural born designer when it came to pleasing herself. Still, even if you recapture your latent abilities and preferences, you may find yourself hesitant about taking the next step and buying furniture for your living room.

Why the doubt? It might be that you still don't completely trust your sense of style or believe you can trust your innate taste.

AN ARCHAEOLOGICAL EXPEDITION

Searching your past for clues to the sensory experiences you enjoyed as a child, along with reconnecting to your earliest memory of pure experimentation and creativity, are both important steps toward regaining your sense of style. Reflect on how you presently decorate your home, and how this has been influenced by the preferences and habits of people who shared your environment. For most of us, this means our parents, but it could mean some other guardian. By knowing which parts of your taste have been influenced by others, you can better decide which influences are right for you, at this point in your adult life, and which are better discarded.

No matter what your home looks like today, you can be assured it didn't get that way by accident. You personalize your space based on your character, which means, in great part, on ingrained habits that originated earlier in your life. You tend to avoid certain colors and things, or feel attracted to certain colors and things, because of their association with people, events, and experiences from your past.

Most of the time, however, we unconsciously re-create (or rebel against) influences from our early lives. There are people who wouldn't be caught dead wearing lace, or decorating with pastels and floral prints; those who can't seem to rest until every last dinner plate has been washed and put away; those who insist on placing the same brown couch against the same wall in every living room they inhabit; those who can't stand having a single thing out of place in the kitchen cabinet or utensil drawer.

The list is endless. We all have certain things we do a certain way, again and again, purely because that is the way we *learned* it should be. Sometimes, this behavior or preference works out fine. The only time it becomes a real problem is when you maintain habits and preferences that make you unhappy, that are contrary to what you really desire in a home.

Are you living the lifestyle you want and need? Or are you living by, and with, someone else's sense and standards?

If you suspect you are being unfavorably influenced by people in your past, it is important to get to the root of those influences, and face the *actual* impact they have on you now. Only by recognizing the hidden influences of your old, possibly obsolete images of home can you truly free yourself to decide what will constitute the true home for your heart.

You can use the following exercise to help you find out the answers to these and other questions about your past.

THE HOME METAPHOR MEDITATION AND EXERCISE

Get into a comfortable position, shut your eyes, and prepare to take a meditative journey into your past.

I want you to travel back in time to the first home you can remember. Where was it? What did it look like inside? Outside?

Visualize the front door, and then step inside. Now, begin in your mind to mentally tour it, moving slowly from room to room.

Notice the colors . . . objects . . . the overall atmosphere of the space. What activities do you recall doing in those spaces? What do you feel when you are in each space?

Walk toward your childhood bedroom and enter. Once inside, picture it in detail, visualizing the elements of it that you loved or hated or had little reaction to. Re-experience some of the things you did there.

If you moved around a lot during childhood, relive that experience as well. How did it feel to leave the place you'd called home up until that point? What were your initial impressions of your new home?

Travel, in your mind's eye, to every home in which you lived with your family. Call up images of good and not-so-good times, of conflicts, changes, or re-decorating projects that took place. Recall important milestones that took place in those places.

When you are ready, return to the present, open your eyes, and spend a half hour or so recording all you remember about your journey. Use sketches, key words, poetry—whatever you feel best expresses what you remember . . . what you felt . . . what you experienced.

After you complete the mental touring part of the Home Metaphor Meditation and Exercise, you can complete the following statements:

1. The region of the country I was raised in was _____

2. I would describe the socioeconomic class I grew up in as _____

3. The family members I lived with were (names, birth year, relationship to you) _____

4. The other people I lived with were (names, birth year, relationship to you) _____

5. Of all the people I grew up with, the one person I feel had the most influence on the home I lived in was _____ because _____

6. The person who made the most decorating decisions was _____

7. The most negative effect that (insert appropriate name) had on my childhood home was to _____

8. The most positive effect that (insert appropriate name) _____ had on my childhood home was to _____

9. Because there were _____ people living in my home, the space in that home felt _____

10. As a child, my first bedroom was decorated with _____

11. I remember purposefully decorating (personalizing) my bedroom space with _____

12. When I was in my bedroom, I felt _____

13. When interior decorating or any type of house maintenance was discussed in my home, it triggered the following types of emotions and events _____

14. The areas of my home I was allowed in as a child were _____ but only during special events was I allowed in _____

15. The way my childhood home reflected my mother's taste was _____

16. The way my childhood home reflected my father's taste was _____

17. The colors, styles, and atmospheres each person preferred were ___

18. My childhood home was sloppy _____, neat _____, cluttered _____ organized _____, other _____

19. My family felt it was important ____ (or) not important ____ to decorate based on the way other people or design professionals felt our home should be decorated.

20. I felt comfortable ____, uncomfortable ____ bringing my friends into my home because _____

21. Another home that had an effect on me when I visited belonged to _____. When I was there I felt _____ _____ and I wished I could have had _____ _____

in my home, just like they did.

FINDING THREADS TO OUR CHILDHOOD HOMES

As you work through this personal home history, you'll begin to notice threads connecting the homes of your childhood to the places you've lived in as an adult. For example, if your parents always purchased brand name appliances and refused to settle for anything less than top quality items, then you may have taken on this value system. If your mother was a neatnik, and drove you crazy with her meticulous cleaning habits, you may find yourself doing that with yourself and your own family. Or, if your childhood bedroom was always decorated in country Wedgewood blue with white, quilted spreads, you might find that same combination in your present bedroom! The way you set the kitchen table, the order you use to spice your foods during cooking, even the brand of window cleaner you use, may have become customs.

On the other hand, you may find you have an absolute obsession about ironing your clothes, and in looking back, recall your mother never ironed—something that embarrassed you as a child. Some of the most powerful, unseen forces in our lives are the result of forgotten vows to do anything but what our parents did.

The more you search for such connections, the more you will understand your present preferences. Therefore, I suggest you do the exercise of journeying back to your childhood home a few times (just as you should return to your angel home) until you develop a clear image of that subconscious part of your home life. When you are satisfied you have learned all you can, start making detailed lists of the things you automatically adopted, or rejected. Such lists might include:

- DECORATIVE ELEMENTS, such as choosing certain colors, arranging rooms in a particular way, or leaning toward one style of furniture.

- HABITUAL BEHAVIORS, such as thoroughly cleaning your apartment every Saturday morning (just as your mother did); creating messes because you were never allowed to do so as a child; or hoarding collections (and clutter) because you had little or nothing to call your own during childhood.

- ATTITUDINAL THROWBACKS, such as feeling it important to establish a happy mood during holiday meals, or finding that no holiday in your adult life has ever seemed as happy as your childhood times were.

Attitudinal throwbacks, in particular, exert powerful influences on our present-day lifestyles, our decorating decisions, and the types of priorities and values we ascribe to interior design, often reaching beyond the realm of habits into barriers.

While some of the threads that you unravel in your quest through the past are negative, there is much good to be found there as well! For example, when I realized my own inclination to move furniture around regularly was connected to my mother's penchant for yearly decoration, I uncovered one of my purely positive memories of time spent with her! I recalled sitting back with delight as decorators gave my mother advice, and then, when they left, being asked my opinion on colors and style—or joining her on a shopping spree. I felt important at those moments. I felt respected, acknowledged, and valuable.

On a deeper level, I now realize that as a young girl, I believed my mother had the best style. I wanted to have a style exactly like hers because I felt that if I had her sense of style, if I replicated her, then I would have her love also. If I acted like her, dressed like her, chose her favorite colors, then I would also get something I needed emotionally from her. On one level, it wasn't hard for me to replicate this style because I did appreciate her sense of elegance and gracefulness. But it did become confusing and frustrating when it came to actually expressing this grace. My mother liked things more formal, very French, and very antique, while I enjoyed things more whimsical and playful. But for a long time, I tried to replicate her anyway.

It didn't work according to my plan, though. When my emotional needs were not automatically satisfied, those needs started to manifest themselves in rebellion. I spent a good part of my adult life attempting to totally divorce myself (and my sense of style) from my mother's.

Later, when I was out of my rebellious stage and redecorating my New York apartment, I found myself thinking: "This is something my mother would like." Soon after I also realized that I *had* inherited my mother's sense of style. I was drawn to the same colors, the same fabrics, even the same contours of furniture. That awareness disturbed me at first, especially since I had worked hard to rebel against my original feelings and my upbringing.

But then I made a delightful discovery: Although I could select those things for myself, I did not *have* to choose them. I had endless options, and as an adult, I had the power to decide what I would and would not bring into my home.

You may have inherited a flair for decorating from your parents, an eye for color, for finding the perfect spot for a chair or sofa. Knowing and accepting such inherited skills can free you to explore, enhance, and consciously draw upon those qualities in ways you could not when you were unaware of them.

Uncovering hidden influences from your past that hold you back, or show up in your living space, gives you power to overcome those that are negative, and capitalize on the positive. You are then free to do, and be, what fulfills your unique, present-day needs and desires. The entire process can be tremendously liberating.

So, take the time to ask yourself: "Now that I'm a grown-up and in charge of my life, what would I rather do?" Revisit the place your soul calls home and consult your "I love" lists to help generate answers. In addition, make other lists of pleasant memories: the busy, sweet-smelling kitchen on a holiday; the big, overstuffed chair you used to crawl into on a rainy day; the sounds of music flowing through the home in the evening. Revel in these memories, and then see if you can re-create them in your present home, with your own family.

Most importantly, know that you are the true purveyor of "good taste" in your life. Know that you were born with natural creativity and can recover it, and always, always, trust your unique sense of style.

*U*SING WHAT YOU HAVE TO CREATE WHAT YOU WANT

"We contain within us all universal truths, all universal knowledge. Everything that is, is known to us. Our soul self has limitless capacity."

—MACHAELLE SMALL WRIGHT

By this time, if you have been doing all of the exercises and meditations I have suggested, you have a journal full of insights, full of visions, and full of ideas. You also realize that you have ready access to the lost part of your being that may have been stifled in childhood.

I also have a feeling that you are anxious to understand how all of this information can be combined to create your sacred space and help you begin living the life you have only previously dreamed about. How can you combine this information and apply it to your goal of living in your true home for your heart?

In this and the next two chapters, I am going to explain the three phases of creativity, and show you through example and inspiration how to understand and further identify your natural talents. You will soon be able to synthesize all you have learned about yourself, to pinpoint your own personal, evolving sense of style.

Some of you are on a creative high, so to speak, reading this book with enthusiasm and already being very productive. If you are one of these people, then much of what we are going to cover now may seem unnecessary, and you might be tempted to jump to part two of the book and begin the actual interior/life design process. Still, I suggest you continue reading, and continue the exercises. You may be surprised about what new insights you will uncover.

For the others among you who are still experiencing doubt or uncertainty, this might be because you think you have not created much lately, or have been feeling stifled. Well, there's a good chance that you're feeling blocked because you've been confusing artistry (or technical skills) with creativity.

Creativity is a process, a way of looking at the world and consciously choosing the results you want to see. Anything you produce with your own hands—a cheese soufflé, a floral arrangement, a term paper, or a pile of neatly folded bath towels, is a creation.

You may not picture yourself as a true artist. But you are!

When you accept this idea of yourself and lean into it, both the energy you put out into the world, and the energy you attract changes. That energy is then transformed into the material things you need to turn your ideas into realities. New opportunities come your way from this energy shift. At this point you are able to see them, and use them, to get what you sincerely desire and yearn for.

The best thing about all of this creative energy is that it doesn't run out. The more you use it, the more you'll have. In time, you will become what I call "creatively oriented." You will devote more energy and attention to what truly matters to you. You will live in accordance with your highest values, electing from moment to moment to be true to yourself and the direction in which you sense and envision your life going. No longer will you see yourself as a victim of circumstances. You'll recognize circumstances for what they are: starting points to help you grow.

Think of a sunflower seed. Better yet, find one, and hold it in the palm of your hand. Look at it carefully. Fold your fingers around it and feel its vibration. This tiny bit of nature contains the basic ingredients for growing into a sunflower as tall as you are! Under the proper conditions, it will be transformed into all it can be.

Now, picture yourself planting that seed and tending it. Give it fertilizer and water; pull the weeds from the area surrounding it to give it space and air. Even though you have no proof that your efforts will pay off, do it anyway. You can't see it, but that seed is growing, and because you are nurturing it, because you have faith in it, you continue to do what you can to help it grow.

Soon, the tiny seedling pushes through the soil. It grows taller, sprouts leaves, then a bud. The bud opens. The yellow sunflower petals unfurl. You can now see, touch, smell, even obtain nourishment from the end result of a process that began (and will begin again) with a tiny seed!

In *The Path of Least Resistance,* Robert Fritz divided this process into three distinct phases.

I have taken his structure and enhanced it here to enable you to better understand how all this relates to your home for your heart, or to anything else you really want to create!

First, you come up with an idea, and through thought and visualization, endow it with all the basic ingredients of the outcome you desire.

Second, acting on faith, you do what is necessary to bring about the results you want, even though no tangible results are yet in sight.

Third, as the fruits of your labor become apparent to your five senses, you complete the process by accepting the results as real, and by allowing yourself to fully appreciate and receive them.

When your dream is fully grown, you then work to keep the flower of your creation alive and healthy. You take good care of it by *allowing it to continue to grow and change* as your needs and desires change.

A CLOSER LOOK AT THE THREE PHASES OF CREATION

Every creation starts as a seed, a kernel of an idea, a flash of insight. It's usually accompanied by a great burst of energy which sets the process in motion.

For Claire, a fifty-three-year-old widow, that seed was a sudden impulse to turn a spare room into an artist's studio. "I'd always wanted to paint and sculpt," she told me, "but I'd never gotten around to it. My husband, raising children, cooking, cleaning, and volunteer work always seemed more important."

When I met Claire, her husband had recently died; her children were adults living on their own. She'd sold her house in the suburbs, made the family's former summer home her full-time residence, and decided that, "It was the perfect time to take art classes and try my hand at painting seascapes or throwing pots." Claire recalled that the notion first came to her when she'd walked into the spare room, saw the sun pouring in the skylight, and realized she could make that space into her dream studio. Brimming over with enthusiasm, she began to think about where to set up her easel and paints (which she didn't have yet) and how she would use an old cupboard as a storage area for art supplies. She imagined her Victorian lounge repositioned in the east corner of the room, which would allow her the best possible view of her outside garden during quiet moments.

For Claire, as for all of us, her new ideas took on a magical quality. Her seed was planted and its energy was already building, moving her to transform her space and her life.

Pondering possibilities that you've never before considered sends a rush of excitement coursing through your veins. If you allow yourself to go with this rush, any number of mental pictures will begin to take shape in your imagination. You mustn't stop there, however! You need more than creative impulse and a bevy of ideas. You must also have a coherent vision of what you hope to manifest in your surroundings.

$\mathcal{T}$HE INNER CRYSTALLIZATION OF NEW IDEAS

The clearer and more definite your vision, the clearer and more definite your completed creation will be. The inner crystallization of your vision of the result you want has the power to carry you past the ordinary, into the extraordinary. If you hold it in your heart and mind, it will, in time, become a part of you, and finally, your life—if you develop it in the right way.

For example, Claire's first major step was simply to dream about a warm, inviting, functional artist's studio. It then became equally important to begin working through the details. She had to take action, to delve deeper into her imagination for ways to expand upon those ideas. As I explained to Claire, if she didn't do this, wonderful ideas would continue racing through her mind for a while, but they would then begin to lose their luster. Her vision would eventually become less than satisfying, less than inspirational, without signs that it was attainable through incorporating specific details. Therefore, I suggested that Claire go to the store and gather up all the paint chips, catalogs of art supplies, and other studio accessories. Then, I told her to bring them home, lay them out all over her bed or floor, and just concentrate on them . . . meditate on them until ideas began to form in her mind. Ideas did indeed form, and soon she had an even more detailed image of her completed studio, even though not one piece of furniture was in place! The small steps she took had an enormous impact on Claire; she was able to truly visualize results and see it was all possible.

The process of a seedling growing into a fully developed flower takes time, but you already have an idea of what your sacred space should look like, and you can now expand upon it. All the notes you have generated, along with the pictures and scribblings you placed in your design journal, can now become part of this stage of phase one of creative development. It is time to refine your vision.

REFINING WHAT YOU HAVE ENVISIONED

With your creative process flowing freely, you can endow your vision with the basic ingredients you need to move you into the next phase of the creative process. In doing so, you will also develop your first tangible blueprint for your own personal style.

What you will do now is to bring forth and start blending the results of the activities, meditations, and exercises you have completed. Don't panic! This is not the stage of the creative process where you make final decisions. It's a time to become aware of connections and themes that have risen naturally in your design process. By taking steps along the way to organize what you already know and feel, the final stages of decorating will not only go faster, they will also find you focusing more on action than on sorting through piles of ideas.

So, take out the folders you have organized for each space or room you plan to redecorate and begin to look for tangible connections. Choose one of the folders and spread its contents across a table or floor area where you have plenty of room.

Look at the clippings, the photos, the notes you jotted down after your Angel Meditation and your journey back to your childhood home. Study the "I love" lists, gratitude list, irrational or fantasy floor plans, and all of the other lists you have completed.

Turn to the "evolving personal style" table at the end of this section; and refer back to your journal to help you answer the questions on the table. You should also start an entirely new page in your journal for listing any themes and similarities you find that are not listed in this table. Even if they are only remotely similar, the thoughts and design elements you've gathered should be clustered together as much as possible.

If, for instance, you find that the color green or mauve is predominate in your file or you continue to yearn for large spaces with lots of windows, then make a note of these things.

Some people use highlighters to help make this task easier. You can use different colors to indicate ideas or preferences that go together: For example, you might highlight in yellow any notes or references you made to creating an open, brightly furnished space, or highlight in blue any notes that indicate a preference for antique objects.

While you are doing this, set aside all thoughts of financial limitations or assumptions about what is practical. Simply reach out to what you have already envisioned, collected, and sensed, and look for any similarities in your preferences. Continue this process until you have matched up with each other all the elements you can. You'll probably also have some odd clippings or notes left over; put them aside for later.

RECORD OF MY EVOLVING PERSONAL STYLE

Date: _____

The colors I seem drawn to are _____

_____

Do I like bright colors or subdued colors? A blend of both? _____

The furniture styles I seem to like are those that _____

_____

The period(s) of furniture I prefer is (Victorian, Modern, etc.) _____

_____

The wall adornments that please me most are _____

_____

I seem to choose pictures or images of the following types of natural materials

_____

Of man-made materials _____

_____

I continually envision spaces that are open and airy, sheltered, etc. _____

The shapes and contours I prefer are _____

The textures I sense again and again in my visions are _____

The smells I repeatedly experience in my imagination are _____

The sounds I repeatedly experience in my imagination are _____

The things I know, for certain, that I do not want to be a part of my sacred space, are _____

My environmental concerns are (list them). The ways I feel they are influencing my development of my personal tastes are _____
_____

Address them by _____

If I had to summarize my overall personal taste at this point, I would say I prefer a look that promotes a feeling of _____

VISUALIZING THE RESULT

In front of you lie the first shoots of your sunflower seedling, in the form of thematic folders, your design journal, and your table of taste. This collection of papers and notes is tangible proof that you are on your way to making your vision into a reality. It is based on your inner self: You are now beginning to make it connect and merge with your outer self. You are making the transition between phases one and two of the creative process.

To strengthen your vision and bring it to flower, you need to re-envision it. This time though, you will guide your vision by incorporating into it the thematic styles and preferences you have chosen.

Close your eyes, relax, and picture the space or room you are designing. Visualize the colors that you seem to prefer, visualize the types of furniture you seem to prefer, visualize the space with the configuration that appeared in your fantasy floor plan.

Now use your other senses as well! Imagine yourself touching the wood of that chair . . . running your hands along a new, smooth kitchen counter top . . . positioning the drapes on your bedroom walls . . . fussing over the floral arrangement on the dining room table. And don't forget your sense of smell! Can you smell the bread baking in your new oven? The aroma of mixed potpourri in your bathroom? The odor of fresh paint in the hallways as you are putting the finishing touches on that hard-to-reach corner? Hear the birds singing outside your bay window . . . music playing softly as you test out the new carpeting in the recreation room . . . your children laughing as they play in their newly decorated bedroom.

Your sixth sense should now come into play to complete the experience. Experience the mood, the energy, the spirit of your new surroundings. Picture yourself already enjoying the results of your work, or entertaining the guests you would like to have in your home at a later date . . . allow yourself to feel the excitement, the drama, the satisfaction of being in a place you created!

Feel how you are capable of making your imaginings clear and tangible, and of manifesting any result you imagine. Believe that what you envision you can create.

As you embark upon these more detailed stages of your preparation, continue to visualize the results on a daily basis. After each visualization, get those folders out again. Continue to fine-tune, to look for new connections, to sensitize yourself to your unique, personal sense of taste and style. This process works as a steady affirmation that one day the home for your heart will really be a part of your daily life.

A COMMITMENT TO SELF AND TO YOUR VISION

You have envisioned and experienced the seeds and shoots of your creativity—now it is time to make a commitment to the flowering of your vision. That does not mean committing yourself to an exact chair or style of cabinet. It means committing yourself to the fact you are going to make concrete decisions about your preferences, and to believing that the home for the heart will one day be yours. You do that by consciously choosing to have, and to go after, whatever you visualized—even though the thought of commitment might sound a bit scary to you!

As you will learn in the following chapter, you can achieve this by acting as if it were already here!

Chapter Five

SOARING TOWARD YOUR SACRED SPACE: "ACTING AS IF . . ."

". . . open your heart, convey your intent and spirit will quickly work to communicate what it knows and you need."

—MACHAELLE SMALL WRIGHT

Grace, a thirty-year-old special education teacher living in Morris County, New Jersey, had moved back into her parents' home after going through a messy divorce. When she felt she had been at her parents' home too long, she began to visualize her own space. She pictured a carriage house with a stone exterior, a large, open living area, and two cozy bedrooms. Her dream dwelling had a "rustic, pioneer feel to it." Every night, before she went to sleep, Grace thought deeply about this as yet unfound place. She even started purchasing odd pieces of furniture and artwork to furnish the rooms. At the time, though Grace didn't realize it, she was experiencing the first phase of creation; nor did she realize when she naturally moved into the second phase:

"I arranged to take the big, rust-colored, sectional sofa my mother wanted to replace," she explained. "I bought a terrific brass headboard, packed my books, and sorted through boxes I hadn't opened in years, searching for accessories. Finally, all I needed was the place. People around me thought I was crazy as a loon, but I didn't care. I just acted as if it was a done deal. I was determined to find that house, and to be ready when it showed up!"

After a few months went by, and the realtor still didn't come up with anything even remotely similar to Grace's dream home, she began to wonder if she was indeed crazy. Maybe that dwelling didn't exist after all. Maybe she *was* fooling herself. Still, Grace didn't allow this temporary wave of self-doubt to get in her way. Instead, she went out and purchased flower seeds for the garden she was going to plant at her dream home.

Then one afternoon, Grace was forced to take a detour home from work. "That's when I saw it," she said. "*My* house, with a 'for rent' sign hanging on the mailbox. And there was someone I presumed was the landlord, walking out the front door with two prospective renters in tow."

Intrigued, Grace pulled into the driveway. She asked to be shown the home. It wasn't exactly what she had pictured, but it was very close. Even the color of the living room carpet matched the vision in her mind.

As it turned out, the two other people she saw didn't take the carriage house. But Grace did. "I immediately paid a security deposit and moved in within the week," she said with a satisfied smile.

Although not always so dramatic, what Grace experienced was the magic which evolves during the second phase of creation. Grace found almost exactly what she wanted first by envisioning it, and then, by having faith that it was forthcoming. Grace "acted as if . . ." it were already in her life.

Nourishing your vision

Soaring
toward your
sacred
space:
"acting as
if . . ."

———

87

In pursuing your sacred space, your home for your heart, a lot will be happening to you, but you won't always be able to see it happening! Like a seed germinating underground, or a baby gestating in its mother's womb, the end results of your creative efforts and all your imaginings will begin to take shape before they become visible to your eye, or even your consciousness. Many of your experiences during this phase will manifest through your *spiritual,* or *energetic* reality. This is often the least obvious reality, but it is extremely powerful.

In essence, phase two of the creative process is the growing season that brings the seed of your inner vision to its realization. It draws you steadily closer to turning your fantasy floorplan, your angel home, and all your other visions, into a tangible home for your heart. During this transition, your role isn't to make everything happen, but rather to clear the area, nurture the soil, and allow them to happen: to trust in the process, and trust yourself. I have coined the term "juicy spirituality" to describe this transition, this moment when your spirit and matter come together as an integration.

As I've already mentioned, this type of trust involves more than idle hoping and dreaming, wishing and waiting. Passivity can never bring about real or lasting change. Therefore, as you work through the more challenging moments of the "acting as if . . ." stage, you will need to call upon your blind faith for the energy you'll need to continue *until it does become visible.*

To accomplish this, you must positively embrace your vision. Nourish it, pay close attention to it, and believe that what you want is already out there. You will do exactly what you would do, if you knew, without a shadow of a doubt, that your dream was going to become a reality.

While guiding you through this second phase of creation, I will illustrate how you can better use, and balance, the three levels of realities we discussed in chapter two: *physical, perceptual, and spiritual.*

Most important of all, you will be encouraged to take as many preliminary steps as you can to support and nurture your creation, as it is taking form and to lean into it.

Magic magnets

Once you start taking action, the "magic magnets" you experienced during phase one will become even more powerful. This will enable you to attract the guidance and resources you need to manifest your inner vision. You will see opportunity when you least expect it, and notice that previously obstructed paths will be cleared. A colleague might suddenly be transferred to a distant branch office and decide to leave behind a leather sofa that would look terrific in your den. Your accountant may call and tell you to expect a larger tax refund, enabling you to purchase that new convection oven. A neighbor will hold a garage sale, offering a vintage four-poster at a drastically reduced price. Sometimes, you will be inexplicably drawn to objects, or feel an urge to re-explore a back room that you haven't used in years for anything but storage. When this happens, no how much the voice of reason tries to convince you not to, you should respond to that inexplicable desire to move a coffee table, to take a closer look at the armoire your Aunt Sophie is thinking of donating to a charity, or to begin clearing out that extra bedroom. Such actions will generate a momentum that will trigger other actions, and help your soar through to the third phase of creation, until you are actually receiving the results of your efforts. You may experience mixed feelings at this point. Part of you might want to stay where you are. But do keep choosing what you want. Say "yes" instead of "no," even if this seems to go against your usual or negative patterns.

Having faith doesn't mean that you will be totally freed of the responsibility of looking for opportunity, however. You must still pay attention to keep opportunity from passing you by. And all the while, you must strive to move past any unproductive thoughts, or any fear of uncertainty. Just like Grace, you'll need to continue the positive thinking path, no matter how far off or far-fetched the results you're looking for seem to be either to yourself, or to other people.

In Norman Vincent Peale's highly acclaimed a *Get Confident Living,* he discusses this connection between fear and faith: "How do we develop faith? . . . Affirm the positive thought. Faith, too (like fear), begins with a thin trickle across the mind. Repeated, it becomes habitual. It cuts deeply into the consciousness until finally, you have two basic channels of thoughts—one of fear, and one of faith. But fear can never defeat faith." Peale also says that eventually, the fear will dry up: "The faith thought overflows and becomes the deep, flowing, primary thought of the mind. Then every thought about your business, about your family, about the world, is touched by the thought of faith and comes up bright, resplendent, optimistic."

I have personally seen this magic of positive thinking and action work wonders, in my own life, and in the lives of my clients and students. Frequently, positive definitive action paves the way for spiritual and material miracles.

Whether they're as big as a carriage house or as small as the missing

Munchkin in your *Wizard of Oz* collection, as momentous as an unexpected inheritance, or as casual as striking up a conversation with a "color expert" at a party, the necessary elements for reaching what you envision will begin to show up, *if you believe they will.*

Inspiration to create a home for your heart, and to carry that inspiration through to fruition, begins with the step of inner seeing, of imagining interiors and exploring them with your mind's eye.

In essence, you are going to create the "what" in what you want by making it up, and then daring to picture yourself having it.

ACTING ON FAITH: HAVING THE COURAGE TO TAKE THE FIRST STEP

By "acting as if . . ." you will have a chance to take back some of the aesthetic control that has been taken away from you, or that you gave up, in the past. This phase is about your ability to align yourself *with yourself* and prove to yourself that you can count on yourself.

The actions you take here will also function as emotional and psychological reinforcements, or as spiritual replenishers. For example, let's say that you place a special "dream box" on your dresser, and you begin putting your pocket change in that box with the express goal of saving up for a home water spa. In doing so, you are not just taking a monetary step, you are taking an emotional and spiritual step. You are proving to yourself that you believe in your vision of having that spa in your home, even though it might take a long time before you will actually see it on your back patio, or before you are able to ease into the warm water of the spa after a long day at work. Now, if the others in your family feel that this spa is a frivolous idea, or insist that you will never be able to save enough money from your already strained budget, then naturally, you might experience second thoughts. But if you go ahead anyway, if you make the decision to stay in motion instead of giving up, then you are reinforcing your commitment to your dream. Your family might not understand that the spa represents luxury or comfort to you, and that to enjoy such comfort is important to who you want to be. But you know.

By continuing to save money in that dream box, by sorting through catalogs and choosing your ideal spa, you are "acting as if . . ." you will one day have it.

You are showing the courage of your convictions. The longer you continue on this path, the more your courage intensifies, the closer your dream is to being realized.

In simpler terms, if you maintain an attitude, behavior, and belief long enough, it will eventually become part of your reality.

SERENDIPITY: TAKING THE WINDING PATH

One of the most unusual and exciting side effects of "acting as if . . ." is that often, a seemingly simple task can lead to an entirely different approach. Or even to a completely new, but equally satisfying direction!

For Terry, a woman in her early fifties, the prospect of acting as if her vision was already achieved was both daunting and memorable.

I met Terry two years after she had inherited her parents' house, full of boxes and furniture she didn't know what to do with. Terry's inclination was to wait until she could think more clearly, so she had done nothing for twenty-nine months. She had her parents' furniture jammed in every available space (usually beside her own furniture, which she could no longer enjoy), with one room completely brimming over with boxes. She'd hung her mother's collection of artwork in the hallway, even though she really didn't like it. "I put it there so it would be in full view, and planned on having dealers in to see it, hopefully to take it off my hands," said Terry. "But I never invited a single dealer in to see the paintings!"

One day Terry realized she had to do something. She began with the artwork, purely because she couldn't stand it glaring down at her for another minute. She took down the paintings and brought them to a nearby dealer, who purchased them at a fair price. With some of the money she received, she went out and purchased a high quality latex paint for her hall. She then had the dark blue hall painted a soft rosy beige. Almost immediately after she took these steps, she noticed that she didn't rush down that hall anymore, and what's more, she was no longer rushing past the storage room that happened to be located off that hallway.

In fact, one morning she actually walked into the overflowing room, and carried one of her parents' boxes into a spare bedroom for sorting. Over the course of the next few months, she made frequent trips back to the storage room. Eventually, everything she had wanted to sort or sell was either in the back bedroom, awaiting her attention, or completely out of the house.

"Once it was out of that storage room and in the back bedroom, I didn't have to see it or think about it every time I went down that hallway. By getting myself started and moving one box, I immediately felt I was able to breathe better. I started to feel that there was hope. I could almost picture the room empty and ready to be redecorated. This thought of redecorating surprised me, because until that point I hadn't even thought about it. Suddenly I wanted to make this extra room into a giant walk-in closet, something I always dreamed of having in my home."

At this point, I urged Terry to do a fantasy floor plan for that room, as well as encouraging her to continue working. As Terry continued, she also realized that some of the furniture pieces her parents had left her weren't so bad. One piece in particular, a small, ornate dresser, was the perfect size for a walk-in closet. It was what she had envisioned in her fantasy floor plan, but as she told me, "It was something I thought I would have to buy, yet it was in my midst all along!"

Terry discovered the power of taking small, but continuous steps in pursuit of her goal. She also found that the steps she was taking were subconsciously related to her dream of having a walk-in closet. If she'd stopped to intellectualize every detail, or waited until she'd mustered up enough time to schedule dealers to see the artwork, she probably would have continued feeling paralyzed longer. As it happened, the process only took one more year.

I worked with Terry after she'd cleared the storage room and together we designed a closet suitable for a queen. Terry had plenty of space to hang her seasonal clothing, she used the small dresser for accessories, and we found a beautiful beveled antique stand-up mirror at a store in her area. Terry chose thick, luxurious white wool carpeting for the floor and used her extra wall space for a collection of antique hats. When we were finished, Terry could barely remember how skeptical and frustrated she'd felt in the beginning, but she understood the power of small actions and positive thinking.

Although, like Terry, your first inclination may be to wait until there is more time, more information, more skill, more whatever, the fact is that you'll probably never have every resource you need—at least not all at once. At some point, just be optimistic, dive in, and do something to set the process in motion.

If you cannot do everything you want to do all at once, you can manifest temporary solutions to keep you going. This way, you will be open and ready for opportunities when they do arise. Even simple changes, such as clearing away clutter, moving the furniture around, or purchasing a few carefully chosen home accessories, can nurture your spirit and motivate you to continue to "act as if . . ." Let's say that you long to have a beautiful, comfortable dining room, a place where you can invite your reading group over for lunch every week. The problem is that your present table is too small, and too worn for you to feel that it is even remotely acceptable. To make it worse, money will be tight for at least another two months. Well, what you can do is visualize the dining area of your dreams. Then go out and buy the exact type of table linen and dinnerware you want. Purchase lovely napkins to go along with the set. Then simply act as if the entire room were as lovely. Put away the paper plates you were using to serve your guests and use the new china. Dress up in a flowing silk pajama set and serve champagne with lunch. You would be surprised how this type of temporary solution, and your new behavior pattern, can alter your entire perspective on your dining room, and yourself!

THE CREATIVE BALANCING ACT

For some people, the "acting as if . . ." concept is not an easy one to grasp, especially since so many of us have been raised with a "prove it to me right away" attitude. The motivation to take on an inner vision and move ahead on faith is more naturally vested in some people, yet it involves actions that seem difficult or downright silly to others.

Maybe you are one of these people. If so, then you might resist the "acting on faith" theory because you fear you'll waste valuable time and energy to achieve something elusive at best, only to find out you didn't really want it at all. Or worse, you believe that you could never possibly have that item, or that lifestyle, or that type of personality. You further reason that, since you cannot see the total result with your five senses (at least in the beginning), you have no guarantee that it will be exactly what you want. Therefore, why should you even attempt to bring it about?

What you should really concern yourself with is not that the end result will be different from your original vision, but that without taking a risk and acting on faith you will never know what you truly want!

On the other side of the spectrum, there are those who embrace the blind faith approach to interior design with such an overabundance of enthusiasm that, in the end, they miss the mark. Say, for instance, that you're walking through a furniture showroom or antique shop, obsessed with the feeling that you just have to buy something new. In this case, your desire stems from a feeling of needing to buy, not from a desire to buy something specific, or even necessarily to enhance a particular room in your home. If you don't allow that feeling to be balanced by the logical part of you, you may end up making a disastrous purchase. So, you should use your feelings as only one barometer for decorating.

As you can see, there is a fine line between taking steady, thoughtful steps toward "acting as if . . ." and rushing headlong into a project without the leveling factor of patience to accompany you. It is important that your desires be valid and based on real needs. It is also important that the way you attempt to fulfill them is an outgrowth of careful consideration.

Creativity is part logic, part feeling, and part divine inspiration.

It's when all three of these components combine to form a balanced blend that you achieve the most harmony. If you lean too heavily toward the logical side of creating, for instance, you might get hung up on details, or on constantly demanding tangible proof that what you want to do will actually work. You run the risk of focusing on what couldn't possibly work, while missing out on countless opportunities that would.

In attaining a creative balance, it sometimes helps to have increased knowledge understanding of your right and left brain processes—the blend of your *natural* and *acquired* skills.

YOUR LEFT AND RIGHT BRAIN PROCESSES AT WORK

In focusing natural skills I am referring to intuition, the sixth sense, the understanding of what is not yet a tangible reality, and other skills we call on by using the right side of our brain. Some of us feel perfectly at ease with our right brain processes, and are well aware of their power. We rely upon and trust our intuition, allowing circumstances to unfold as they will, following our gut instincts as a matter of form.

Others, however, are left-brain dominant, meaning that they are more comfortable with processes that are logical, time-sequenced, and organized (linear). They like a concrete plan, a clear-cut road map to follow, just like a set of printed instructions for putting together a bird cage or prefabricated table. If you are one of these people, there is much to commend about organizational traits, but you must make certain that you also leave out a few pieces in your master plan so that there is room for growth and discovery.

All us need room to blend the powers of our right and left brains. Don't marry yourself to one method, one goal, one set of strategies. Different circumstances require different solutions, and changing circumstances require changing solutions. One key to turning your inner vision into an external reality lies in choosing to do what is necessary and appropriate to the task at hand—at any given moment.

Tapping into your emotional realities, for example, and looking at your surroundings based on how you feel, helps to keep in balance your purely logical, "prove it to me," side. This is especially vital if you are considering major, or costly, changes in your home or lifestyle.

The creative process, when experienced fully in all three of its phases, also challenges us to admit when we are not getting the results we want—if that time arrives. It allows for the fact that we might be wrong, and counsels us to willing to be wrong. You need to learn to feel comfortable with the process of not knowing, with the fact you might have a few wrong starts. This is not something to fear, but to accept. Accept it because it can be fixed.

You may discover halfway through your project that certain elements of your fantasy floor plan really don't suit you at all. You originally pictured a bedroom bedecked with furniture crafted of dark woods, accentuated with Regency period carvings. Then, as you are browsing through antique shops, you realize that a lighter wood or simpler style would fit the space better. Fine! At that point you have the option of abandoning, or altering, your original preference, but you probably wouldn't have purchased anything if you hadn't been searching to begin with!

ORGANIC DECISION MAKING

Given a comfortable balance between your logic and feelings, you can make better decisions. Your intuition will help you clearly envision the outcome that will serve the highest, most meaningful purpose in your life. This spiritual element of creation frees you from the limitations of both logic and feelings. It enables you to temporarily suspend disbelief, fear, and self-doubt. You can then find a true picture of your potential, and of the way your dream home, and your life, can be.

The activities and exercises you do along the way while creating a home for your heart, can ensure you, to a degree, that you are on the right path. Even though that path might be a winding road. Yes, certain things will change as you progress in your decorating project. Yes, you will experience growing pains. And no, as we discussed in chapter three, the actual design process itself is not perfect. But by going through the process, step-by-step, you allow your-self ample time to adapt or alter your strategies as your vision evolves.

Even with these assurances, you still might find yourself wondering how to make the most of the "acting as if . . ." phase of creativity, or wonder how you can learn to use both your right and left brain processes, and how you can maintain the creative balancing act.

One way is to view this as a relaxed, organic process that unfolds gently. Think through your decisions, keeping in mind all three levels of reality. After you have really looked at your goal (dream) on these levels, you can then con-fidently take steps to "act as if . . ." it were already here, without feeling nervous about making the wrong choice.

ℰXERCISE: MAKING DECISIONS BASED ON THE THREE LEVELS OF REALITY

The first thing I want you to do is write down the object you want to buy, your basic redecorating vision for a particular room in your home, or even the life-style you want to be living.

I want _____

_____

Now, I want you to complete as many of these sentences as you feel apply to this particular decision:

- MY PHYSICAL REALITY: If I get _____ it will affect my tangible, physical reality in the following ways:

  I will be able to touch _____

  I will be able to hear _____

  I will be able to smell _____

  I will be able to taste _____

  I will be able to see _____

  I will be able to feel _____

  I will be able to sense _____

- MY PERCEPTUAL REALITY: I want this because I believe my life will be different in the following ways _____

I have always dreamed of having this because _____
_____

* MY SPIRITUAL REALITY: I want this because I just know that if I
  have it I will _____

  My inner voice is telling me to get this, or that I need this because _____
  _____

Which of these realities is more important to you right now? Go back to your gratitude lists and your resource lists and see what you already have to achieve what you want. What are you willing to do, right now, to make this dream a reality? What can you do, right now, to "act as if . . ." this is already a reality?

Exercise: Creative Structure

After you have completed the decision-making statements, you can move on and take yet another step.

Review what you have just written. Now review your journal, from start to finish, then look carefully around your living space.

Identify specific actions that could bring it closer to the space you want it to be. Don't view these actions as drudgery, or as punishment for having neglected your surroundings. Instead, think of them as proof of your love for yourself and those around you.

You might want to start by simply dusting your furniture. By repairing a window sash, cleaning a musty carpet, airing out a blanket. Whether you envision a large or small task, that task will be a confirmation, an act of faith, showing that you are committed to improving your home life.

Now, make an organized list of these actions. Begin each action with the words: "I can . . ."

From that list, make another. This time, identify things you can reasonably do in that space within the next three months. Now, from that three-month list, pick one or two actions you can achieve within the coming month.

When you are done with this part of the exercise, you will have developed a structural foundation to express your creativity. After you have finished, allow yourself to savor the sense of energy, freedom, and accomplishment you get from the momentum you've created.

As you complete your tasks, check them off your list. Continue this process and soon, "acting as if . . ." will no longer seem like an elusive goal. It will become a part of your everyday existence. By trusting your intuition and knowledge of yourself and your surroundings, and then coupling that with action, you will fly through phase two of the creativity process.

It is this type of careful, organic decision making that will help you gain confidence during the "acting as if . . ." phase of the creative process. This way, you can be assured that what you see in your inner vision is not arbitrary, because *your heartfelt desires aren't arbitrary.* They are aspects of your truest being, aspects which you are admitting into your consciousness and choosing to bring into the world.

Having the courage to explore your vision, to admit to yourself what you really want, and then dare to picture yourself having it, is an accomplishment in and of itself! And even occasional diversions in judgment are part of the learning aspects of your journey. The trick is to remain flexible and open.

Here are six more things you can do to make certain you remain on the right path to your dream.

- Say, "I want this or something like it in my life; I choose to have it." Know that you are going after a dream, but also realize it will continue to develop along the way.
- Set timelines for yourself, but not necessarily deadlines. Leave room within your schedule for exploring and reaffirming what you want along the way.
- Ask for help; but when asking for help, keep in mind that you are the true arbiter of taste in your life, and home.
- Leave yourself quiet moments, when you are not actively pursuing. Listen and pay attention to what you are shown.
- Leave yourself open to seize opportunities.
- If you encounter changes or alterations in your vision, make note of these changes in your journal or alter your floor plans accordingly.
- Pay attention to the information that you find in your heart and mind, and write that information down so that you can act on it at the most appropriate time.

Most of all, keep the energy moving!

"ACTING AS IF . . ."
IN YOUR EVERYDAY
LIFE

So far in this chapter, I have been discussing the "acting as if . . ." concept in direct relation to your home, your spatial environment. But that is not where the creation strategy begins, or ends! In designing a home for your heart, we are talking about a *cyclical process.* We are talking about life design, and this extends to your personality, your dress, even your speaking patterns. Remember our discussion in chapter two about human, spiritual energy and its connection to the power of objects? As you change your environment, your personality and lifestyle changes, too.

If your goal, for example, is to be more financially affluent, then your environment will change you begin to attain that goal. If you decide to do away with the more material side of life, and enter a more spiritual realm, your environment will reflect that as well. As a matter of fact, I often counsel people to "act as if . . ." in their everyday lives, while they are making spatial or object changes in their home.

If your ultimate goal is to make your home more of a soothing haven, but you don't yet have all the resources you need to purchase certain objects or to make architectural changes to effect this transition, then start by "acting as if . . ." in your everyday life. Think soothing. Once a week, take a long, relaxing bubble bath instead of a fast shower. Play calming music and light candles scented with aromas that make you feel calm. On the other hand, if you long for a dramatic, fun, upbeat home, then change your habits and behavior to reflect this change as well. Play pulsating music while you're cooking, start wearing clothes you feel reflect the mood you want to create in your home. Become that wild or soothing person. "Act as if . . ." you are already there! The everyday part of you is what you already have to work with. Sometimes, these small but important changes in your personality and behavior can lead you to your ultimate goal.

I knew a woman named Kristen, a talented fun-loving journalist who had a dream of becoming a bestselling author. In Kristen's mind, there was a great distinction between journalist and author. She respected both types of writing, but saw authorship as her ultimate goal. By the time I met her, Kristen had already published numerous articles and short stories, but she was ready for "the book." Kristen longed to be recognized for her creativity. She also longed for the public attention, the book signings, the media appearances, the acclaim—all traits that she felt were perfectly natural extensions of her Scorpio sun, Leo rising personality.

Not one to procrastinate, Kristen set a deadline for completion and started on her great American novel.

While she was engaged in this task, she also happened to join a regional writing group. After the very first meeting, which featured presentations by some of the published big-name novelists in that group, Kristen realized that these authors emitted a certain aura, a certain feeling of confidence and accomplishment. They exuded this in the way they talked, the way they dressed, even the way they postured in front of the audience.

From that moment on, Kristen decided she was going to "act as if . . ." she were already a published novelist. She was convinced that this would help her achieve her goal. She dressed in business attire, she straightened her posture, she even took a mini public speaking course. She didn't lie about her present status, but she did accentuate, and discuss, her journalism credentials, whenever someone asked "what she'd done."

The day finally arrived that Kristen published her book. As was customary, she received congratulatory flowers at the meeting following her acceptance by a publisher. When she rose to accept these flowers, several people protested: "But she's already a published author! Why is she getting flowers again?" The fact of the matter is, that Kristen had "acted as if . . ." so adeptly, that most of the group just assumed she was a novelist. They treated her like a novelist. They accepted her in this role. And this attitude was responsible, in part, for getting her book published as well.

So, you can see through Kristen's experience, how the "acting as if . . ." concept can be transferred to virtually every area of your life.

Another example of this concept in action can be found in an entirely different realm: the inner city, and with much younger players, financially disadvantaged teens. There is man named John W. Downs of New Jersey, who operates Venture & Venture, Inc., a human skills training center. Downs has developed a unique, trademarked "casting process" which he and his staff use to help inner city youth overcome seemingly insurmountable barriers to become the person they truly want to be. His system, called Attitudinal Experiential Training™ (AET) has worked wonders with youth and adults across America. Although the actual training process is quite complicated, I want to highlight part of it to illustrate the power of "acting as if . . ."

When Downs brings in a new group of young adults for supplemental training (students who have, for all means and purposes, been deemed unemployable or at-risk by the traditional educational institutions), the first thing he asks is: "What is your name and what does it mean to you?" The second question is: "What do you want it to mean *in the future?*" The answer to the second question then becomes the ultimate employment or life goal these students strive

SOARING TOWARD YOUR SACRED SPACE: "ACTING AS IF . . ."

99

DESIGNING A
HOME FOR
YOUR HEART
FROM THE
INSIDE OUT

100

toward during the training, and often, throughout their lives. But what makes this process so special, and so unique, is that Downs guides students toward acting out their chosen roles in class.

One sixteen-year-old, named Joseph, said his dream was to become a "big-time executive" for a blue-chip company. Once this goal was stated and written down in a personal contract, Joseph was then assigned the task of researching the way executives act. So, with the assistance of Venture & Venture guide/counselors, Joseph headed out to the library. He looked through business magazines, he studied the types of careerwear men wore in *GQ*, he even interviewed local business executives. He returned to the training one week later (the training was conducted in a businesslike setting, complete with a conference table) and gave a complete report of his findings. His next assignment was to take a field trip to the local thrift shop and purchase a suit. (He was compensated for this expense.)

From that time on, Joseph was expected to dress as an executive, to do away with his slang, to act the role as best as he could. The amazing thing about Joseph's metamorphosis was the speed at which he started to evolve. It took less than sixty days for Joseph to start becoming this polished executive-type. He was expected to act a certain way, he was given total support in this quest, and, as a result, he did achieve a startling behavior change—one that impacted on the way he inter-related to his fellow trainees, his teachers, and his family. He graduated from the Venture & Venture program in the spring, with a certificate stating that he was "a professionalized, job-ready worker."

Joseph landed a part-time job as a mail courier for a corporate firm in his area the summer after he completed Venture & Venture's program. And I have no doubt at all, that one day Joseph will reach his ultimate goal!

As you are working through this second phase of creation, I cannot stress enough that when it comes to creativity, in your life or in your home, there are no wrong answers and no wrong solutions. Whether positive or negative, clear or presently incomprehensible, moving quickly or at a snail's pace, whatever is happening at any given moment is right, as long as it feels right to you.

You may not like where you are at times, you may not always see the benefit you're getting from whatever isn't occurring (or is changing), but the process is working, and will continue to work, if you continue to "act as if . . ." And "act as if . . ." based on an organic decision-making process.

The universe is infinite in its abundance. It runs on its own timetable, and you will get what you need and genuinely desire if you actively cultivate patience and faith.

Even while you are still developing this faith, "act as if . . ." you already have that too! Commit yourself to your choices again and again. Acknowledge the obstacles that appear in front of you. Say, "I'm doubting myself and having trouble trusting the process right now, but I am willing to resolve the problem and move on."

Realize that you are entering unknown, previously unexplored territory, and that to do so is frightening. *But do it anyway!*

Test the waters. Experiment. Pay attention. Soon, you'll see more and more of the beauty within and all around you. "Imperfection" can often be the very path you need to lead you to satisfaction. So, be willing to take alternative courses of action to bring about the results you desire. And always, always, respect your unique, changing style.

And if, as you are en route to your quest, you find that you, or those around you, still seem skeptical, then you should repeat this affirmation:

An Affirmation

I am not just merely wishing for this to happen. I am thinking it into the realm of possibility by infusing it with power sources: *positive feelings, energy, and intentionality.*

Chapter Six

RECEIVING THE RESULTS

"One of life's most fulfilling moments occurs in that split second when the familiar is suddenly transformed into the dazzling aura of the profoundly new."

—EDWARD B. LINDAMAN, *THINKING IN THE FUTURE TENSE*

You can make your heart's desire become a reality only after you have admitted this desire to yourself. Once you do, you must then accept it as something that is *yours to keep* for as long as you want it. That is the essence of the third phase of creation, "receiving the results."

For many, this can be the most exciting and personally satisfying phase of all. If you are one of these people, then you

DESIGNING A
HOME FOR
YOUR HEART
FROM THE
INSIDE OUT

———

104

also know that this is the moment you've been waiting for. After all, you've been envisioning your desired results for a substantial length of time. You have affirmed that you really want it, and you have "acted as if . . ." it were already there by taking preliminary steps to bring it into tangible form. So, when it finally arrives, you open your heart and freely, unabashedly receive. You plunge right in and revel in your efforts, happily enjoying and using all you have created.

I have been with numerous clients as they were positioning the last, framed painting on the wall; applying the final brush stroke to a refurbished antique; or tapping the last tack into a lush new living room carpet. I've seen them actually dance with glee, celebrate their accomplishment with a toast, or rush right in to prepare a lavish meal in their new kitchen. Such people are comfortable with the results of their efforts, and visibly grateful for them.

Yet, for others, receiving the results isn't an easy task at all. Not everyone is adept at graciously accepting the good that life has to offer. It's a challenging, confusing, even frightening experience. Generally speaking, most of us are more used to dreaming of and striving for our goals, and more comfortable dealing with the obstacles that arise along the way, than we are to having achieved them! Because of this, when the magic moment finally arrives, so does apprehension.

People usually exhibit this kind of apprehension during the transitional stage, right before they embark on phase three. Let's say that you have only one more thing to do before your vision is achieved: for instance, you have to buy and apply paint to one more room or bring a new sofa into the otherwise fully decorated living room. You might simply need to plant the last rose in your beautifully landscaped flower garden. But instead of performing that task, you panic and stop the process, as if you were afraid of finishing the job.

We've all seen this type of behavior, or at least heard about it. How many manuscripts of the great American novel are lying in drawers, awaiting the last chapter? How many completed novels are waiting to be sent to the publisher's desk? How many oil paintings are stacked in attics, missing a few, final brush strokes that would make them complete? How many lyrics are short of the last line . . . photo albums missing pictures of the final year of an offspring's childhood . . . mail order catalogue forms completely filled out and placed in an envelope that is never mailed?

In other cases, you may experience a strong, negative, emotional reaction at the actual moment of completion. With the vision already realized, there in tangible form, you may suddenly feel angry or discontented with the results. You *thought* you really wanted this. You worked for it, but now that it is here, you decide that maybe it wasn't what you wanted at all. You begin to second-guess your earlier decision, wondering what if you had picked a different color wallpaper for the bathroom, or a better quality of carpeting for the mud room, or a brighter curtain in the kitchen. Suddenly, you are dissatisfied. Or you want more. Or you begin to downgrade and doubt your instincts.

What is happening here?

What is happening, in part, is that some of the belief barriers that we discussed in chapter three can come back to haunt you during the third phase of the creative process. In order to bring your ideas to fruition, to manifest your entire vision and complete your design project, you might be called upon again to let go emotionally. Fortunately, this bout with belief barriers is usually much less powerful the second time. Actually, I have found that getting past this hurdle, and getting back on track, most often requires you to reaffirm to yourself— what you have already done. In doing so, you also return to the right and best frame of mind for receiving: the positive state of mind!

Just like a Broadway actor who feels butterflies right before going on stage, you too can learn to move beyond your last minute doubts and emotional butterflies, and give a memorable performance to get the applause and recognition you deserve, that you have worked long and hard for. And just like that actor, you may need to quietly run through the lines you already know, and contemplate what you have already achieved, before you step on stage for what just might be the greatest performance (accomplishment) of your life.

I feel it important to stress that feelings of anxiousness are common when making the transition from phase two to phase three of the creative process. Like labor during childbirth, our experiences immediately prior to the big moment are strenuous, even scary. Mothers-to-be are often so anxious at that point that they wish they could just turn back the clock to nine months before, so they could undo what they started and avoid having to deal with the next step at all! But the natural birth process continues, of course, and as soon as the baby is born, euphoria replaces anxiety. The reality which began as a seedling takes on a life of its own!

Remember, too, that it is all a matter of positive thinking and of being in the right frame of mind. When you approach creation with your mind and emotions in a quietly confident, calmly expectant, unhurried, unworried way, you will be able to embrace your metamorphosis.

DESIGNING A
HOME FOR
YOUR HEART
FROM THE
INSIDE OUT

———

106

SELF-UNDERSTANDING AND SELF-AFFIRMATION

*"Today we learn a lesson which can save you more delay
and needless misery than you can possibly imagine.
It is this:
You make what you defend against, and by
Your own defense against it,
it is real and inescapable. Lay down your arms,
And only then do you perceive it false."*

—EXCERPT FROM *A GIFT OF PEACE*,
"RELEASING JUDGMENT AND DEFENSE"

In preparing yourself to receive, one of the most important things you can do for yourself is to keep any feelings of apprehension in the proper perspective. Do not allow them to take over, to overpower you. You are stronger than these feelings!

Accept the fact that these are probably temporary feelings and you can help keep them in perspective by first, understanding them: *Where are they coming from?*

Possibly, you are relating the notion of the process being completed either to *responsibility* or *vulnerability*. Now that the dining room is actually completed, you know in your heart that it's time to follow through on those previously made promises to entertain frequently. Or, to have the giant family holiday dinner at your home, or to maintain that beautiful space so it doesn't get ruined. You may find these to be daunting realizations. You fear success because of the consequences, even though you have been working toward this outcome all along. And even though these consequences will surely be wonderful!

Further, since the redesigned space you have cultivated is a reflection of your inner self, you might suddenly start resisting the step of actually showing this space to others, fearful of exposing your inner self.

But if you really think about it, although it may seem easier to conceal your true internal self, to hide it from the world rather than have your self out and exposed, it is actually the *most freeing experience of all.*

The reasons why people respond in a negative way once they've accomplished what they set out to do are complex and varied. The truly important goal here is to learn how to enjoy the moment that your reality comes alive, to learn the importance and pleasure of gracious acceptance.

Therefore, if you feel you resist results, or even success, yet you truly long to embrace and fully accept the fruits of your labor, *then your limited frame of reference will need to change.*

You must change your self-image to fit in with your new, more balanced and harmonious surroundings. You need to realize, yet again, that you are deserving, that what you have created is not a foreign element in your spiritual, emotional, or physical self. It is a part of you.

To do this, begin by reviewing your journal. Look, really look, at all you have accomplished so far! Review your clipping journal, your floor plans, your personal style sheets. Take another trip to your angel home. Try to regain the enthusiasm and excitement of discovery that you experienced before, and let this carry you through. Be proud of the fact that you have reached this point in the process! At the beginning, you might have thought the exercises you were completing were difficult too, but you did them. You got through that barrier and you can get through this one. Reward yourself in some way—celebrate it.

PRACTICING HOW TO RECEIVE

Receiving with gracious acceptance is a learned, human skill. Some of us learn this skill earlier, or easier than others, but we can all learn how to receive. What exactly is it about this skill that makes you feel uncomfortable? It might be that you simply need more practice. But before you start practicing, I suggest that you define what receiving really means to you, in your life.

What is receiving, really? What does it mean to you? Is it a chance to accept something that is offered to you? Is it your ability to partake in what you want and deserve? Is it your ability to allow something or someone to enter your life?

Receiving doesn't always involve objects and things. Receiving also means taking in all that is around you that you love—your family, your friends, your environment. It is the act of giving yourself permission to enjoy. Whatever receiving means to you, it often helps to break it down into simple terms. Write down your reflections and your answers in your journal. Then, I suggest taking the following steps to work past the strongest feelings of resistance you are experiencing:

- FURTHER EXPLORE AND DISCOVER WHAT IS PERSONALLY IMPORTANT, NECESSARY, AND NOURISHING TO YOU: Take opportunities to fully activate, and fully enjoy, your physical senses. Observe forms and textures, listen to the sounds of natural settings, revel in the

DESIGNING A
HOME FOR
YOUR HEART
FROM THE
INSIDE OUT

108

aromas of nature, or your kitchen on baking day. Go for walks in the woods, along the ocean, or on the banks of a river. Drive through the country to watch the change of seasons. Stop and really notice the things you usually take for granted: the patterns of icicles or cloud formations, the beauty of a neighbor's lavish garden—or even of her simple hedgerow. Visit your local florist and ask about the various types of flowers in season, then purchase some to enjoy when you return home. Develop an appreciation and affinity for man-made objects as well. Collect fabric swatches and color samples. Make drawings and add to your clippings and photo files, all the while envisioning the objects and styles you already like, or want to have, in your home.

- **GIVE YOURSELF CHANCES TO EXPERIENCE AND TRUST THE PROCESS OF BECOMING:** Rearrange a few pieces of furniture. Place items that usually stay out away in a drawer. Display new ones. Reverse your sofa cushions. Move your area rug. Try something new every day. Experiment with almost everything in your life. Give yourself permission to leave it in the new way—even if you've been living with it in the old way for decades.

- **THE ART OF PLAYING:** Play with things you're thinking of bringing into your home. Introduce colors and textures by tacking fabric swatches to a wall, or painting one section of an area in a new color. Update items you already own. Put a lacy doily on a beat-up antique or a colorful throw on an old chair. Use scratch polish on your slightly damaged cabinets. If you have a collection of dolls, games, or other such collectibles, play with them for a while: Enjoy what you have, and remember why you started collecting them to begin with.

- **ENJOY YOUR PRESENT SPACE:** Actively accept and receive the things you already like about your present space and life. If you haven't had people over for a while, throw a small party. If you are nervous about purchasing an entirely new kitchen set, then at least try preparing a new recipe, using ingredients that are already in your kitchen. If you always work on Saturdays, then stay in your pajamas and watch television for a change. Enjoy the solace that can be found in any special space in your home, and take time to daydream about what you will do when you are ready to receive the new in your space.

- **TREAT YOURSELF:** Go out and buy that bottle of perfume you've been wanting, get a massage, or take a one-day vacation. Choose a gift for yourself and actually get it. Once you have it, sit back and revel in

the wonderful feelings that treat gives you. Practice receiving and accepting in small ways, become comfortable with the act of receiving.
Step by step, work up to the larger things you long for. In this way, you
can become accustomed to receiving at your own pace, in your own
way. Just keep reminding yourself that by bringing beautiful things into
your home, for yourself or your loved ones, you will be able to achieve
a sense of balance and harmony that will enhance your spiritual development, not detract from it. Know that everyone in your home will
benefit from those changes as well!

A TIME FOR GRACIOUS ACCEPTANCE

After you have completed the steps above and further defined your meaning of
receiving, there's a good chance that you will begin to feel better about the entire process.

I also suggest that you remain open to the possibility that at least part of the
reason for your resistance is that you haven't given yourself enough time to adjust to your new surroundings, your new objects, your new thought processes,
your new lifestyle, whatever it is you are trying to receive! Mixed feelings that
manifest themselves at the moment of truth are sometimes really reactions of
alarm at the new. Humans are creatures of habit. *If you give yourself time to adjust,
many of these feelings will disappear.*

As you are taking this needed time, also continue to cultivate encouraging
thoughts. Saying or thinking "I won't" (get what I want, ever be happy, find what
I'm looking for), or "I can't" (get organized, get a beautiful home, create a positive energy pattern) is not productive. Neither is "I shouldn't," which usually
translates into last minute cries of: "I shouldn't spend all this money; I shouldn't
indulge myself so; I shouldn't even begin to think I deserve all of this."

But you should. And you *do* deserve it. You have worked for this. You can use
whatever types of affirmations you choose to return to the frame of mind you
were in during the first stage of the creative process. "You must learn to change
your mind about your mind," reads the *Gift of Peace: Selections from a Course in
Miracles.* "Only the mind can value, and only the mind decides on what it
would receive and give. And every gift it offers depends on what it wants."

You know what you want in your heart of hearts. You have written it down
and made decisions about it . . . you have called upon your natural artistic sense
to visualize it . . . now is the time to embrace it.

DESIGNING A
HOME FOR
YOUR HEART
FROM THE
INSIDE OUT

110

You need not postpone your joy any longer.

I am reminded here of Eve, a woman who experienced (and then success-fully overcame) a deep-rooted feeling that she did not deserve the bounty in life she was offered. Eve was a commercial artist, specializing in layouts for various lines of perfume and jewelry. At forty-eight, she was soft-spoken, with a gen-teel personality and a vivid imagination. A Piscean native, Eve was the kind of person that everyone liked; she had a soothing quality about her that put oth-ers immediately at ease.

One summer, during a mutual colleague's garden party outside of Stamford, Connecticut, Eve met Charles. Charles was a multimillionaire bachelor, an en-ergetic, fifty-five-year-old entrepreneur who had transferred his uncanny nose for scents into a highly successful fragrance empire.

They immediately fell in love. Although they were from extremely diverse worlds, they shared many similar interests, including running, classic movies, and reading. In many ways, it appeared to be the ideal storybook romance. They were married within six months and Eve moved out of her tiny one bedroom in Hartford into Charles' expansive estate in southern Connecticut.

That's when the trouble started.

Charles told Eve to decorate the estate in any style she desired. Aside from his library, he was eager to see Eve's stamp on the home, and he wanted to give her everything and anything she had ever wanted. His only requirement was that she choose "only the best of everything."

I was called in, along with an architect, to assist Eve with her task. Eve was very nervous during our first consultation. I encouraged her to do breathing exercises and led her through a simple meditation. Eventually, she was calm enough to talk openly. Eve told me that she felt like Eliza in the play, *My Fair Lady.* "I am a fraud!" she said, her green eyes wide with anguish. "I do not be-long here in this great home, with this wonderful man. It's too good for me."

When I delved deeper, I learned that Eve had been raised in a poor rural community in Washington state. Her parents had always told her she would never be anything special, and that she shouldn't even try to be like "the rich folks." At one point she had been on welfare. And although Eve had worked her way to the East Coast, had put herself through art school, and had established herself as a respected commercial artist, she still felt she had never (and could never) really fit into this upscale lifestyle. She certainly didn't feel comfortable choosing only the best, as her husband had directed.

"I love Charles with all my heart," she said. "But I don't think I can do this." In spite of her uncertainty, Eve wanted to make Charles happy, so she agreed to join me on a shopping trip to Manhattan. "Just to look," I assured her, "so I can get a sense of what you like." That day, we went in at least ten top-of-the-line antique stores, and in each place, I asked her to tell me when she saw something that appealed to her.

As it turned out, Eve had a remarkable sense for what Charles called "the best." She was drawn to, among other things, a William and Mary marquetry chest, a large Stiffel brass lamp, a pair of imperial cinnabar garment boxes, and a priceless Russian seating arrangement in Karelian birch veneer.

When we were driving home, I told Eve that she had easily selected furniture and accessories that would, if she purchased them, cost over one million dollars. She was shocked. She'd just thought they were pretty.

It seemed that Eve had a natural leaning toward exquisite, beautiful, and pricey objects. At least beautiful in the sense of what was considered classic in the design world. And even though her background was modest, she had instinctively chosen objects that we both knew would please her husband. She also realized they pleased her as well—tremendously in fact! Of course, it took another few months for Eve to actually bring any of these objects into their home. She just could not readily accept such luxury in her surroundings. (I even had to arrange for Charles to write the checks to the dealers.)

Eve started by choosing a smaller item, like the Stiffel lamp, and allowing herself time to become accustomed to it in her space. Then she moved onto a sidechair, a painting, and a tapestry. Eventually, she became much more confident about her choices. With Charles' gentle support, she even began to feel she might deserve them around her. Finally, she redecorated an entire wing of the estate.

One thing that did mystify both of us, however, was where this natural taste of such high caliber had come from. I suggested Eve go for a life reading from a woman I knew who specialized in reincarnation readings. When regressed, Eve learned that she had once been part of the British nobility, a woman who loved (to excess) all that was ornate and beautiful and expensive! Eve was also told that she had been born into a poor environment this time around to teach herself humility, a trait that had been lost during her reign as a lady of the *ton* in England.

Whether it was a karmic necessity or not, Eve did learn much about herself during her interior design experience, including the skill of gracious acceptance. As of now, Eve has still not had her parents into her new home; she is nervous about their response. Although she has a good relationship with them, they don't feel comfortable with the idea of a visit either. But in time, I have no doubt that both she and her parents will overcome this hurdle.

DESIGNING A
HOME FOR
YOUR HEART
FROM THE
INSIDE OUT

112

Accepting your Higher Self

In summarizing this phase of the creative process, I urge you to remember that the life you've led up to now, and the influences that have come into it, were the results of your choices, and that you manifest different results by making different choices. If you remain receptive to the part of you that says, "Go for it, release your fear, enjoy the bounty you've created," you will open yourself up to peace, prosperity, and pleasure. Accept whatever serves your highest self and your sincere, heartfelt desires.

Ambivalence, insecurity, and conflict are part of being human. We may manifest them differently, but we all go through them and need to go through them in order to fully appreciate our efforts. Every aspect of your personality has its own energy, and you can't alter the current until you've listened to and experienced the noise, so to speak, discerned its meanings and examined the beliefs behind it. So take time to reflect and examine the beliefs behind it. Reflect upon your life and what you've been creating, and then accept what is.

At the first hint of an opening, take action for yourself and your highest good. Take another step. Enjoy the results. Take another step, then rest. Reflect and take in more.

Know that it is just a matter of time for you to have what it is that you want and need. As the soul grows and changes within the physical body in the material world, the physical body needs time to adjust to the new and the different, and to the flow of energy that comes with them.

At this point, manifestation evolves in a new way as well. Our homes and our lives are the natural outgrowth of our inner dynamic, one that we were creating all along. When we see the results of our efforts, it is a natural outgrowth, a creative explosion of what we have been striving to create. But it does take time to adjust to!

There is one more challenge that might be keeping you from receiving the results of your labor thus far: the need to reclaim your space. Since this particular topic is so important, and so common to all of us, I have decided to deal with it as a separate chapter.

Let's move on to the next step, and learn about the need to cleanse the parts of your home, and life, of all that is no longer needed, *to make way for the new.*

Chapter Seven

RECLAIMING YOUR SPACE

"The master sculptor begins with a dream.
A dream of something beautiful, or striking, or symbolic.
She gathers the tools of her trade, a block of granite, a chisel, a silver hammer. Then, one step
at a time, she chips away at a block of granite, removing the excess, in search of the treasure below.
She can't see it yet, but she knows it is there.
As the midday sun wanes, she labors on, slowly, mindfully. Chip. Chip. Chip.
Bits and pieces of granite fly through the air as the original form makes way for the new.
Finally, all that remains is a pattern of indentations and contours.
A form: beautiful, or striking, or symbolic.
Her dream. Her art. Now a reality. Is set in stone.
To enjoy."

—KAREN PLUNKETT-POWELL [1994]

In a way, we are all sculptors. Sculptors of our life and of our homes.

And just like a sculptor, you will reach a point in your creative process when you are challenged to chip away at

Designing a
home for
your heart
from the
inside out

114

the old to make way for the new. To unclutter. To simplify, and keep only the things which empower and enhance a home for your heart. To sculpt a new environment, keeping only those parts of the old environment that still have meaning and real use to you, and for you.

To reclaim your space.

This is not always an easy task. Frankly, whenever we reach this point during my home for your heart course, I find that many of my students have similar responses, in varying degrees: 1) a realization of the need to pave the way for the new; 2) feelings of uncertainty about how to begin to achieve this task; 3) physical and mental resistance to *letting things go;* and 4) a belief that they will cease to exist without their possessions.

You may have already experienced this resistance.

Let's say that you have worked hard to envision your dream home and your angel home. You've completed the fantasy floor plans and answered a myriad of important questions. You've even developed a good sense of your personal sense of style that feels authentic for you. You are bursting with energy and are ready to receive. You want to commit to doing something about your home, beginning with your bedroom. So, as a first step, you finally call up the manufacturer and order the lovely mahogany wardrobe you've always wanted. You hang up the phone and walk into the bedroom, still brimming over with excitement.

Suddenly, a realization strikes. There is not enough space for your new wardrobe! Objects permeate every corner of the room; the top of the dresser is littered with bills and correspondence; the closet is so full that you cannot fit another item inside.

The thought of getting rid of anything is unsettling and feels impossible.

You do need all of these things. Don't you?

Or do you?

Chances are that you do not need everything in your home. What you really need, perhaps, is to accept the fact that you are going through a transition point in your life, one that is extending into your environment. Your inner voice is urging you to grow, to allow the new you to manifest itself in your space.

You should try to think positively about this transition. Know that this is not a process of discarding, but of *cleansing*—a deep, energetic, spiritual, cleaning.

There is something else at stake here too, that I want you to keep in mind throughout this chapter.

If you insist on holding onto every single tangible part of your past, then you are telling yourself that your past has been more important, and more interesting, than your potential future will be.

If that is the case, then your vision will never have a chance to become a reality. And that would be sad indeed. You should strive to make room in your future rather than putting all of your energies in the past.

It is a spiritual law, and a natural part of your material life as well, that in order to grow personally, and enhance your present living environment, you must be open to that growth. And there must be room for it. If space is not made for the new to come in, it can't. So it's limiting the future as well.

Let me give you a simple example of this concept: I could not easily attract new clients, or even add to my design photo collection, if my business files were jammed with excess unnecessary papers. There would be no space left for more clients because the past would be stopping it up.

Therefore, it is vital to learn to let go, when it is time to let go. And it is best to let go lovingly with ease and grace. It's all part of life design, you see. And it is intrinsically related to the creative process, of moving closer to your vision.

Effectively dealing with excess is a challenge. But resistance to letting go of things can be easier to overcome than say, a primarily psychological barrier such as perfectionism. At least you can see excess objects; they can be moved. When you decide to unclutter, you can see immediate results. You can then stand back relieved. You've unburdened yourself, as well as the area. Also, the moment a space is cleared, old energies are released, and that space is ready for the new. This is all very energizing. And, it is all part of the natural cycle of growth.

Still, you may be wondering: "If this is such a natural process, then why am I so paralyzed? So confused? So torn? Why am I still so inexplicably attached to these extra objects around me when I realize they serve no purpose in my life?"

Feelings about letting go, and of reclaiming both our inner and outer space, manifest themselves on many levels: psychological, emotional, spiritual, and physical. To utilize your space most wisely, you need to understand these feelings. You also need to understand exactly how you consciously and unconsciously view your space, and how to safeguard against allowing your space, or objects, to control you.

POWER AND ENERGY IN OBJECTS

The objects in our space can exert an enormous amount of power, both perceived and unperceived. Soon after you place a sofa, a desk chair, a pile of mail, or a cluster of figurines in your home, you incorporate it into your *perceptual re-*

Designing a
home for
your heart
from the
inside out

116

ality. You become accustomed to it being in a certain position. You walk around the sofa, toss your coat over the chair when you come home, or you dust the figurines without altering their original arrangement. You're not thinking about what you're doing, or about the objects involved, yet it doesn't take long for these actions to become habits that you engage in on a regular basis—sometimes several times a day!

When home-based habits become too ingrained in us, we are no longer mentally or emotionally free to make the best decisions about our living environment. We lose our objectivity, and therefore miss important environmental clues that might be telling us our living spaces need updating now—before it becomes too painful, or before it becomes a monumental task.

Sometimes this surfaces in the form of being angry and frustrated about our clutter, other times as an unexplained bout of depression; at still other times, it manifests itself in behavior (often unconsciously exhibited) that holds us back from making changes in our lives. Due to clutter our homes are not supporting the best of us.

About ten years ago, I worked with an elderly woman named Margaret, who had fallen into just such an unconscious pattern of resistance. During my first visit to her cottage, we strolled from room to room to get a sense of her present environment. As we did this, I casually moved some of her things: a spice jar here, a vase there, the angle between two living room chairs. The next time we passed by those spaces, Margaret returned whatever I had moved back to its original position. When I pointed this out to her, she was shocked. Not only wasn't she consciously aware of her actions, she had never even consciously noticed that I had changed anything to begin with. Both of us realized, right away, that in redecorating her cottage we would first have to break her of certain habits, and gently overcome her resistance. We would have to ease her into accepting new objects, and a fresh new placement of old objects, if she was going to achieve her goal of a new look in her home.

Another client, who had had a similar, automatic reaction when I moved his childhood collection of miniature toy soldiers, used to say jokingly that those objects were really magnets that were pulled back into place by a giant force field. His tongue-in-cheek theory wasn't far off base. Objects that stay in one spot for a long time can get rooted in place. After a while, it seems as if they have the power—not you, the owner of the objects!

In fact, you can grow so desensitized to your living space, *that you continue to see it the original way, even after a change.* How many times have you moved a wastebasket to a different corner of the room, and then automatically tossed trash into the empty space where the wastebasket used to be? I have even seen people land flat on the floor after they sat down on a sofa that the carpet clean-ers had moved a few feet to the left of its usual position!

Further, the actual location in the room where you place an object creates an energy field that affects you. It affects your mood, as well as the activities that take place in that room.

Bill, a salesman in his late twenties, summarized this phenomenon well, after he'd completed his irrational floor plan activity: "There's this spot in my living room that's like a black hole. It pulls me toward it and once I'm in it I can't seem to move. I lose my energy. If I lie on the couch in that space I fall asleep almost immediately."

For whatever reason, that couch, in that space, was acting like a black hole! Needless to say, we made moving that couch a priority in Bill's decorating plan. These days, a nice, simple bookshelf occupies the space, and the couch is on the opposite side of the room. Bill hasn't had any further problems about falling asleep there—except when he wants to take a nap, of course! I've also seen cases where the actual object causes the problem. For example, if you get a dining room table from a relative you don't like, or have a chair left over from a past re-lationship you are trying to clear out of your life, then those objects may be giv-ing off feelings, energies, that are creating this feeling of a black hole.

These are physical, kinetic examples of the ways object energy can control or take over our space, and our life. But there other, deeper forces at work here, which you need to become aware of before you begin any large-scale project that involves reclaiming your space.

THE NEED TO CLEAR SPACE FOR NEW MEMORIES

Items and objects with memories attached to them usually give off the strongest energy in your home, and are more prone to control you and a given space. If these are good memories, this can work out well. You may need or want to reposition your grandmother's antique bookshelf to create a more aesthetically pleasing space; or regroup your child's doll collection to allow more space for other items. Generally, we easily adapt to such minor changes, because the orig-inal objects are still with us.

The true problem arises with people who are what I call *memory-attached* or *dependant*. This type of person places an equal emotional attachment on every

DESIGNING A
HOME FOR
YOUR HEART
FROM THE
INSIDE OUT

———

118

ticket stub, ever dried flower corsage, every copy of every utility bill that they have ever received, and of course, saved. These objects have worked their way into the person's view of the world, and deeply into their emotional reality. It is often difficult for such people to let go of even the most minor objects, such as an old paper clip or worn ball of yarn. Even when this behavior, this attachment to the past, is not that extreme, it is still rooted in the memories and feelings associated with those items.

When organizing for a garage sale for example, you may find it almost impossible to put a price tag on items that belonged to your relatives, especially deceased relatives. Even though the object no longer serves a practical purpose in your home, you may feel it represents an emotional link with that person, and to part with such items feels like severing that tie. Of course, it is not the actual object that allows us a spiritual or emotional connection to others (although it can assist us at times), but even when you realize that, it isn't easy to break down and part with the object.

The object is giving off its energy, and that energy strongly affects you.

These unseen energies feel meaningful and have very specific effects: They can be fun, serious, romantic, or anxiety-provoking. A new down comforter just doesn't *feel* the same as the one you made love under with a old boyfriend—not even if it's the exact same style, brand, and color. Something given to you by friends, lovers, parents, or spouses will exude a particular energy as well. This energy is real, as is your mental association with an object and the person who gave it to you. When they selected it and gave it to you, they did so with a certain intention or love—and those thoughts and emotions are now contained in the object as part of its vibration. But the end result is a stockpile of objects all vying for space and attention in a limited area.

People stockpile in every room of the house, but closets, basements, and attics seem to be the preferred resting place for old objects. Many psychologists, including Jung and Bachelard, have written of this tendency among humans. Bachelard said: "It is these subsidiary regions that make the house such an effective shelter for our imaginations . . . thanks to the house, a great many of our memories are housed, and if the house is a bit elaborate, if it has a cellar and a garret, nooks and corridors, our memories have refuges that are all the more clearly delineated."

You may see the attic or garage as the perfect spot to house your child's broken or unused toys, your worn towels, your outdated dictionaries, even the pile of old uniforms from your last job. These objects might not all have sentimental value. You might be keeping them on the off chance they might come in handy one day. Or, maybe you'll have a garage sale and make some money on them. Even if this amassing of things gets completely out of hand, to the point where you can't even walk from the garage door to the circuit breaker box in the back of the garage, for example, you may still find yourself allowing these things to accumulate.

Another reason you may be finding it so difficult to let go of objects, is because you perceive them as tangible symbols of who you are. When your living space starts to look more like a clutter museum than a home, you're often, subconsciously, establishing an archive of your life. You may feel that if you clear out certain things and make room for the new (even if the new is pleasing and life affirming) then you'll lose a part of yourself as well. You'll forget who you know yourself to be.

We are constantly going through transitions that affect our possessions. You may walk into your closet one day and find that your wardrobe which felt right before now feels totally wrong. Out of sync. This is usually a clue that you have changed a lot recently. Perhaps you purchased a stunning scarlet cocktail dress during your flashy stage and now that you have settled into a new lifestyle, you are leaning toward more subdued, understated clothing styles, or vice versa.

This same principle applies to our other possessions; we reach a point where they no longer represent who we are. We long for new items that represent our catharsis, the new self. But how do you know the difference?

One way to know is to get in touch with the current feelings you have about your possessions. If you are going through your closet and pick up a piece of clothing you loved last year, but now, as you touch it, you feel annoyed, out of sync, antsy with "what is"—that is a real indication that something has changed. Perhaps you want it to change, but aren't sure how. The important thing at this stage is to trust your response, to trust your sense of being connected. Allow your spirit to be connected to the outside world. It is part of the natural growing process. When you grow a lot, you no longer feel in sync with what was fine last week. Whether that be your clothes, hairstyle, furniture, whatever!

Begin by walking through your home, and really looking around at and sensing the objects in your space. Bring along your journal and write down any special feelings or memories triggered by the sight of any objects you even *suspect* you no longer need. Now ask yourself the following questions:

- Does everything I see here truly reflect who I am now?
- What does my living space, and the things in it, represent to me?
- What beliefs about myself, fears, and assumptions about what I can't or shouldn't do, does the present state of my space reflect?
- If I removed this object from my space, would it really change my life?
- Would this change be positive or negative for me where I am in my life now, and why?

DESIGNING A
HOME FOR
YOUR HEART
FROM THE
INSIDE OUT

120

- How might my beliefs about these objects be holding me back from my future?
- What kind of person, family, lives here?

As you're walking through your home, it might also help you to realize that *as long as all of these objects, with their respective memories, are completely filling your present space, you are not allowing or encouraging new life memories to be created.*

Letting go of objects that no longer represent who we are, or who we want to be, is not a final act. It is a first step. Getting rid of obsolete objects is often exactly what you need to release yourself from obsolete attitudes that are re-creating a life that you may not want. In this way, it is a spiritually cleansing process. A freeing process. It is important to free up space to pave the way for a fresh new direction in your home and in your life.

Each of us has the ability to transcend our present circumstances, the power to be born anew and make a fresh start. We can all learn to cleanse ourselves and our environments so we can begin with a new slate.

We are the spirit; we are the light. We see ourselves a certain way—not that we necessarily *are* a certain way. This type of thinking can free you. What we are is a lot more flexible than most of us realize. The physical world is not set in stone. Who you were is not set in stone. Who you can become is not set in stone. This is an important distinction. You might not have to work as hard as you think you will to change or grow.

The cleansing process involves the tangible, emotional, and spiritual levels of our psyche. In the next few pages you will see exercises and meditations to help you make decisions about your possessions. I have also included a step-by-step strategy to help you decide what to do with the objects, after you decide to remove them from your space.

EMOTIONAL CLEANSING EXERCISE

Throughout your farewells, and throughout your redecorating projects in general, you'll need to be constantly aware of your attitude, and do a bit of *emotional cleansing* as well as object cleansing.

If, as you're attempting to unclutter your environment, you feel overwhelmed, tense, or distracted, then the energy you generate can further upset the fragile balance in your environment. As you learned in chapter three, it might even create delays, and perhaps lead you to settling for less than your heart's desires, to lose the courage to actually take concrete steps to clear your space.

To avoid this, you can start by planting positive affirmations in your mind:

- I deserve a beautiful, elegant, special, fun, uncluttered home.
- My home can be living art, born of my true self.
- I can have an incredible space, the kind I've always wanted.
- I want and need to reclaim my space and make room for the new me.

You can now take another important step. You can release any negative energies that have gotten stuck in your living space, that may be suffocating you, and keeping you stuck.

I have found that the following energy cleansing exercise, taken from Machaelle Small Wright's, *Behaving As If the God in All Life Mattered,* works wonders.

Energy Cleansing Exercise

Adapted from *Behaving As If the God in All Life Mattered*
by Machaelle Small Wright

1. Choose and diagram one area (or object) you want to be cleansed. Place the diagram or basic sketch in front of you during the cleansing process. If you need to clarify your visualization of what you're cleansing, you'll easily be able to look at the diagram and refresh your memory.

2. Sit or lie quietly. Focus on relaxing your body. Focus on your inhaling and exhaling as you prepare to go on.

3. With your eyes closed, see a bright, white beam of light above your head. This is the Light of the Christ (the term used to describe that evolutionary dynamic contained within us all). See the light rays from that beam move downward toward you and totally envelop you in white light. State to yourself, "We ask that the Light of the Christ aid us so that what we are about to do will be for the highest good. We ask that this light help us by transmuting the lower vibrational energies released to us humans and that we be protected fully during this process. We welcome the presence of the Light of the Christ and thank it for its help."

DESIGNING A

HOME FOR

YOUR HEART

FROM THE

INSIDE OUT

———

122

4. Focus again above your head. See a second beam of light—this time the light is green. Stay with this focus until you see the light clearly and brightly. The quality of the light simply depends upon the quality of your focus. If the light isn't very bright, see it brighter. Or will yourself to see it brighter. The green light is the Light of Nature. See its rays come toward you and also totally envelop you, comingling with the white light that is already surrounding you. State to yourself, "We ask that the Light of Nature aid us in collecting and transmuting the energies absorbed by the nature kingdoms, including the realm we describe as 'inanimate objects.' We also ask that the Light of Nature aid us so that what we are about to do is for the highest good. We welcome your presence and thank you for your help."

5. State, "At this point, we ask that any inappropriate or darkened energies allow themselves to be totally released from this area. We request that in gentleness and love, knowing that the transmutation process we are about to be a part of is a process of life, of evolution—not negation."

6. Visualize the area to be cleansed. If you are having trouble, sneak a peek at your diagram. Visualize the shape of the area, especially the outside boundaries.

7. Visualize a thin white sheet of light forming five feet below the area. If it's a house or piece of land, see the sheet form five feet underground. See the sheet brighten and become whiter. Focus on it until it's bright and clear. Allow the outside edges of the sheet to extend slightly beyond the outside boundary of the area.

8. Once the sheet is fully formed, ask that the Light of the Christ and the Light of Nature join you, as together you begin to slowly move the sheet up and through the area to be cleansed. See the sheet move slowly, evenly, and with ease. Remember, energy moves easily through form. Stay focused on the sheet and watch it move through the area. If the sheet begins to sag, stop its movement and, by using your power of focus, lift the sagging area. Once it's even again, allow pockets of darkened energy to collect on it. Don't feel you have to fantasize the darkened energies. They will automatically collect in the sheet. All you have to do is recognize their presence.

Allow the sheet to rise five feet above the highest point of the area you are cleansing. The top of the roof. A tree. The ceiling. The highest hill.

9. Using your visualization, carefully gather the edges of the sheet forming a bundle of white light totally enclosing the collected darkened energies. To the left of the bundle, see a gold thread. The thread is from the Light of the Christ. Take the thread and tie the bundle closed. To the right of the bundle is another gold thread that is from the Light of Nature. Take this thread and tie it around the bundle with the first one.

10. Declare that, "The bundle now be released to the Light of the Christ and the Light of Nature so that the darkened energies can be moved to their next highest level for transmutation and the continuation of their own evolutionary process." Watch the bundle as it moves out of your range of sight.

11. Important. Bring your focus back to your breathing. Inhale and exhale through your body and out your feet. Repeat this three or four times, each time feeling the exhale through your feet.

12. Spend a moment recognizing all the energies that came together via your focus, and cooperated with you throughout the process.
    • the white Light of Christ
    • the green Light of Nature
    • the white sheet
    • the gold threads
    • the energies that were released

    In the spirit of gentleness and gratitude, allow these energies to fully release from your focus. Focus on your breathing once again and see comforting darkness.

13. Focus on the room around you. Sense the walls. The floor. Feel whatever your body is touching. Wiggle your toes and fingers. Slowly move your hands and feet. Open your eyes and make a deliberate effort to see the room around you. When you're ready, slowly rise to your feet. Walk around. Look out a window. Drink some water if you desire it. Give yourself a moment before continuing your day. Be sure you feel absolutely present to yourself. If you feel spacey, walk outside and put your hands on a tree or a rock, focusing your

DESIGNING A
HOME FOR
YOUR HEART
FROM THE
INSIDE OUT
———
124

sensation of touch with it. Just continue moving your hands until you can clearly feel it. Or spend time smelling a flower. In essence, simply ground yourself by restoring your five senses. Focus on being physical.

By using your choice of a spiritual and emotional cleansing exercise, along with all the other activities and natural creativity available to you, you can begin to feel more motivated, energized, and optimistic. Such exercise can prepare you for the physically draining parts of the cleansing such as moving boxes or packing up bags of old clothes for your local charity organization.

There is another plus to the cleansing rite as well: Soon after you mentally and spiritually release objects, you may find that you synchonistically encounter people who need these very objects! This is directly linked to the magic magnets phenomena I discussed in chapter five. By letting go with a positive attitude and the positive intention of simplifying and beautifying your life, you put out energy into the universe, that attracts forces to help you accomplish your goal.

TOOLS AND TECHNIQUES TO HELP YOU RECLAIM YOUR SPACE

Many of us just need to learn to distinguish between what objects we really need and want around us to be happy, and what objects we truly don't need or want. Cleansing doesn't always means throwing out or totally removing objects from our home, either. We might simply need to become better organized. Most of the time, however, we need to use a mixture of both these methods in order to achieve our goals.

To begin the physical aspect of the cleansing process, you should go into each and every room in your home and take definite, purposeful steps to free up space. Since this can be a daunting experience, especially if you have been accumulating objects for a long time, it helps to think of this as *a continuing, ongoing process.*

Learning to unclutter, and to be more selective about the possessions you accumulate, is similar to learning any other subject. You study the basics, and then slowly make what you have learned a part of your everyday lifestyle. Eventually, you will master the subject.

But in the beginning, especially in cases where letting go of objects is truly traumatic, you should approach it one step at a time.

Make a decision, right now, to allow fifteen or thirty minutes a day to clear away a particular space. Even five minutes a day over a month will begin new habits.

But how should you actually use that time? I suggest that the first thing you do is take an inventory of present space and of all the possessions that occupy it. Lean into this new behavior, make lists, think about new ways to structure your space.

TAKING INVENTORY

In taking inventory of your home, you will find (sometimes by rediscovering) countless objects that tell your personal story. They keep bits of your history alive, and remind you of who you once were. You also have possessions that make you feel secure, stable, grounded, or in control. We want and need familiar things around us. Without them, we can feel disoriented or uprooted. As I have already mentioned, you do not need to give up everything that connects you to your past, or speaks of who you used to be, and still feel yourself to be, but it is important to understand the nature of the connection that each object symbolizes for you.

I feel it important to stress, one more time, that as long as memories associated with objects, and our emotional attachment to them, remain unconscious, they can dictate or control our houses and our lives. By allowing these unseen forces to move to the surface and show themselves for what they represent, we also allow ourselves to mindfully, actively recognize what we have outgrown, what we no longer need, what we have to alter in some way.

Therefore, as part of your inventory, you need to look at the objects and contents of your space as if you're seeing them for the first time. You should really try to tell the difference between what you think you need versus what you actually need.

DESIGNING A
HOME FOR
YOUR HEART
FROM THE
INSIDE OUT
———
126

INVENTORY EXERCISE ONE: TAKING STOCK OF MY SURROUNDINGS: MY INTERNAL AND EXTERNAL RESPONSES

First, copy the chart below onto a larger piece of paper (or use it as is) and then fill it in with the following information:

IN COLUMN 1, list the names (and a brief description) of all items you're attempting to see with new eyes.

IN COLUMN 2, use your immediate, gut response (your natural intuition) to decide whether this object should be a keeper or a discard. If your initial reaction is clouded, then simply write down, "not sure."

Your answers in this column are especially important, because they will allow you to make decisions that take into account feelings separate from variables

MY INVENTORY CHART

Column #1 (name of item/ brief description)	Column #2 (my gut response: keep item; discard item; not sure)	Column #3 (history of object)	Column #4 (feelings about object today)
_____	_____	_____	_____
_____	_____	_____	_____
_____	_____	_____	_____
_____	_____	_____	_____
_____	_____	_____	_____
_____	_____	_____	_____
_____	_____	_____	_____
_____	_____	_____	_____

such as "Aunt Mary gave me this." No matter who gave it to you, you may still want to dispose of it. So, when filling in column 2, just go with your *immediate* feelings about whether or not something should stay or go. Don't ponder the deeper issues until column 3, and beyond.

IN COLUMN 3, summarize the object's history: When did you get it? Where? How? From whom? Note special memories associated with that object.

IN COLUMN 4, describe how you feel about that object and the person who gave it to you, if that applies today.

..>

INVENTORY EXERCISE TWO: MY OPTIONS

Now that you've completed all the columns, you can move ahead and think about each of the options you have regarding those objects:

OPTION ONE: KEEP IT AS IS

Some of the furniture, accouterments, and memorabilia in your home bring you joy and reflect the real you. You may have already itemized them as keepers: those you consider helpful, healing, or valuable to you as you go along the business of your life. Naturally, you will definitely want to incorporate them into your newly designed interior.

OPTION TWO: KEEP IT, BUT ALTER IT

There are any number of possessions that don't quite do it for you in their current condition, but might become more right for you if you rearranged them, applied a fresh coat of paint, re-upholstered, or otherwise improved their status in your eyes. For example, collections you take pride in can still retain that effect without taking up so much space.

Weeding out a few items, rotating items in a given display area, or moving them to any unusual or unexpected place, are possible alternatives. After all, how many spice jars, primitive baskets, or deco animal pitchers do you really need on display at once?

DESIGNING A
HOME FOR
YOUR HEART
FROM THE
INSIDE OUT

———

128

OPTION THREE: REMOVE THE OBJECT FROM YOUR SPACE

While taking inventory, you're apt to find items that no longer serve any practical, spiritual, or emotional purpose in your life. They don't enhance your environment and, in fact, may be detracting from it. To feel more in sync with your surroundings, and to make room for new or different objects and energy, you'll want to clear these outdated things from your space.

Now, return to your inventory chart and write the words, "Option 1," "Option 2," or "Option 3" beside each item.

Cleansing through Organization

If you chose either option one or two in the previous exercise, then you still have the objects, or series of objects, in your home. That is fine, and I have no doubt that you made a mindful decision. But the dilemma remains. Where do you place this object? How do you keep your entire collection of artifacts and still leave room for new objects, new memories?

It is at this point that you will be need to find alternative ways for storing or displaying your objects. Take heart! There are literally hundreds of books on the market about organization with ideas about everything from how to take advantage of the height of a room by installing shelves, to ways to group thematic objects in one location, to space savers such as placing seasonal clothing in storage. There is also much out there on the topic of clutter psychology, and there is even a national support group forming to help people deal with the emotional and psychological aspects of clutter obsession. Also, with the renewed interest in wide, open spaces, and the "less is more" philosophy, home design magazines also feature these topics.

You can certainly benefit from the ideas in these books and articles, although I, personally, will not be going into detail about organizational techniques. That is not the focus of this chapter. But I do hope that I have helped you to understand the connections between energy and objects, options and choices, and between who you have been and who you want to become.

SPIRITUAL AND PHYSICAL RECYCLING

There is one more group of objects you'll need to deal with now, those you have flagged "Option 3," the objects you've decided to let go.

Some of these objects are those for which you feel no special attachment, and the remainder are probably made up of things you are still having difficulty parting with.

If an object is truly in bad shape, for example, a blanket riddled with so many holes it can't even be used as a dish rag, then it is best to throw it away. If you cannot bear to throw an object out (such as that wedding gift you received twenty years ago that you never used) then I suggest that you give it away to someone who will use it. This is a form of spiritual and physical recycling: You can give your object a new home. One of the most wonderful ideas for giving away objects that I've ever heard was in the book *The Learning Annex Guide to Eliminating Clutter* by Susan Wright. Wright said that her husband uses the technique of placing a grab bag near their front door. When guests are leaving he tells them to take a look and see if there is anything they need.

You can also donate things you no longer need to an organization that serves the homeless, or you can seek out a needy halfway house, or a neighbor going through rough times.

I also urge you to take advantage of recycling opportunities. There is absolutely no reason to have stacks and stacks of bottles, cans, newspapers, or plastic containers crowding your home when they can be better served by being transformed into new objects for the world at large.

As you can see, there are many positive, helpful ways to cleanse your space. And if, by any chance, you are still left with one box of objects that you are especially torn about letting go, I suggest you allow yourself a transition period. Put the items in a box or loan them to a friend for a moderate length of time. If, by the end of that period, you have not missed using them or seeing them, then you can be certain that you no longer need them in your space.

Also, a word of caution! In terms of recycling, a lot of people make this process harder, more complex, and simply more difficult on themselves than it has to be. You need to be careful of an extremist attitude toward recycling. Don't become obsessed with the idea that everything has to be recycled every day every minute. Actually, I've seen several people use recycling as an excuse to retain their clutter. This seems like a good time to remind you that if you intend to *make* these processes go smoothly, gracefully, and easily, then they will.

DESIGNING A
HOME FOR
YOUR HEART
FROM THE
INSIDE OUT
———
130

FAREWELL RITUALS

When letting go of things that have been with you for years, and that meant a lot to you at one time, or that have memories associated with special people in your life, it is often best to take one more step to make peace with these objects and to say good-bye.

Farewell rituals and blessings take many forms. The best way to actually say good-bye to an object is something only you know in your heart of hearts. I have worked with people who chose to say good-bye lovingly, and others who have used their farewell as more strident, venting process. The latter is especially true when the holder of an object retains feelings of fear, resentment, or anger toward the person who gave them the object to begin with. Some of my clients have ritualized this by actually burning, ripping apart, or shredding objects during their final farewell. For them, the physical cleansing process was directly linked to an energetically symbolic emotional cleansing. Negative thoughts and feelings associated with the person who gave the object a negative memory to begin with, are also tossed out into the universe.

However, you might choose to release objects in a spirit of forgiveness and gratitude, acknowledging the purpose they've served in your life. You should develop a farewell ritual that you are comfortable with, and view the release as a celebration.

For example, if the memories attached to an object are *positive,* but you know you simply do not need it anymore, then you might take pictures of it before you give it away. You can then retain at least part of that object to ponder in the future, but the actual object can be set free.

You might choose to say a warm, heartfelt good-bye to the object, or even throw a new beginnings party on the eve of your garage sale or the afternoon of trash pick-up day. You can write a poem or song about the object, or draw a small picture of it in your journal.

A farewell ritual might simply be a case of sitting down with the things you will soon part with, and meditate on the memories they evoke in you, before you pack them up, thank them, and say good-bye.

Whatever your choice of farewell ritual, know that this cleansing is the beginning of something new, different, and exciting in your life. Through the act of reclaiming your space, you are yet another step closer to creating a home for your heart, your sacred space. Do understand that you *don't have to say good-bye* to objects. Only if you truly feel it is important, and feel a strong need to take this time for the good-bye ritual is it necessary. Don't take any more time than you need while letting things go!

PRELUDE TO PART TWO: A CURE

In this first part of *Home Design from the Inside Out*, you have learned many things about yourself and your relationship to your environment. Through the meditations and exercises in chapters one through seven, I have attempted to guide you through the interior design process from the inside out. Now it is time to move to part two of the book, which approaches design from the outside in. When combined, these two very different but very connected areas can help you create a sacred space that reflects the life that you yearn to achieve.

Thus far, I have asked you to revel in your many natural resources and inborn talents, but I have also urged you to face and deal with barriers and belief blocks. I have done this in the first part of the book so that when you reach the second part, and are asked to actually make decisions about your space, such as the type of colors to use in your kitchen or the style of furniture to purchase for your den, that you are emotionally, psychologically, and spiritually prepared for these steps.

I sincerely hope that you are clearer about your barriers at this point, and are already moving them out of your way. But just in case you are still experiencing a level of uncertainty about redesigning your home, I am going to share one more meditation with you.

This meditation, called "Four Red Strings Cure," has its roots in ancient Chinese folk and medicinal cures. It is taken from *Living Color: Master Chin Yun's Guide to Feng Shui and the Art of Color*. This cure is beneficial for people who are experiencing blocks and barriers in their lives, even those that seem insurmountable.

To begin the "Four Red Strings Cure," I suggest you set aside a day when you can be alone in your bedroom, and a time during which you will not be disturbed.

In each of the four corners of the room, install a red string from ceiling to floor. These four strings symbolize the legendary four columns that hold up the canopy of heaven. They also represent a sort of mystical phone line linking heaven and earth, invoking the power of heaven to intercede on your behalf on earth and remove your difficulties. Then on each length of string, at the point midway between ceiling and floor, attach a nine-inch red string, fastening it at its center. This nine-inch string symbolizes human beings—the string when held out at a downward angle resembles the Chinese character "ren," 人 which means "human."

Now you should perform the Three Secrets Reinforcement, which adds ex-

DESIGNING A
HOME FOR
YOUR HEART
FROM THE
INSIDE OUT

———

132

tra strength to any cure. First, you should assume the ritual hand pose of the expelling mudra (pictured). The mudra is a form of body language, a silent physical invitation. Next, you should begin a mantra chant. If you are familiar with yoga, this will be a natural next step. You may use the six-true-syllables-mantra: *om mani padme hum*. If you are not yet schooled in mantra, then I suggest you choose a "hum" noise that you feel comfortable with, and allow this to ease you into a spiritual state of mind. Third, you can begin your visualization, which, in this case, would be a silent wish or a prayer asking to be released of your barriers.

You can also visualize yourself being confronted with the barrier you want to be freed of, and then picture yourself actually being freed from it. With your wants and needs clearly imaged, continue to assume the expelling mudra and continue your mantra, until you feel ready to move on to the last part of the cure.

Envision that you are at the junction between heaven and earth and thus will receive universal ch'i to help you overcome all your obstacles.

Part Two

Designing a Home for Your Heart from the Outside In

Chapter Eight

SPACE SCULPTING

"Consciously blending and mixing the senses of home, creating an environmental life sculpture soufflé that rises and falls, undulating, can be a full, rich, conscious dance as our senses meet and interact unexpectedly with the varied physical materials of life."

—ROBIN LENNON

ARCHAEOLOGIST OF THE PSYCHE

I think of myself as an archaeologist of the psyche. In this role, I guide clients toward uncovering and then thoughtfully sifting through the layers of the past and their inner selves, so that they can be brought forward to the step of *now* to build *new visions.* After this initial discovery process, I seek to act as a lens, focusing spirit, time, energy, space, and

I went to a most intriguing lecture last night at the Open Center, given by a woman, an interior designer. The class is called "Home for Your Heart" and it deals with the metaphysics of aesthetics, and the impact of one's surroundings on the psyche and the soul. I am the one who becomes saddened in a room with florescent lighting. I feel bad in office environments because I am withdrawn from sunlight and fresh air for so long . . .

The lecturer spoke of something called Feng Shui—the ancient Chinese art of sacred placement. She spoke of finding the right place and time for all things. These ideas thrill me. Somebody is talking about something I have always thought about, yet my heart grows utterly chaotic when I attempt to move an object from one corner to the other. At home, that is . . .

A FEW MONTHS LATER

Reinventing Home! Already I am reinventing home and the inventing will go on and on and on. This is a good journey, a path with a heart, and I set out upon it with ecstasy and anticipatory joy. I am happy to go there. My heart wills it and my hands feel God's hands.

The Home I have come to feel is an extension of my body. The body is where the spirit dwells; the home is where the body dwells. Why it is so hard for some of us to house the body is still a mystery to me. However, I wanted to share some of the writing I've done these past few months that relates to our journey. These are just bits and snatches.

This process is ongoing, there will be more bits and snatches in the future.

SOME TIME LATER

I am coming home. Little step by little step. Heaven wills it; Earth supports it. There is a place for me on this Earth and I am not worthless upon it.

I will do anything now to push through my resistance.

I will take any workshop, make new friends, form networks, make phone calls. And it's working!

matter into a graceful reflection of individual and collective needs, wants, and desires—a reflection that can be manifested as a tangible reality in a person's living or work space. *And now, I want you to think of yourself in the same way.*

To achieve that goal, you will need to switch gears in terms of your own mental and emotional lens. You will now learn how to tap into your creativity, not only from the inside out, but from the *outside in.* You will take all you have learned from the inside/out exercises, such as your angel home meditation, your irrational and fantasy floor plans, your evolving personal style charts, and others from part one, and begin to use this knowledge of self to sculpt your home living space.

In part two of *Home Design from the Inside Out,* you will learn even more techniques, meditations, and exercises, along with hands-on information about how to craft specific rooms of your home to achieve specific moods and lifestyle goals. I will help you become more aware of environmental hazards and how to overcome them; even how to involve your entire family in the home of your heart design experience. At times, I will guide you toward using helpful, traditional interior design techniques, such as floor plans, to bring your dream to fruition. I have also included less traditional methods like color healing, Feng Shui, and aromatherapy. From all these methods you can choose those which work for you and pass on those which don't.

A lot of information will be imparted in the following chapters, but I feel it important to state, once more, that my goal is not to fill this section with pages and pages of decorating tips. There are hundreds of books on the market about how to choose antiques or how to choose carpeting. That is not the purpose of *Home Design from the Inside Out.* It is true that I have included several idea sections to joggle your creative juices, but my focus will continue to be on the underlying elements of design. Elements that surpass pure aesthetics and form, and move into areas of function and emotion; of deeply felt needs, desires, and secret yearnings.

This section of *Home Design from the Inside Out* is about *possibilities.*

When you combine these possibilities with what you have already learned, you will naturally, ergonomically move from envisioning to performing. And although you will be moving into another dimension of interior life design, the ultimate goal remains the same: to create a home that gracefully reflects, and satisfies, the individual and collective needs, values, and personalities of the occupants of your home.

And it all begins with *space.*

$\mathcal{D}$EVELOPING A SENSORY SPACE IMPRESSION

The first thing that you see when you walk into an empty room is . . . space. And if you have recently cleared out your home and let go of objects you no longer need, then you have yet another addition to your life: more space. Space, like energy, is everywhere. (Actually, space is energy!) Space is something that must be considered in every design plan. And the question of how to best use space is often one of the biggest dilemmas facing homemakers.

Most professional designers, and a good number of do-it-yourselfers, view space as simply a void, an emptiness that one places objects in, to achieve a specific aesthetic effect. But I am going to take that a step further. I want you to view your space as an object, a thing, something you can work with, as well as in . . . to consider the seemingly invisible space in your environment as a live *tangible entity.*

Space is both receptive and receptacle. As a receptor, it can become a mental

DESIGNING
A HOME FOR
YOUR HEART
FROM THE
OUTSIDE IN

138

image formed in your mind, seen through your perceptual reality, which is your view of the world. As a receptacle, space holds or contains the other objects in a room. But just like an electrical outlet which is designed and positioned in a particular way to allow a plug to be readily received, so can space be arranged to be receptive. Space is composed of energies, and both energy and space can be changed, and controlled, just like a table or chair can be moved.

I call this process "space sculpting." It is a technique that has boundless options and offers boundless opportunities for creating a home for your heart. Through it, you can better pinpoint the best way to use a given space to your advantage. It is generally accepted that a room's space should reflect and accommodate the types of activities that happen in it, as well as the aesthetic tastes of the user. Space can be sculpted to create a particular feeling, such as intimacy, airiness, coziness, intrigue, or drama. And many designers firmly believe that the energy comprising a space can be channelled in such a way that it helps to achieve life goals. You can sculpt space, both aesthetically and energetically to achieve a specific purpose, in a specific place, at a specific time in your life.

How you actually use, design, and fill your space, combined with how you channel its positive ch'i energy (through Feng Shui, which will be discussed in the following chapter) can help you attract a new relationship, make more money, or spawn a business promotion.

To illustrate the powerful effects of combining aesthetic, energetic, and functional use of space in your home, I want to share one of my favorite client stories.

When I met him three years ago, Elliot was forty-five, a successful securities exchange specialist; a conservative Wall Street type, as are many of my clients. Elliot had recently moved into a new, larger apartment on the West Side. In doing so, he'd simply transferred all of his belongings from one space to the next, and set them up in almost the exact spots they'd been in before. Actually, as he told me during our first consultation, his apartment hadn't really changed at all since his New York University days. It was simple and sparsely decorated, full of both useful (and no longer useful) objects and mementos, with several pieces of worn furniture that had seen better days. The color schemes of the curtains, table coverings, and area rugs had been chosen by various girlfriends along the way, and he had kept them all. Not because he wanted to prolong the memory of that person in his mind, but because he really didn't know what to do about it. Overall, Elliot's home was rather scattered and messy, a total contrast to his organized work environment.

Elliot was suddenly feeling tired of the state of his home. He said he was finally ready to settle in, to grow-up in his home. He also told me about his family, adding that he wanted to re-create some of the hominess he'd experienced living in New England in his youth. But most of all, Elliot wanted to draw romance into his life.

We began by reclaiming his space, discarding objects that no longer represented the new Elliot, as well as performing several spiritual cleansing exercises and the sensory space impression exercise (page 141). He also did a lot of physical cleaning and/or altering of the larger material objects.

To re-create the New England feeling, we chose folk art antiques, paintings, and plants of the dark rich greens he remembered from Massachusetts. He purchased a large wooden four-poster bed, which was promptly adorned with valuable, local, handmade quilts. We even redesigned his foyer by adding mixed, antique, decorative tiles. Elliot had an extra room off the living room which he used as his special room, a place where he hung college mementos and sports trophies, where he kept his sound system and vast collection of record albums, and where he worked out every morning on a weight machine. Within six months time, Elliot's apartment had been transformed—except for one room, the kitchen, which we'd saved for last.

As I said, Elliot longed for romance and marriage with someone who could share his many interests, his new lifestyle, his future. And one of the traits Elliot wanted this person to have was a love for cooking. Elliot enjoyed a good meal, especially the mood of a warm kitchen and the experience of dining with someone he loved. But he could not stand the actual cooking process, and in fact, was a terrible cook himself.

Together, we set out to draw such a person into his life. We created a kitchen a gourmet chef would be proud of. A beautiful, modern, stained glass window was added to his rather dark kitchen, the counter spaces were painted in shades of soft rose and mint greens, and every conceivable accessory was incorporated, including an elaborate ceiling structure from which hung copper pans and cooking utensils. I also advised Elliot to concentrate on the energy in his space, and to use geomancy to further empower his kitchen. For example, we moved the refrigerator so it did not face the stove, thereby assuring that the elements of water and fire were not opposing.

Six months later Elliot fell in love. And yes, she happened to enjoy cooking. As a matter of fact, when she first entered Elliot's kitchen, she felt instantly at home there . . . as if it had been designed just for her.

Through Elliot's story, you can see how space, and your use and configuration of that space, can greatly impact your life. Elliot's story also illustrates how the aesthetic (how it looks), the function (how it will be used), and the energy (how it feels or vibrates), can be combined into a successful design project.

DESIGNING
A HOME FOR
YOUR HEART
FROM THE
OUTSIDE IN

140

To design for a purpose, one must remain focused but flexible. I don't walk into a client's home with the preconception that I will use only Feng Shui, or only antiques, or only a new storage system, for instance, to make that space amenable to my client. I use a combination of all three elements, and many more.

So, how can you start getting to know your space? You will begin by envisioning your space, not just as an empty void, but as *an energetic totality,* as an environmental entity comprised of many aspects. Space aura, flow of energy, lack of or too much space, blocked space, the objects in that space, and certainly, the activities your space will be used for, are all facets of your environment, and of this thing called space.

Your immediate goal is to become even more attuned to the energy and space around you. To learn how you are using it now. You can begin by viewing your home with new eyes, and by keeping your lens focused on the physical, multidimensional facets of each area. This includes all the tangibles: furniture, appliances, decorative accessories, wall treatments, flooring, etc. There are strong connections between a person's living space, his or her personality, daily habits, activities, and the objects and energy in a given space. This connection now needs to be defined as it applies to you in your home. Your awareness of space itself can be greatly heightened by re-examining the objects in that space. In order to achieve the best results, you need to do this as objectively as possible.

Therefore, I suggest you perform the following exercise *as soon as possible,* before you shop for any more major furniture pieces, rearrange existing objects, or perform similar tasks that will substantially alter the arrangement of your living environment.

This exercise will provide you with an entirely new perspective on your space. It will provide you with a *sensory impression* based on an objective viewpoint. This exercise is designed to shadow your visual stimulation, so you will be forced to concentrate on your other sensory reactions. It will help you become more connected to your body, your senses—the spot where your spirit comes out from. Again, in our culture we are so pressured into figuring everything out in our head, that we are taken away from our sensory animal self. This exercise can help you remember how much luxury there is in experiencing your senses. Sometimes, an act as simple as sitting on the hardwood floor, rather than on a soft chair, can make us more attuned to our senses. You will then be able to combine these new insights with what you already know (and have) to find the right spot for the right object at the right time. When you arrive at the point where you realize that space is a receptor, and an integral part of your perceptual reality, you will automatically begin to think in terms of space sculpturing.

When you have completed the exercise, write down your responses and all you learn about your environment. Record this information in your design journal. Keep the notes from your exercise close by you as you move ahead, so you can incorporate them into your final assessment on page 147.

EXERCISE: SENSING MY SPACE

Enter your home or apartment at night (preferably after a relatively prolonged time away from your home) and leave the lights off. In this darkened environment, begin to slowly wander freely or even crawl about your space. Use your tactile senses, and also pay attention to smells and feelings that certain places evoke in you. Be aware of the freedom of movement, or lack of freedom, you are experiencing. Allow the animal part of you to explore this space. Picture yourself as a cat or dog who has never been in this space before.

Do you find yourself bumping into objects? Tripping over things on the floor? Or can you maneuver relatively unhindered from room to room?

Do some spaces seem open and comfortable? Does the energy seem to flow faster or slower in certain areas? Do you detect aromas you would like to savor? Others you would prefer to remove from your space?

In touching objects along the way, which ones please you? Which ones irritate you? Why? Concentrate on smells, textures, the sensory feelings about this space.

Do you feel the need to move through a more expansive space or the need to add more objects into your space to make it more intimate?

Continue this process for at least ten minutes, depending on the size of your space.

Some people even close or half-close their eyes (as in meditation) to better sense their space and focus on the energy. It's a bit like running a sensuality workshop in your own home!

Through this sensory exercise you may have already pinpointed some ways your present arrangement is not working. For example, if you bumped into objects, regardless of which way you turned in the darkened room, that's an indication that there is not enough space to maneuver in that room. Someone I know coined the term *dysfengshui* to describe this experience. When you walk by an object, like a piece of furniture or sidetable and you keep hitting it with one side of your hip, this actually unbalances your nervous system. This sensory awareness is allowing the animal part of you to notice, to react. But because our head works overtime thinking, and our eyes analyzing visuals, we are not always

DESIGNING
A HOME FOR
YOUR HEART
FROM THE
OUTSIDE IN

142

aware of our reactions to things. We are somewhat disconnected from our physical selves, our natural, animal self. Or, if you touched objects you found displeasing, they should be replaced with others you find more amenable. People feel various sensations while doing this exercise; they actually sense areas of the room that feel empty or crowded, or spots where the space needs life or rejuvenation.

You should repeat this exercise at various points in your remodeling process as your space will be changing along with the other objects in your environment. You can stay aware of these subtle changes, especially the positive ones, and use this experience whenever you feel a need for physical replenishment or reinforcement.

With a better grasp of your space from a sensory viewpoint, you are ready to combine this tactile information with a more technical impression.

Space Perspective

At this point, I am going to ask you to make a list of the exact number of rooms, or spaces (such as walk-in closets or foyers) that you actually plan to redecorate. You probably already did this, to some degree, when you developed a preliminary inventory chart in chapter seven. Now you will begin to fine-tune this and other lists and diagrams. Set one or two pages of your journal aside for each room, and write the name of the room at the top of the page. You will be making notes on each room as you move along.

I want you to walk into every area you have chosen for remodeling or redecorating, and stand in that room. It is best to view a room that is empty of furniture, but if that is not possible then simply enter the room, and notice details about how the space in that room is structured or divided. What do you see? Feel? Now move two feet to the left, then to the right, until you have covered the entire room.

It is important to study that room from as many angles as possible. When you stand in the middle of the living room, for example, and then pivot to face the window, do you like the view? If so, then you may decide that your sofa should face that wall to take advantage of that view. Similarly, if you pivot left and find yourself staring at a blank wall or a less than soothing view, you may want to position the sofa away from that angle.

You will immediately begin to notice that the moment you change position, even slightly, your entire perspective of the room changes. If you are staring across a narrow room, your impression will be of a space that is short and wide.

Another angle will seem long and perhaps roomier. Unfolding space will appear expansive. The placement of windows and other fixed objects such as radiators also contributes to the impression.

Which angle or perspective did you prefer? Why? Concentrate on what you are feeling as well as what you are seeing. If, during your sensory exercise, you felt uncomfortable while moving around in the dark, find those areas and view them in full light. What do you think it is about that space that is making you feel that way? In the same way, find the spaces you had sensed as warm, inviting, and positive, and try to determine what it is about that space that might have made you feel that way. Before you leave each space, take measurements of the size and dimensions of each room and write down the results in your design journal.

REFINING YOUR FLOOR PLAN AND ADDING DETAILS TO YOUR VISION

Equipped with a multifaceted space impression, you can now translate your knowledge into an even more organized, focused form.

In chapter three, you began crafting irrational and fantasy floor plans. I want you to pull them out and look at them again, incorporating into your observations the new insights you've developed (since then) about your space. You are ready to take the best, most useable, and practical components of your irrational and fantasy floor plans and create a floor plan.

The floor plan is your map to sculpt your space to meet a particular need. They are extremely helpful in any design project because they allow you to visualize the results better. The most wonderful part about floor plans is that they can be changed again and again until you are satisfied with the results.

An old-fashioned and highly effective way to make a floor plan is to take out a fresh piece of graph paper and draw the outline (frame) of one of the rooms you would like to redecorate. Draw the frame of the room in miniature while referring to the measurements you jotted down in the previous exercise.

In creating this framework, you can use a scale of one-quarter or one-half inch to represent every foot of actual space in a room, but that isn't absolutely necessary. Basically, I want you to create a simple visual framework to use as a foundation for placing objects in your space. Don't worry that your floor plan is not a mastery of artwork, but do indicate clearly that one area of

DESIGNING

A HOME FOR

YOUR HEART

FROM THE

OUTSIDE IN

———

144

the room is longer than another, for instance. If necessary, use a ruler to measure adjoining walls. Also, you should sketch in openings in the room, such as windows and doorways, along with symbols for electrical outlets. You will need that information later, when you begin to determine the best place for your favorite lamp or other objects requiring electricity. Complete a preliminary floor plan for each of the rooms and spaces in your home that you would like to redecorate.

But before you make your final decision about where to place the objects, or actually draw in these objects on the graph paper, you will need to learn more about the traffic patterns, the activities, and the actual physical parts of your body that are connected with your space.

Activity Cores

"The floor plan is like a map. There are usually many
different ways one can get
to one's destination. Organizing and arranging furniture in a
home is like playing
with and moving shapes on the map. They are not stuck;
they can be moved
again and again."

—ROBIN LENNON

Most of the time people don't have any problem evaluating or measuring their space, or even drawing a preliminary diagram, but they do experience a level of confusion when trying to decide where exactly to place objects, such as furniture, wall fixtures, and paintings, in that space. It isn't always easy to decide which configuration is best for you and yours, but you can make the process less taxing, and more enjoyable, by writing an *activity assessment* of your space.

Activity assessments represent the way people actually use, or plan to use, the space in their home. A room or space, however lovely, loses its luster, and its purpose, without people moving around in that space. Your home is not a museum, or simply a place to visit, it is a place to live with, and in. So in constructing your activity assessment, you need to remain honest and positive about how that space is presently being used. Even in cases where you are not particularly satisfied with the activity that goes on there, such as your nightly ritual of watching your favorite shows on an outdated TV (you want to replace but

The understated elegance and subtle sensuality of this bedroom which overlooks the Hudson River in New York—with its washable, silk bedding and iridescent window treatment—blends celadon and sage green with creamy chartreuse to create a soothing retreat.

The humor and playfulness of the inhabitants of this room are reflected by the mix of warm colors, from fuschia and lilac to salmon and orange. The honey-colored wood juxtaposed with the dark periwinkle leopard carpeting adds drama to their everyday lives.

Sultry jazz tones mingle with rich, jewel-tone velvets and ultrasuedes, creating a space for casual weekend entertaining.

Unique, handmade Moroccan side tables coexist playfully with the sumptuous area rug and the vibrant Arabian-style seating.

The unusual wood grain of this custom kitchen is stained plum and accented with a russet granite countertop and back-splash. The multicolored African slate floor provides an interesting texture to the space, resulting in an inviting combination of materials and cultures.

This updated deco living room, with its elegantly curved seating arrangement, overscaled chartreuse-veneered radiator cover/storage unit, and plush, floral wool carpeting, possesses a youthful exuberance ideal for lively entertaining.

A Tuscan feel permeates this New York City entryway with warm and earthy sage and olive greens. The large scaled natural wallpaper and the dramatic, hand-painted Venetian silk chandelier set the stage for the exotic texture of the African slate tile in the next room.

In this funky yet elegant dining area the handmade beaded fixtures hang from cable lighting like ornaments, creating a festive atmosphere.

*I*n this dining area, blue-gray coloring provides a tranquil backdrop for hand-hewn furniture. The original clock watch-plates are hung on the wall haphazardly to create a relaxed eating environment.

*R*ich, teal blue mosaic tiles interact with the coral colored walls and the hunter green stained cabinet to create an atmosphere that cleanses, nurtures, and replenishes.

The warm taupe and sepia tones of late afternoon light cast a unifying patina over muscular antiques and a slender, iridescent standing lamp.

This inviting, extra-deep, custom-made couch contains subtle fabrics and textures that reflect the inhabitants' changing moods. The warm, masculine mahogany tones of the table and lamp combined with the soft, creamy velvets of the couch create a comfortable dynamic that welcomes friendship.

$\mathcal{A}$ whimsical chandelier juxtaposes green patina metal against the velvety apricot walls. The angular window frames the cool, blue winter scene, while the multicolored dining chairs and clear glass dinnerware set the stage for dinner.

can't) while sitting on a chair that you really want out of your home. Or how you or your spouse perform the less than exciting task of doing laundry. But you still need to make note of that activity and how much space you have, and need, to make it less taxing and more pleasurable. These activities are all part of your lifestyle, and part of what makes your home unique. "Home is the one place in this world," said Frederick W. Robertson, "where hearts are sure of each other. It is the place of confidence. It is the place where we tear off that mask of guarded and suspicious coldness which the world forces us to wear in self-defense, and where we pour out the unreserved communications of full and confiding hearts."

A thorough activity assessment calls for both honesty and communication. Take the time to really think about your daily habits. You may even want the others in your home to share their insights. This would be a good idea, in either case, especially since you will be asking for their involvement on a grander scale when you reach chapter thirteen and deal with family centers.

Through the activity assessment exercise, perhaps more than any other, you will learn the difference between the notion of idealized, picture-perfect interior design and the equally beautiful but nurturing and real *lifestyle design*.

It's time to move ahead now. I'd like you to concentrate on the types of activities that go on in a given core of space. While viewing these activities from both a physical and emotional viewpoint, answer these questions:

- What is the major activity that goes on in this room?
- Is this room used often or only occasionally?
- Is this room or section of the room a high-traffic area? Low traffic area?
- When you are moving around the room do you feel cramped or comfortable? Do the activities that go on here require more or less open space?
- Do sections of the room seem to make people feel uncomfortable? Relaxed? Especially happy?
- Is there a section of this room you would really like to keep neat and orderly almost all the time? (Such as a space for guests?)
- When you are performing daily tasks, such as moving from the chair in the living room to turn on the stereo, do you feel you can do this unhindered? Or do you feel the space is cumbersome? Do objects or furniture attack you, trip you etc.?
- What mood would you like to experience in this room? Expansive? Warm and inviting? Bright and busy and encouraging communication?
- What objects in this room would you like to keep? Remove? Alter? Move elsewhere?

DESIGNING
A HOME FOR
YOUR HEART
FROM THE
OUTSIDE IN

146

These are just a few of the questions that will lead you to answers about your space, but they are vital to creating a design scheme that will be emotionally satisfying, functional, and pleasing to the senses.

On page 147, you will see a sample form you can photocopy and use to write down the results of your assessment. I suggest you actually write down your information on this type of structured list, including the types of activities you perform in each room. Beside that, list the kind of mood or activities you would like to create to accommodate that activity. Your lists of mood and atmosphere can be used later in choosing decorating accents and styles to convey a particular sense of style. In *Home Design from the Inside Out* all the information that you gather will be used at some point during the design process!

What you will have when you are finished compiling your list, is an extremely clear idea of the heaviest traffic areas and zones in your home, and an idea of the types of special needs for each room.

You will find that by viewing a room in terms of how it is used that where you will actually place furniture into that space becomes self-determined (to a degree) by practical necessity.

PLACING OBJECTS INTO YOUR FLOOR PLAN

With your completed assessments in front of you, you are ready to return to your floor plan and decide where each piece of furniture should be placed in each room. You can now sketch in symbols for each piece (and label them) or create basic drawings of each object.

It might be even better to create a configuration you can alter until you are comfortable with the final product. Almost every home center store has prefab kits for constructing room diagrams (many of these are designed like the Colorforms games you played with as a child) in the do-it-yourself section of the store, and current technology allows you to design entire rooms on your personal computer. But I usually tell my students to make their own cutout symbols (circles or squares or small renderings of furniture). This process of thinking about how and what to cut, and the actual motions of cutting and creating, seems to add a new, more fulfilling dimension to the entire creative process.

To accomplish this, you can cut out small pieces of construction paper or

```
┌─────────────────────────────────────────────────┐
│              ACTIVITY ASSESSMENT                  │
├─────────────────────────────────────────────────┤
│        (insert name of one room or space)         │
│   The types of activities      The mood or        │
│   that I want to happen        atmosphere         │
│        in this room          I want to create     │
├─────────────────────────────────────────────────┤
│   _____           _____       │
│   _____           _____       │
│   _____           _____       │
│   _____           _____       │
│   _____           _____       │
│   _____           _____       │
│   _____           _____       │
│   _____           _____       │
└─────────────────────────────────────────────────┘
```

graph paper to represent sofas, beds, chairs, etc., and actually move them around your floor plan. You can cut them to the scale I suggested earlier. Even if you are going to work with a professional designer, you should do your own preliminary floor plan and use your own cutouts to decide where furniture should go.

Now, pick up your cutouts and move them across the page. Experiment with different positions, different furniture groupings. You might also want to buy a glue stick (the type that uses removable glue, like on Post-it notes) so you can keep the object symbols in place while you study them.

Now continue to experiment. Enjoy yourself. Try to find the best place for the objects in each room. You can change the paper layout as many times as you want! I sometimes suggest that people come up with incredibly strange ideas. This often opens things up. Actually, a lot more things can actually happen than we imagine.

In a recent consultation, I rearranged a couch and placed it in front of a full-length mirror that ran across one wall of the client's living room. The client's boyfriend was in the room and said: "You can't do that, it's not supposed to be

DESIGNING
A HOME FOR
YOUR HEART
FROM THE
OUTSIDE IN

———

148

done that way." In actuality, because it was placed about eight inches from that mirror, the couch looked better since the reflection emphasized the wonderful detail on the back of the couch. But the client's boyfriend insisted there was only one right way to place that couch. There is no one right way. In my office, for example, I often move my desk around the room to move or use the changing energy. Many people think that there is one right way to arrange furniture in a room, but with rare exceptions, there are numerous ways and you should feel free to experiment!

Even with your list of activity zones, your sensory space impression, and all the notes in your design journal from part one of *Home Design from the Inside Out,* you might still feel somewhat uncertain about the best configuration of objects. Therefore, I want to give you a bit more food for thought to get you over this hurdle.

In helping people make major decisions about room layout, many designers present the analogy of thinking of a room as a city block. Your entire home is the block and each of the rooms inside represent sidewalks and streets where people conduct their daily business. In thinking of your home this way, you can arrange the furniture to accommodate that flow.

For example, you know that your kitchen needs a clear flow of traffic from oven to table and back again, so you should leave empty spaces in your floor plan to accommodate that flow. Equally important, consider what obstacles are

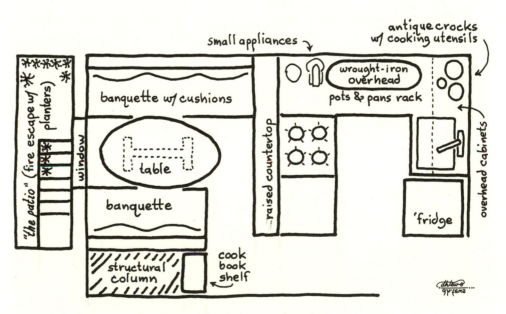

Sample of a freehand, colored pencil sketch for a kitchen/dining room area.

now in the way that you can remove to make walking through that space easier. If, right now, you have a large plant obstructing the walk from the oven to
the kitchen table, then you should remove that object from your floor plan.
Such obstructions need to be eliminated because they stifle smooth activity,
almost like the way a work crew in the middle of a street makes you walk
around them!

If you are constantly walking between the television set/home entertainment unit and your sofa, then leave the space between them free. If objects that
require electricity, such as your coveted Stiffel lamp or multimedia entertainment unit, are the most important objects in a particular room, then place them
in your floor plan first by concentrating on spaces near or around electrical
fixtures.

In essence, your furniture should serve a purpose, not act as an obstacle!

You may want to draw arrows showing the traffic flow of each room first,
then place primary and secondary furniture pieces in the picture.

USING SPACE AS A GALLERY FOR OBJECTS

Along with the city block analogy, I often ask people to imagine a particular
room or space in their home as a gallery, a place to hold sculptures or shapes.
Looking at it this way, you can view the walls and floors as backdrops for three-
dimensional objects. This mode of thinking creates many possibilities. For instance, if you have an architecturally interesting feature in your living room,
such as a fireplace, then this may be the perfect spot to nest two chairs and a
table and create an intimate zone. If you have large double windows and a
breathtaking view of a garden, you may want to face your dining room table or
your sofa in that direction to take advantage of the view.

Taking the idea of the gallery one step further, I want you to think about the
following question: As a physical human being, how do you want to move
around these three-dimensional objects?

Do you like to have a lot of space around your body as you move through
the room? If so, then in placing furniture symbols in your diagram, you should
leave more empty space. Generally, this initiates the less is more theory, where
you might want to limit the number of additional pieces of furniture you place
in that room.

If you prefer a closer, decidedly cozy, and intimate space, then your furniture

DESIGNING
A HOME FOR
YOUR HEART
FROM THE
OUTSIDE IN

150

should be nested both around you and in terms of the way the chairs, for example, act as a cocoon for your body. If your living room is a shared space, or a high traffic area, you may need a mix of designs. One side of the room may hold a couch and video center, while another corner might hold a wing chair flanked by a reading lamp for quiet moments reading.

At times, some sections, or zones, in your room will have to perform double duty. It is not always possible to have a room divided into an entire reading area, seating area, viewing area, or home office area. In such cases, experiment with your floor plan to determine which activity blends best with another.

THE PATTERN LANGUAGE OF YOUR HOME

Whatever technique, or series of techniques, you use to determine the best placement of objects in a room, it is also important to design a "pattern language" in your living area. It is no doubt obvious by now, that this language should be conducive to the activity that goes on within that space, but you should also strive to create a particular mood or atmosphere. That is why I asked you to make mood and atmosphere part of your activity assessment.

This will take some additional planning and thinking on your part, but will be well worth the effort in the long run!

To get you started thinking in this direction, I have included a couple of diagrams on page 151, which illustrate furniture placements that have been proven to reflect a specific mood. There are numerous books available to help you with such standardized approaches to design.

If you do a little research, you might be surprised by how much you can accomplish unassisted by experts by concentrating on your own responses to your space and using your common sense. Even if you are working with a professional decorator or architect, you should still perform many of the steps outlined in this chapter before the professional arrives at your door. That way, you will have your personal decorating preferences ingrained in your heart and mind, backed up with a working floor plan to use as a starting point.

If you have followed all the steps in this chapter thus far, then you now have your floor plan relatively finalized.

It's time to test the grounds, and see the results of your planning!

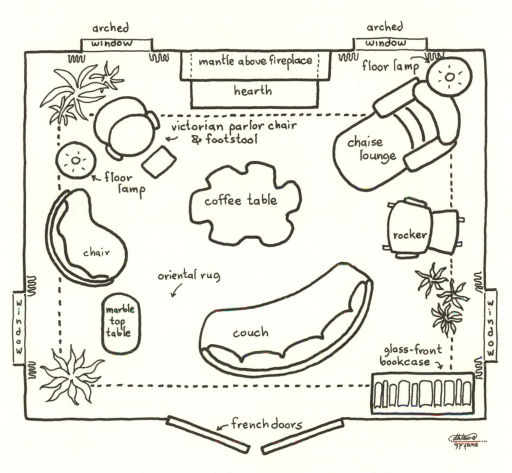

Furniture grouping in a living room which creates an intimate, cozy feeling

DESIGNING
A HOME FOR
YOUR HEART
FROM THE
OUTSIDE IN

——

152

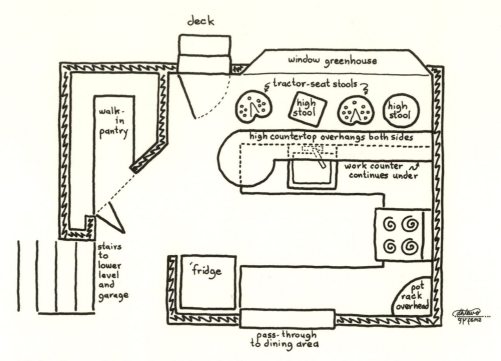

Kitchen layout that promotes high levels of communication and organized activity

TESTING THE GROUND

Your completed floor plan is your map to find the most harmonious, sensible design. But to determine whether or not your ideas are truly workable you need to actually begin making changes.

I do not suggest you stop everything else in your life at this very moment and rearrange your entire living space. That would take a great deal of planning, including getting people to help you move the heavier furniture pieces! But I do want you to begin "testing the ground."

Walk back into one of the rooms you plan to redecorate and take yet another thoughtful look around you. Then, choose a fairly light object, such as a side table or chair, and *move it*. The simple act of moving objects from place to place will allow you to know where things belong. The placement will feel right when you get to the right spot.

Now move that object to another place in the room. Try angling the object in various directions. If it is a chair, stop and sit on it and view the room. How does it feel when it is in a particular spot? If you are staring at a blank wall do you want that view? Or would you prefer a window view? Position the chair until it is exactly where you want it. If you are working with wall areas, then choose a painting or print. Take it off the wall and hold it up against the other walls of the room. Raise it, lower it, angle it, until it seems right.

Continue this process of experimentation, preferably moving at least one object in each room.

So far, we have concentrated on the concept of objects in relationship to you and your family, as users of those objects, with heavy concentration on preliminary planning. But in the next chapter, you will learn about the energizing effects of your space, and your ability to control that energy.

It is time to learn about the ancient, sacred art of object placement, *Feng Shui*.

Chapter Nine

FENG SHUI

"Being in the middle of the stream of life, we can either go with the current or against it. Feng Shui can help us balance the life living around us so that we are in a co-creative process with our own life."

— ROBIN LENNON

REDISCOVERING AN ANCIENT ART

In the past five years, Feng Shui (pronounced *Fung Sway* or *Fung Shway*), the ancient Chinese art of object placement, has been featured in many lifestyle magazines and in the home design columns of major newspapers, even on many television shows. More and more, Feng

DESIGNING
A HOME FOR
YOUR HEART
FROM THE
OUTSIDE IN

156

Shui and other sacred arts, such as color and fragrance healing, are being accepted as viable alternatives in the often traditional world of home design. An
increasing number of established designers and architects are tuning in to the
importance of placing objects in specific relationship to their surroundings—of
taking into account the energy of a building's site, foundation, and shape; of using object placement to counteract nonproductive (sha) energy and enhance
good (ch'i) energy. A treatment of Feng Shui seemed a natural addition to *Home
Design from the Inside Out,* especially on the heels of discussing space sculpting.

Since 1967 I have been studying Western sociology and the sociology of
many cultures around the world; all cultures have a deep strong mysticism and
meaning to them, many of which have been obliterated. I have observed that if
you step back, reflect, contemplate, and analyze them, many of these mystical
systems dovetail. This is a way to enjoy, appreciate, and utilize the truths and
gifts of supposedly opposing ideologies.

Our homes hold patterns and vibrations. Feng Shui is a life force, and in par-
ticipation with it, we can move into a co-creative process with our own life.
Feng Shui is rich in metaphors and strong in its cause and effect. Feng Shui can
help you access your power in the universe. It is learning to listen metaphori-
cally.

There is a lot of life living around us. Our house is a live entity. Feng Shui
sees all construction as surgery. Therefore one can prepare the house spiritually
and psychically, in addition to physically, as the house is undergoing transfor-
mation.

There are invisible patterns of energy and they shape our expression in life
and in our home. Energy vibrations are sent out into the universe and shape our
expression in life and our home. Feng Shui is acupuncture treatment for the
home. The closer the universal ch'i can get to us, the stronger our human ch'i.

To the trained eye of a Feng Shui practitioner, our floor plan is an X-ray.
Feng Shui uses the forces of nature to support us. We align with existing energy
patterns instead of swimming against the current. We participate in our destiny.
It has been described as cutting-edge spiritual technology—an understanding
of what is magic.

Ironically, this Eastern art has been in existence for over six thousand years
yet it has only recently gained popularity in the West. Perhaps its time has come
again. Now that information about Feng Shui is more readily available, it has
caused quite a stir among consumers. Why the sudden acceptance?

One reason is that Feng Shui incorporates concepts that simply make good
sense. It is considered unfavorable Feng Shui, or dysfengshui, for example, to
position a second-story bedroom over a garage, as the seeping fumes and vapors
of objects stored in the garage might prove harmful to the sleeper upstairs. Feng

Shui also appeals to people who are reassured by structure and rules. Feng Shui is an art of multiple rules, all clearly mapped out for the experienced user to apply to his or her space—room by room, nook by nook, wall by wall. Another reason for its surging popularity is that Americans, in general, seem to be leaning toward disciplines that offer hope for increased prosperity or happiness—particularly if that discipline allows them to experiment almost immediately in their homes. With Feng Shui, the mere act of repositioning a bed or sofa can change the entire dynamic of the room at large.

Yet on a deeper level, the widespread interest in Feng Shui is in keeping with our current quest for answers. As we move closer to that question mark, the year 2000, people across the globe are seeking answers of all kinds. And they are seeking them in previously uncharted or previously unexplored realms—mental, physical, and spiritual. For the first time since the cultural revolution of the 1960s, people are actively accepting new and alternative religions, alternative lifestyles, even alternative astral dimensions.

Feng Shui, unlike some ancient arts, believes that humankind can intervene in the direction their fate is taking them by manipulating or working with their environment, and being in tune with the natural forces of the universe. In that sense, Feng Shui is an art of hope and practical magic.

But it is a complex art as well! Therefore, in this chapter I will only be able to cover the most general principles of Feng Shui, leaving it up to you to continue your study using the numerous books and classes now available on this most fascinating subject. Over the years I have investigated and experimented with the myriad of possibilities that Feng Shui and other ancient arts have to offer us. I often called upon Feng Shui specialist Nancy Santo Pietro to help me analyze the space in a home and to help clients determine the exact placement of furniture or accessories to attract a specific response.

Through Feng Shui, you may find answers to otherwise unanswerable questions about your home and your life. There may be dysfengshui structural problems that may be affecting your life without your knowing it, as there was in my home. You might decide, as did Sarah Rossenbach (author of three books on the topic), to think of Feng Shui as "a pair of extra eyes." Whatever your decision, Feng Shui, when used wisely, sensitively, practically, and in conjunction with other techniques in *Home Design from the Inside Out,* can enhance your already bountiful creative process.

DESIGNING
A HOME FOR
YOUR HEART
FROM THE
OUTSIDE IN

——

158

THE HISTORY AND EVOLUTION OF FENG SHUI

Feng Shui, originating in China over six thousand years ago and then traveling through Nepal, Tibet, picking up various rituals along the way, is a mystical book of knowledge that is still intact and is a pre–Christian-Judeo nature-based religion as is that of Hinduism and our Native American traditions. There are three schools of Feng Shui.

Feng Shui started in the ninth century in Kuang Hsi, a province in southwest China. A brilliant scholar named Yang Yun-Sung compiled the first systematic approach to Feng Shui. Yang Yun-Sung was both impressed and intrigued by the landscape of his area. He studied the undulations of the landscape of Kuang Hsi, and the various routes taken by the streams, hills, mountains, and water courses. He was convinced that placement of these natural structures greatly influenced the residents. His teachings eventually became known as the *Form School* of Feng Shui.

One century later scholars in the north decided that the Form School of thought was too subjective. Therefore they developed the *Compass School* of Feng Shui, its name derived in part from the actual Feng Shui compass. Luopan (or Lo Pan) is the Chinese name for this tool which is used to determine the actual flow of ch'i and helps determine the most favorable site for buildings, rooms, and furniture. There are many types of Luopan. Some are very simple, consisting of only a few rings with a magnetic needle in the center. Some are more complicated and contain thirty-six rings. The originators of the Compass School developed precise mathematical calculations and detailed schematics for future practitioners to follow. They placed great emphasis on the fact that certain directions exerted greater or lesser beneficial influences at particular times, for particular events.

These days the lines often blur between the Form and Compass schools of Feng Shui, and many experts incorporate both schools in their practice.

The other main school of thought which is growing very rapidly in popularity is the *Black Hat Sect Tantric Buddhist School* of Feng Shui, led by world-renowned Master Thomas Lin Yun. This school of thought has drawn so much attention from Westerners in the past ten years that the Metropolitan Institute of Interior Design in Plainview, New York, has created the country's first department devoted solely to Feng Shui studies. Nancy Santo Pietro, Feng Shui expert and department chairperson, has designed comprehensive training programs in Black Hat Sect Feng Shui for lay persons, architects, and interior designers alike. Santo Pietro says, "Feng Shui is here to stay. It's not just a passing trend but a way of thinking and understanding how we interact with and are affected by the energy patterns that surround us."

In America the practice of Feng Shui in interior or exterior planning is still considered a novelty, but in countries like Singapore, Hong Kong, and Taiwan, geomancers are employed—often at great cost—by home and apartment owners and by large companies. Sometimes huge corporations hire geomancers before the ground is broken and business managers consult Feng Shui for the best placement of everything from office windows to employees' desks and chairs.

As was pointed out in the article in *New York Newsday* on August 25, 1994, this ancient art is now moving into the American mainstream. A lion's share of Feng Shui schools and experts are based in California, where Feng Shui master and Chinese clairvoyant, Tin Sun, along with others, now offers private consultation services. There is an American School of Geomancy, based in Sebastopol, California, which offers workshops developed by Richard Feather Anderson, an internationally recognized pioneer in the revival of geomancy. The American Society of Interior Designers now offers formal classes in geomancy, as many clients were asking their designers about this approach to design. The East Coast also has its share of experts and users as well, from all walks of life and all levels of income. In fact, when WNBC anchor Chuck Scarborough and his fiancée Ellen Ware reopened their Southampton, New York, summer home, their cottage was blessed in part using Feng Shui ceremonies by architect Ronald Chin. Such stories are everywhere, and it is not only celebrities that are using Feng Shui.

Even if you do hire a professional geomancer, I suggest you study the art yourself to enable the knowledge to remain with you beyond the time the expert leaves. In a way this makes even more sense, as Feng Shui places responsibility upon the *individual* to understand the forces of nature and energy and to learn the ways he or she can influence them.

When I was fifteen I had a boyfriend who gave me a small magic box with magic powder in it and gave me the mantra *om mani padme hum*. I have since found out that this means *I bow to the jewel in the lotus blossom*. I promised myself that when I came across this mantra again, I would pay attention. I did not.

Hearing about Feng Shui many years ago, for some reason I resisted it. I thought somehow that this Eastern direction was in opposition to my tendency and propensity toward the European mystical traditions that I felt more drawn to. That was an unnecessary opposition on my part. In studying with my friend and teacher Nancy Santo Pietro and then using myself and my home as the guinea pig, I have been repeatedly surprised by the strength and power of this seemingly confusing and convoluted system.

Feng Shui is a full and rich system that people study for years, so in this chap-

DESIGNING

A HOME FOR

YOUR HEART

FROM THE

OUTSIDE IN

———

160

ter I will only give examples of aspects to hopefully spark your interest and conceptually give you an overview. Feng Shui is also a growing art; it is always changing.

THE SCOPE
AND LANGUAGE
OF FENG SHUI

There is no exact translation of Feng Shui in the English language, but *Feng* means, loosely, *wind,* and *Shui* means *water.* The term Feng Shui is often used (especially in the West) interchangeably with the term "geomancy." "What you might refer to as the 'feel' of a place—good or bad," says Derek Walters, "is called by the Chinese its Feng Shui."

Feng Shui practitioners believe you can control the flow of positive energy (called ch'i) through object placement. You can add, delete, or move certain objects from your home to draw in beneficial fortune. You can even attract wealth or love by positioning your residence in direct harmony with the surrounding landscape. Feng Shui is far-reaching in its scope, and its principles can be applied to everything from the proper placement of a flower vase, to the position of indoor plumbing, to the type of roof you choose for your home. Entire cities can be oriented in such a way as to capture the positive energy of the earth. The afterlife is also a concern of Feng Shui. Several experts, including world-known Professor Lin Yun, have pointed out that America would be a lot happier if George Washington, the father of our country, had been buried in a more auspicious spot. It seems that the present site, Mount Vernon, is placed too low on a shady hillside, without substantial sun or positive ch'i flow, thereby making "an arrested development" our nation's destiny. Further, "Sitting our ancestors' graves in a spiritually advantageous landscape," wrote Susan Morgan in *Mirabella* (February 1995), "provides good life insurance for all future descendants."

Along with the position of tangible objects, the actual direction of energy is considered in Feng Shui. The direction of energy determines whether the energy is beneficial or unfavorable. The Chinese believe that there must be perfect balance of the positive (yang) and the negative (yin) aspects of this energy in the human body to attain perfect health, and in the earth, the vibrant ch'i. Further, they feel that in the earth, positive ch'i regenerates spirit and promotes growth and harmony of natural forces. In simple terms, people can benefit from this revitalizing ch'i and make use of it to fulfill their goals.

The word "ch'i" was created even before the art of Feng Shui was formalized. It was used by ancient astronomers to describe meteorological phenomena. As a matter of fact, Feng Shui is almost always used in conjunction with astrology, as this is also a science of energy and placement. When Feng Shui experts are analyzing the ch'i of a new home, for instance, they construct the natal astrology chart of the head of the household as part of this assessment. Generally in the art of Feng Shui it is believed that there is no separation between one's personal spiritual growth and one's geometric design practice. Therefore the best of geomancers are usually skilled in at least one other human art, such as astrology. Geomancers are much concerned with color and color healing as well as object placement.

GEOMANCY IN YOUR HOME

Just as traditional interior designers use texture, pattern, color, and light to give space form and character, you can learn to balance the elements to give space an energy vitality. Essentially, good Feng Shui is achieved through a combination of common sense, good taste in the conception of space, placement of furniture, and the best use of structure.

It is probably clear by now that the energy in your home, whether positive or negative, flowing or stagnant, creates the overall feel of your house. The yang (ch'i) gently moves along irregular paths in a given space, while yin (sha), the negative energy, strikes vigorously in straight lines.

In applying the arts of Feng Shui to your own residence, it often helps to think of a public water system. Water flows through the system regardless of how the pipes ebb and flow beneath the ground and in and out of your home, but the quality of the water pressure you receive relies totally on that flow being smooth, uncluttered, and logically designed.

Your goal, then, in working with the energy in your home, *is to place furniture and other decorative objects in such a way as to allow the energy to flow most harmoniously.* The following mental touring exercise will help you to better understand and sense the energy that is presently in your living space.

DESIGNING
A HOME FOR
YOUR HEART
FROM THE
OUTSIDE IN

162

ACTIVITY: FOLLOWING THE CH'I PATH IN YOUR HOME

It is easiest to think of ch'i as a mental energy. Picture your home in your mind, beginning with the entryway at your front door, and then mentally begin to tour your space.

Where does your mind take you?

What road does your mind travel?

Does it move easily from foyer to living room to kitchen? Or do your thoughts stumble when you are trying to move through the rooms? If they do, that is usually an indication that the particular room or space is cluttered or blocked, and space needs to be made to allow the ch'i energy to flow.

Move from room to room, through each hallway and beyond, allowing the ch'i path to determine the direction you take.

After you have completed this exercise, write down what you experienced. Notice if there are any areas missing. They are likely to be missing in your life as well. Then, if possible, take preliminary steps to correct minor energy blocks or problems in your space and adjust and balance the metaphoric ch'i circulation in your life. For example, if you sensed the ch'i moving too rapidly at points in your hallway then place a few objects in the ch'i path to allow it to move more slowly and harmoniously. Or if you sensed places where the energy had stagnated (or was moving too slowly), you can avoid blocking the path of ch'i by taking away objects. Hallways seem particularly sensitive hot spots, and if you have a long hallway in your home, the forces of ch'i will have a tendency to rush through your space. This problem can be remedied by placing carpet runners or several smaller carpets on the floor, thereby slowing the energy.

At this point, I am going to briefly explore more principles of geomancy that you can use in the various parts of your home.

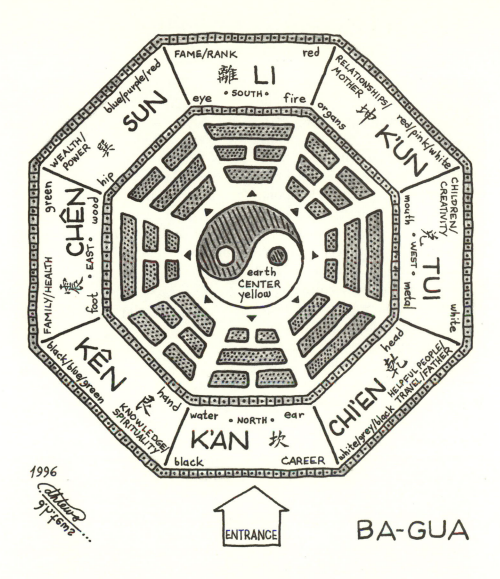

BA-GUA

Use the Ba-Gua as a map. (Legend says the Ba-Gua originated in ancient China and was brought into our world during the mythical dynasties on the back of a dragon-horse. Ba means eight and Gua means trigram; it comes from the I Ching. Half of the trigrams are female, half are male. The Ba-Gua is a metaphor for the essence of our world and a tool to balance our lives with Yin and Yang, incorporating the Five Element Theory of earth, wood, metal, fire, and water.)

DESIGNING
A HOME FOR
YOUR HEART
FROM THE
OUTSIDE IN

164

A GEOMANTIC TOUR

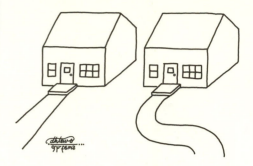

IN HER article, "A Sense of Place" (*The New York Times,* August 21, 1994), Elizabeth Large points out that with Feng Shui design is just like the old real estate saying, "location, location, location is everything." Practices of Feng Shui, or geomancy, should ideally begin from the very moment you are choosing a site to build a home. If you work with a Feng Shui professional, he or she would help select the beneficial site. If you are considering an extension to your existing home, then you should know that it is better to have a home that is deep, as opposed to wide. Depth creates resonance, while widening the home causes more disharmony. Therefore is you are building an addition on your home, try to build it off the front or back of the home (or up) rather than extend along the sides.

The front of your home is also important. The path that leads to it should be curved, not strident (see illustration). In the front yard obstacles are regarded as bad omens and any boulders, mound blockings, or very large trees that block the path up to a house entrance should be physically removed to avoid family troubles or separations. There are exceptions to this rule, which are too varied to mention here, but in general, certain trees, such as evergreens, positioned on the proper side of the home, are considered extremely auspicious.

THE ENTRYWAY

"A threshold is a sacred thing."
— PARPHRUS

Feng Shui isn't the only discipline that considers the entryway to the home one of the most important aspects of a living environment. Often contemporary designers place emphasis on this area, and historically it has usually been a point of focus—aesthetically, spiritually, and emotionally. As architect Stanley Abercrombie pointed out, "Crossing this sacred space can be an anxious experience. The entrance is the point within an interior where inhabitants feel most exposed to the uncertainty of the outside world." In traditional Islamic cultures, the actual entry point of a dwelling occurs at the entrance from the street—the transition point from public to private space.

Feng Shui practitioners believe that ch'i first enters the home through your main entrance. From that point, it spreads and expands into the rest of the home. The positive ch'i gathers strength, undulating throughout the home.

It is believed the entryway or foyer should be bright, airy, and clear. You should visually and physically open up narrow entrances by removing furniture, large potted plants, or anything obstructing the main entrance. Hang wind chimes where there is no wind and crystals where there is no light. (Do you get the metaphor?) The way the doors open and close is equally important. According to Master Yun Lin, the entrance is like the mouth of a person and he advises that doors should open inward because the door acts as a type of valve to beneficial ch'i. If there are two sets of door (a storm door and screen door), they should be in near perfect alignment and open up on the same side. If you see the bathroom as soon as you enter, it can drain finances and create bladder and urinary problems (i.e., your internal plumbing). If the front entrance opens into the kitchen, digestive disorders, problems with the intestines, and food or weight issues can ensue. All of this dysfengshui can be adjusted with Feng Shui cures. Hanging a faceted round crystal in the middle of the kitchen or keeping the door of the bathroom closed and the toilet seat down is also a metaphoric Feng Shui cure.

If, outside your home, especially directly outside the entryway to your home, you sense negative influences or unpleasant vibrations, then place wind chimes outside the door to block the negative influences.

When decorating the foyer or entryway, try to encourage the recommended airy feeling by using light or bright colors, preferably shades of

DESIGNING
A HOME FOR
YOUR HEART
FROM THE
OUTSIDE IN

166

blue/green, pink, and white, while avoiding a lot of browns and grays. The area should be well lit so that when we come home we are made to feel welcome, safe, and renewed.

Feng Shui also acknowledges the relationship between the personality of the owner and the entrance. For example, an introvert should not have a hidden entrance. This would only add to the qualities of introversion. On the other hand, a more gregarious person might benefit from a hidden drive or cloistered entrance. It is all about balance of personality and form.

THE KITCHEN AND LIVING ROOM

According to Katherine Metz, who runs an Art of Placement consulting firm in Los Angeles, the three most important elements in the house are the bed, the desk, and the stove. All of these should be placed where you won't be surprised when someone enters the room. If you are cooking, for instance, the position of the stove should give you a clear view of the doorway leading into the kitchen.

Actually, the stove of a home, the age-old version of the hearth, can be used as a means of attracting wealth. It actually represents the financial condition in our life. Keep it clean and uncluttered. Don't just use one burner; have them all functional and rotate their use. My associate Lawrene used the top of her stove for storage of pots and pans for approximately two years, during which time she experienced tremendous financial instability and depletion. You can place a mirror over your stove thereby increasing the number of burners from four to eight. Eight is the number of money.

Don't put a garbage pail or a litter box in the wealth area of any room. Replace any empty sockets or burnt out bulbs and fill all empty candle holders as a symbol of fullness and abundance for your life.

The great number of energies circulating throughout the kitchen has the potential to start arguments. Laws of geomancy recommend having decorative bamboo flutes and crystals near the stove, as well as a mirror. The bamboo flutes are used to incite safety and peace, bamboo being an element of the earth.

The ceiling of a kitchen or any room should not be sloping if possible. It is generally believed that the kitchen should not adjoin the bathroom, but that is often not practical in this modern age of prefabricated homes. If they are close together, there should be a passage between or at least a cupboard.

Too much red in the kitchen should be avoided because the heat and fire generated from the stove and electrical outlets is fire enough. (It also helps to promote arguments.)

Black and gray should be used somewhat sparingly. Any color that you truly love being in is a good color for your kitchen.

The living room or the family room is the spot the family hopefully gathers for communal activities. Geomancers believe that good Feng Shui is vital to harmonious relationships between members of the family. If it isn't, the family will drift apart.

If you are building a new home, then consider, first of all, which time of the day your family will be using the living room. If you have a morning family, than an easterly view would be beneficial. If you all meet at the end of a long day, then possibly the western view would be better. This way the shadow of the house will not be cast over the view just when it would be most enjoyable.

The ideal living room is rectangular in shape. But with the popularity of L-shaped living rooms in America, geomancers suggest placing a wall of shelves or a decorative screen in such a position as to form the fourth side of a rectangle on the "L." You should have at least one unbroken wall (unbroken meaning no windows or other such openings). The fireplace should be situated in the unbroken wall. If the ch'i of a living room is stagnant, the modern technology of ceiling fans can be used to circulate the ch'i. If you have square beams, round them off.

When it comes to furniture arrangement, there is quite a bit of leeway. One configuration to be avoided, however, is the placement of couch and chairs in such a way that they form a sharp triangle shape, *especially* if the point of the triangle is "shooting" into an adjoining location like a bedroom. No chairs should be either directly facing nor with their backs to any doors or windows. Positioning a chair or sofa against a solid wall is best.

In the living room many colors can be used, along with a variety of shades and patterns. Yellow, beige, tan, green, and blue are conducive to warmth and good conversation. Browns and deeper yellows bring an earth quality to the decor.

If the living room is the room that you and your family use most, then you can use it to attract wealth. Place things in the corners that you value or that are symbolic representations of what you are trying to pull into your life.

HOME OFFICE

Our geomancy tour continues with a discussion of the home office, the room of prosperity and knowledge. The Chinese, along with virtually all Oriental cultures, place an enormous amount of emphasis on work and the work place. Therefore, whether the design involves a home-

DESIGNING
A HOME FOR
YOUR HEART
FROM THE
OUTSIDE IN

168

based office off the dining room, a work nook in the corner of the kitchen, or the grand suite of the president of a corporation, the rules of Feng Shui are readily available to help promote productivity, increase profits, and provide intellectual stimulation.

In America home-based businesses are growing at a record pace. Millions of people now rise from the inner sanctum of the bedroom, brew a pot of coffee or tea, and then head to the job—which may be located only one room away. If you are one of these people, then you already know that this lifestyle presents its share of benefits and challenges.

There are many types of home-based entrepreneurs. You might work alone, with just your fax machine, computer, and phone lines connecting you to the outside world. Or you might have a steady stream of people flowing in and out of your work space picking up reports, delivering goods, or sitting across from you during personal consultations. If you are in one of the "helping" professions such as social service counselor, massage therapist, or astrologer, you also need an area for clients to sit and wait comfortably, as well as an overall atmosphere that reflects a professional image, not simply a personal preference. In such cases, clear, uncluttered pathways between the entry door and the office area need to be incorporated into the design as

both good business sense and good Feng Shui. To have clients weaving past congested hallways or stepping over wayward toys is not the most harmonious way for them to enter your office.

Although they vary in purpose, all home-based careers do have one thing in common: the need for an environment that frees the worker to be most productive, one that doesn't sap valuable energy by being disorganized or chaotic.

No matter what your occupation, the desk (or drafting board), along with its chair, is the primary, perhaps most costly object, that you will choose for your office area. It will probably take up the most space as well, or at least function as the most important space, by allowing you to work comfortably at your computer, handle phone lines, and do your work. The desk is also a symbol of authority.

Geomancers have definite beliefs about the best placement of your desk in order to be most productive and in balance with the universe. The shape of furniture in your work area is also important. To achieve good Feng Shui, it is suggested the worker use a rectangular/oval top shaped desk with rounded corners placed on an angle with the worker facing the door. "This is the most commanding position of the room," says Nancy Santo Pietro, author of *Feng Shui: Harmony by Design*. "It gives the workers the edge they need to sustain success." The window, or outside view, would be preferably to the left of the desk. If you routinely meet with clients, it is considered poor Feng Shui to place your desk in front of a large window because on sunny days your clients may have difficulty looking at you due to the glare. Ideally there should be at least two windows in an office, but they should not be facing each other.

In order to get exact locations for your office furniture or decide on the ideal view, you would need to consult a professional geomancer, a specialist from either the Compass School, Form School, or Black Hat Sect School of thoughts who would use either a special ruler and compass or the Ba-Gua and perhaps your astrology chart to determine where the positive ch'i energy lies in your Western or Chinese space.

In terms of accessories, some geomancers suggest placing pots of bamboo, chrysanthemums, or sculptures of horses (which are symbols of efficiency and vitality) at strategic locations in the home office.

Incorporate whatever stimuli make you and your office area conducive to work. Music playing softly in the background, art prints, or objects interestingly located on your desk, the aromas of fresh flowers—can all help make your work environment enjoyable.

Color is another important con-

sideration in decorating your work area. If you want your work to be more heart-based, more integral to the other parts of your human makeup, then try using soft pinks or greens (the heart chakra color) on the walls to help bridge these two parts of yourself. Or if your tendency is to be a disorganized person running hither and thither without direction, you should use pristine whites and simple furnishings that promote peace. For occupations that involve a lot of reading or study of a serious nature, geomancers feel that brown accents help creative a meditative atmosphere, as do pale blue, light green, and shades of pink. Splashes of bright color such as red can stimulate the worker and add energy to the environment, as red is related to the element fire.

WATER

The element water in a variety of forms plays a major role in the art of Feng Shui. The most obvious places in the home where water is of primary significance are the bathroom, laundry room, and kitchen. But Feng Shui is also conscious of the underground plumbing systems and main water drains. One maxim is that once water has passed by the site, it should no longer be visible, as it might carry off essential ch'i.

DESIGNING
A HOME FOR
YOUR HEART
FROM THE
OUTSIDE IN

170

Bathroom and lavatory water pipes and overflows should be covered or hidden. A window leading to the outside is essential. If there are no windows at all, mirrors should be placed on every single wall. And regardless of the American luxury of having a private bath off the master bedroom, geomancers do not advise this, as the Feng Shui elements of the two rooms are not compatible. The bathroom is the one place where hanging or large plants are not usually placed because anything that blocks the ability of the waste energy to exit is considered an obstruction.

If you live on a waterway, it is most desirable that the water flow in an east-west direction rather than a north-south direction, and east windows should not open to the downstream of a river. Water flowing to the south of a home is considered favorable as it brings wealth.

Water can also be beneficial in the form of aquariums. Have you ever wondered why so many Chinese restaurants have them? Aquariums, especially those containing red goldfish, are often used to counteract the malefic sha in a room or to bring vitality to a business. Many Chinese believe that live fish are able to stimulate beneficial ch'i through their movement and vitality.

Finally geomancers often recommend the installation of a *Ming Tang* in front of the home. The Ming Tang (meaning "bright hall") is a pool of water which the Form School of Feng Shui believes can be fortuitous if designed in the form a semicircle. Since water is flat, it can be positioned in front of the home without obstructing the view of the front entryway. It can be ornamental, such as a pool, or useful as in a reservoir. It can also work to counteract any "secret arrows" heading toward the home.

THE MIRROR AS WINDOW

Another way you can restructure the energy in your space is through the use of mirrors. Although we are taught to think of mirrors as solid masses covered by a material that happens to allow us to see our reflections, Feng Shui views mirrors as clear objects that can be used as tools to open up a blockage in a space and allow energy to flow freely. For example, where a solid wall blocks the flow of ch'i energy, by placing a mirror on that wall, you can create a pathway into the next room. In addition, throughout your home you can use mirrors to free space from confinement, to brighten spaces that seem very dark or foreboding, and to make small spaces seem larger.

Mirrors can create the illusion of space and light and make you feel more comfortable if your back is to the door. Crystals and other bright objects can sometimes be substituted as positive energy sources.

If this brief discussion of the art of Feng Shui has intrigued you, then you will be pleased to know that there are now many books available on this most fascinating subject. Feng Shui has yet another realm of possibilities for you to explore in creating your home for your heart. As Sarah Rossbach pointed out in *Living Color,* "Ordinarily we attempt to reveal a tiny portion of the mystery of our lives by applying certain *ru-shr* (logical) principles, secure within the boundaries of our present knowledge and experience. This effort, while indispensable, is wholly inadequate."

Feng Shui and other sacred disciplines such as astrology and color healing (to be discussed in the next chapter) can allow you, the home designer, to go beyond the traditional *ru-str* and beyond the conventional wisdom, to learn all you can from the cosmos.

Chapter Ten

THE FORCE OF COLOR

"The other side of fear is excitement."

—ROBIN LENNON

Just as water seeps down to the thirsty roots of plants or trees to feed them, you too can be deeply nourished—spiritually, mentally, and emotionally—by color. I believe that color is a door, an entryway, from our material world into the spiritual world of light. The impact of color on our minds, bodies, and souls cannot be overestimated. Color can guide you and take you deeper into your own

DESIGNING
A HOME FOR
YOUR HEART
FROM THE
OUTSIDE IN

174

relationship with your soul. You can ride color, like a winged horse, into the sparkling worlds of magenta or gold, and beyond. Each ride will be different, because the affect, and strength, of a color's vibration varies from person to person, even from day to day.

Never before have you had access to such a wide variety and range of colors. Modern technology can now create virtually any color. You can take a tiny swatch of an heirloom quilt and bring it into a paint store, have it computerized, and it will be generated into a custom paint for your bedroom. The possibilities are boundless!

In this chapter, we will look at the exciting yet paradoxical world of color. What *is* color? How does it affect you? How can you get in better touch with your natural sense of color? Which colors should you choose for your home for your heart?

I feel it is important to note, up front, that I will not be giving you a set of ironclad rules about color. I have not developed a "Robin Lennon's Color System." The reason is, that color is neither purely intellectual nor purely scientific nor purely artistic. What is right and best for one person is not automatically right and best for another.

Color does not always follow the rules.

But as you will soon see, when it comes to choosing color for your home and life, *you can and should make your own rules.*

THE DUALITY OF COLOR

In its essence, color is light. In your essence, you are also light. And in this world, you are also a reflection of light. On a purely metaphysical level you can think of color as a magical tool, here to continually remind you that you are one with the light around you.

Color as light is a phenomenon of *duality*. Color is both physical and non-physical, both external and internal. Further, both the internal and external qualities of color are intertwined through the energies they emit. Let's take a moment to study this duality.

Every day, you witness changes in the physical external qualities of light. You see this in the way the sun's rays shine on your world, or in the way a lamp casts specific patterns of light and shadow in your home. Others around you may have told you that when you wear green, for example, your skin looks markedly healthy, or that a particular blue scarf seems to perfectly match your eyes, making your eyes appear wider, more alluring. In all of these cases, the external effects of color were visible.

The internal, non-physical qualities of color (light) are just as strong, but much more subtle. Hidden, internal color vibrations can greatly effect your moods, your thinking, your health. In the spiritual realm, for instance, color healers believe that physical vitality, especially as pertaining to circulation and the nervous system, depends strongly upon the correct intake of vibrations from the red spectrum.

Generally, I have found that people with artistic minds seem comfortable with this internal/external ambiguity of color theory; while others with more scientific minds are less so. The latter often find it frustrating that the internal, non-material effects of color cannot be readily dissected and analyzed like a living organism under a microscope. Neither can color as light be captured. Like an elf or fairy it is ever-elusive, powerful, surrounding, but never quite in our grasp.

In his study of this enigma, Manlio Brusatin, author of *A History of Colors,* pointed out that, "The field of colors is a territory with ragged borders located somewhere between the sciences and the arts, between physics and psychology, a land whose configuration constitutes a border between these two diverse cultures." Regardless of this ambiguity, experts in these various disciplines have attempted to organize and pinpoint the internal, non-physical aspects of color. Consequently, if you choose to look, you can now find much information about *color theories* and *color systems,* both ancient and modern.

A LOOK AT COLOR THEORIES, SYSTEMS, AND SYMBOLISM

There are probably as many different color theories and systems in the world as there are actual colors in the spectrum. Since ancient times, colors have been used as physical stimuli, medicinal cures, and beauty enhancers. Manuscripts from early India, China, and Egypt show there were complete systems of color science used by healing priests. In ancient Greece and Egypt, people used specific colors in temples, often in conjunction with music, to regenerate the body. In fact, the combination of music, color, astrology, and numerology all formed part of the teaching of what was then known as the *Mysteries.*

By wearing a color harmonious with your astrology sign, for example, it was

DESIGNING

A HOME FOR

YOUR HEART

FROM THE

OUTSIDE IN

176

believed that you could become more in tune with your spiritual, astral self, and in turn, feel more in tuned with your environment.

The following chart, which is a composite of several different ancient theories I've researched, shows that a person born under the sign of Taurus would benefit from the color green, as well as from red mixed with citrine.

ASTROLOGY AND COLOR	
The Sun or Ascending Sign of:	*Would benefit from:*
Aries	*Red, and also white accents.*
Taurus	*Green; also red mixed with citrine.*
Gemini	*Yellow; and also red and white mixed accents.*
Cancer	*Silver; also green and russet accents.*
Leo	*Gold; also red and green accents.*
Virgo	*Brown; also black spotted with blue accents.*
Libra	*Blue; also black and dark brown accents.*
Scorpio	*Deep red; also dark brown accents.*
Sagittarius	*Purple; also light green and olive accents.*
Capricorn	*Black; also very dark brown accents.*
Aquarius	*Vibrant blue; also sky blue accents.*
Pisces	*Violet; also pure white or glistening white accents*

Other systems actually assign colors to particular healing vibrations, such as the aforementioned belief that red increases general vitality. I have read that problems originating in the third chakra, the solar plexus, respond well to yellow, and that problems in the fifth chakra, the throat, respond to green.

More modern variations go so far as to relate specific personality types to specific colors. The next chart, which is exerpted from "Rainbow Personality," developed by Cheryl Birch, illustrates that if you want to feel like, or appear to feel like, an expressive, dramatic personality type (one who is passionate and gregarious) then you would wear the color magenta. This chart, in particular, reflects our current sociological conditioning pertaining to color—a subject I will discuss later in this chapter.

COLOR PERSONALITIES		
Personality Type	*Color*	*Description*
Statement Maker	Red, Black	Assertive, daring, energetic
Expressive Dramatic	Magenta	Passionate, gregarious
Expressive	Yellow	Creative, busy, bright, cheerful, experimental
Casual Expressive	Pastels, Pink	Approachable, gentle, loving, soft, artistic
Earthy	Green, Khaki	Casual, comfortable, nurturing, friendly
Traditionalist	Navy, Green	Conservative, classic, persevering
Intuitive	Periwinkle, Mauve	Searching, in transition, artistic
Sophisticated Outgoing	Gold	Thoughtful, considerate, a good negotiator

Chart taken from "Rainbow Personality" developed by Cheryl Birch

I have been researching such color systems since I was a teenager, and I am constantly adding to this knowledge. I have learned much about the relationship between color and healing from the ancient theories, and have found some of the modern systems inspiring, fun, even useful at times. How many of you recall the widely popular color systems of the late seventies, whereby everyone was walking around in clothes based on whether they were a "spring, summer, winter, or autumn" person?

As you begin choosing colors for your home for your heart, you will probably come across some of these systems, which is why I feel they must be addressed here. Still, I urge you to rely most heavily on your own natural instincts about which colors are best or right for you. It is highly unlikely that an outsider's tastes or preferences will ever totally match your own. Besides, even though color theories and systems can prove helpful in selecting colors and color schemes, you might find, as I did, that they are not always consistent.

For example, although blue is often associated with calmness, plenty of people find the color blue irritating. For others, painting their bedroom in an or-

DESIGNING
A HOME FOR
YOUR HEART
FROM THE
OUTSIDE IN

178

ange hue, which color systems sometimes associate with sensuality, makes them feel withdrawn and guarded when they are in that room. And, although Color System ABZ may swear to its validity, the color yellow might not always make you feel more creative.

It is true that you might find similarities among color systems and theories, but there are no hard and fast rules. It is not an easy task to accurately assign a particular color to a particular vibration. An unusual, more spiritually oriented painting technique, separate from the more popular and well-known faux finish techniques such as sponging and glazing, is the Lazure technique, an outgrowth of the Rudolph Steiner School of Anthroposophy. As we have discussed, color is a vital consideration in "tuning" a room for its intended uses and prospective occupants. The white surface behind Lazure color reflects light back through the layers, making the colors appear to be "in the space," not just "on the wall." The combined colors in the Lazure method weave an enlivening variety for the human eye and spirit, never intruding, always inviting. The colors interplay with the subtle nuances of nature, creating a depth that is not normally present on most interior walls. The walls seem alive.

Perhaps what is most important to realize at this point, is that your awareness of the effect that each color has on you as an individual, is the most powerful system of all! Later in this chapter, I am going to help you begin creating your own personal color system by guiding you through a very special meditation. But first, let's further explore the far-reaching effects of color in your personal life and in creating a home for your heart.

THE FAR-REACHING AND EVER-CHANGING EFFECTS OF COLOR

The colors of the desert. The color of night. The colors of waters, the Mediterranean or the Caribbean. The color of spring, of new young growth. All colors in life. All colors we respond to. But as I have already mentioned, these, and other colors, affect us each differently, and on a variety of levels. Color as light has a different affect on you, your sister, your mother, your neighbor, your decorator. Further, each color in the spectrum has its own personality, its own vibration, and how that vibration is received can transform from year to year, even day to day!

The reason for this diversity is that color is alive and energetic. The actual chemistry of color, of light, is constantly changing in the strength of its vibrations in your immediate surroundings. To add to this enigma, you as a person are always moving and changing. Because of its paradoxical light qualities, the sensations you experience from and through color differ from other types of animal sensations.

In *A History of Color,* Manlio Brusatin points out that, "Color and tastes are sensations that are relative and reflected, whereas sounds and smells are immediate and unreflective. Between these wax and wane our aspirations and desires, our tastes and our memories, our fate and our nostalgia."

Amidst all this "waxing and waning," there is one constant: Colors do affect you in some way.

Everyone has a visceral response to color. Whether you are conscious of it or not, the vibrational energies of various colors alter your moods, your behavior, your physical and mental well-being. Color is the first thing that you perceive when you walk into a room, and it speaks louder than almost any object in a given space. Color is far reaching in its effect on humankind . . . *and beyond.*

Recent studies prove, for example, that even insects are affected by color. Wear clothes of yellow or white and you may be spared from the nips of mosquitoes, but wear dark red or brown and beware! In supermarkets, marketing firms have learned how to use color to attract shoppers to certain items. Veggies are usually packaged in green, yet you rarely see meats and poultry packaged in green (green in this context reminds people of mold). The lighter the color, the stronger the implication that this is a low calorie food—whether it is or it isn't. And in real estate, agents have known for years that a house painted in yellow has the most curb appeal. Yellow makes many people sense warmth; it radiates like the sun.

Due to the far-reaching effects of color, it is important that you give mindful consideration to all the colors you place in your home and around your body. It can extend to the colors of the fruits and vegetables you ingest . . . the type of healing colors you select for the room of an ailing parent . . . the colors you wear when you are attempting to get a new job, or want to set the stage for a wonderfully successful party.

In my own life, I feel and experience color very deeply. I consider myself to be a true colorist and color has always been part of me. From the time I was in nursery school doing my first painting, I've been enthralled by color. As I worked in fine art, it remained of primary importance, and when I became an interior designer this just transferred over. I use color differently than many interior designers. For example, I feel free to mix and use colors that normally are not thought of as being good together or appropriate to a certain space. After years of experimenting and searching, I am now attuned to my own sense of color, and it is a very exciting and satisfying experience.

DESIGNING

A HOME FOR

YOUR HEART

FROM THE

OUTSIDE IN

180

I have, in essence, developed a personal, unique relationship with color. I'd like to help you develop a similar relationship so you can be more comfortable, secure, and happy about the colors you choose for your life and home.

One way to begin that relationship, is to take a magic carpet ride . . .

UNEARTHING YOUR RELATIONSHIP WITH COLOR: A COLOR MEDITATION

The best way to begin making decisions about which colors to add to your home and life, is by getting in touch with your natural sense of *color intuition*.

Although some design specialists make the concept of color selection sound like a rather daunting complicated process; it is really quite simple:

If you are naturally, intuitively drawn to a color, or a combination of colors, then it follows that these are the very colors that you should comfortably have around you.

If you rely on your intuition to choose colors for a given space, it is usually the best color for that area. When it comes to color, people almost always have a favorite color or colors. By age two, we begin to differentiate between colors, even prefer certain ones over others, and these color preferences change and intensify as we mature. Perhaps you've loved a certain color for as long as you can remember, perhaps throughout your life.

You and red. You and blue. You and silver. You and brown.

What kind of relationship have you had with these colors in the past? What kind of a relationship do you have with these colors now? What kind of relationship do you want, and need, in the future?

In thinking about your answers to these questions, you should allow each color of the spectrum to give itself to you, to envelop you in its vibration, to talk to you, and play with you. You already have your own relationship with individual colors and color combinations. You now need to unearth, and then enhance, what those relationships are, and how they can benefit you most.

Identifying your relationship with color becomes even more important when you consider the fact that not only do we each respond to colors differently; we even see them differently. I had one student who did a salmon color on one wall in her apartment in a certain kind of light, and another student who used the same salmon in his apartment in a different kind of light. Observers in both places swore these were two completely different colors!

With all this in mind, I'd like to introduce you to a special meditation, one that is a favorite among my students and clients.

This meditation can help you get back in touch with your basic, intuitive relationship with color, so that you can then make better, more ergonomic decisions about your home for your heart. I call it:

THE MAGIC CARPET RIDE

Close your eyes . . . get comfortable in your body. Take a deep, cleansing breath. Settle back even further inside yourself. Now, imagine yourself in the most comforting, most relaxing room in your home. Or, if you want, you can imagine yourself in the room that you want very much to choose the best and right colors for.

You are in this room, in this space. Take another deep breath. In this space, you look around and notice that a wonderful, personal magic carpet has appeared. The next thing you know, it is beneath you. This magic carpet feels very familiar to you. The colors, the textures, and the size all feel right. It fits your body, your entire person, it feels good to be sitting on it. You feel comfortable.

All of sudden, this carpet begins moving. You are surprised by this, perhaps even excited, but you do not move away because it feels so good, so right being on this magical carpet. Take another deep breath and close your eyes. Feel the carpet moving, more, hear the whoosh of air around you.

When you open your eyes, you find you have traveled. You are now in the world of red. Take another deep breath. Notice in the world of red what type of structures, plants, trees, foliage, smells are here. Notice the quality of the air. Take a few more moments to sense how you feel in this world of red. What kinds of emotions do you feel here? Allow this red to seep into your body, your nerve cells, really take it all in. What might this world of redness offer you? What can it bring into your life? What don't you like about it, if anything? What do you like most? You look up and see a being in the world of red. What kind of being is this? Do you want this being in your life?

Now you notice the carpet is moving beneath you again. You settle back down and close your eyes. You experience another whoosh of air and light. You move for a while in this air, then settle back down. When you open your eyes, you find you have traveled to another place, the world of orange.

You look around and the first thing you realize is that this world of orange is different from any other place you've been. It is different from the world of red. The sky is orange, the flowers are orange, all the structures are orange. Allow this orangeness to soak into your body, and just like before, notice what type of

DESIGNING
A HOME FOR
YOUR HEART
FROM THE
OUTSIDE IN

182

things are in the world of orange. The terrain is unlike any other. Do you see any beings in this world? Are they moving, talking? How do you feel when you are here? If you could take something back home with you, what would you take? What would you leave? What is the best thing about this world of orange?

You experience another whoosh of air and light. You move for a while in this air, then settle back down. When you open your eyes, you find you have traveled to another place, the world of blue.

In this world of blue, you stand up and walk around. Notice all you see and hear and feel . . .

This meditation can be continued using any colors of your choosing. Along with the more common hues of yellows and browns and purples, I also suggest traveling to the worlds of iridescent white, of silver and gold.

When you have finished, write down your feelings about each world. If you were performing the meditation with a group of people, then have everyone share their feelings and responses to each world.

This exercise is simple but immensely revealing. Through this meditation, you can begin to get back in touch with your personal relationship with color. When you are done, the feelings, responses, insights, and notes you take with you can become the first basis for you own individual color system!

THE COLOR POLICE

Before closing this chapter, I want to attempt to answer a question that always seems to crop up in my classes when we reach the topic of color theory and selection. My students often say: "If all of this is so simple, and if I should simply choose the colors that feel right and best for me, then why is it so hard to do this when the time comes to actually do it?"

There are several reasons why choosing colors for your life and home sometimes seems so difficult. But I feel that the most important reason of all stems from our sociological conditioning. I want to mention some of my own thoughts on this topic here, with the hope that you can then understand (and overcome) any resistance to your natural instincts.

Too much, too bright, too bold—is often construed (by the public or the experts) as a sign of having *poor taste*. In a way, this indicates a fear of expressing the self, a fear of standing out, of making a personal statement. Regardless of its roots, the result is that many people are wary of using certain colors in their home, even when these are their favorite colors. They may be concerned that these colors might go out of style or be considered a tacky and disgusting combination of colors to the outside world. Some people are actually frightened by color, especially bold, daring colors.

There is this tremendous anxiety that someone else will come in and say, "The decorator rules state that you should never mix magenta and brown." Perhaps a respected home magazine avowed that a certain combination was gaudy, and then homeowners won't use it in order to remain in vogue. Each season, professional home designers and fashion designers and all other types of designers let the world in on what will be the hottest and best colors and styles for the season.

Such pressures and influences, real or imagined, have taken their toll. Consequently, many will tend to select neutrals like tan, gray, or beige specifically because they are afraid to choose their favorite shade of blue. Generally, Americans believe that neutrals such as beige, ivory, tan, and gray are symbolic of sophistication—while bright colors (or certain color combinations) are garish and uncouth. Neutrals and whites are considered a mark of understated elegance. (I have often wondered: Understated *from what?* I have nothing against neutrals, mind you, but there's a myriad of colors for us to choose from!)

There is an underlining irony in this situation as well. One can readily find a score of designers or homemakers who absolutely love the work of impressionist painters like Matisse (who routinely combined magenta and chartreuse) but do not feel comfortable using these same color combinations in a home. *That's different,* people insist. The powers that be continually advise that is it better to use daring colors and combinations to accessorize. The general rule is to use items like throw pillows to bring the bright colors you love into your home—but don't use them on the walls! I call this the "throw pillow mentality," and although it does work well in certain environments, it can be extremely restricting.

In a way, this type of response, this guarded fear, is understandable, considering our color conditioning. Our contemporary (primarily Western) responses to colors have been formulated in part, because of our exposure, in both subtle and not-so-subtle ways, to various forms of cultural *color police.*

One of the most interesting parts of my research into color theory was my realization that we modernists are responding to color in ways we were conditioned to respond centuries ago! Take a minute to look at the color symbology on the next page. You will see clearly that certain connotations and rules about the meaning of each color started in pre-Christian times, and that these rules became more complicated as time moved on. In the case of the code of color currently being used in American universities, color has also been used to structure society. There is nothing really wrong with this use of color. The problem occurs when people lose their own sense of color amidst these symbols, ancient

DESIGNING
A HOME FOR
YOUR HEART
FROM THE
OUTSIDE IN

184

or modern. Historically, the natural aesthetics and intuition gifted upon our forebears were actually shattered during quests for moral and spiritual enlightenment. This loss was far reaching, and the effects are still being felt in today's society.

In post-Christian times, an "anti-physicalism," or an "anti-life" aspect began to take people away from their natural sexuality, sensuality, and intuition. The reigning tenet was that the good god was non-material; and that the bad god was material in a physical world. To be pristine and clean and non-sensual was the right way to be. To be pagan was not.

The brothers and sisters, the priests and bishops, all wore neutral browns and tans, or black and white. Vibrant colors were used sparingly, only on special holy days. Dullness was considered virtuous and bright colors were branded as sinful. Many pagan rituals, which had emphasized color, free expression, intuition, and interaction with Mother Earth, were suddenly taboo. *When the church was strong, colors were weak.*

In discussing the effects of the ancient Christian conquest of the pagans, Prudence Jones and Caitlin Matthews, editors of *Voices from the Circle* point out, "Thus . . . the rich cultures of yellows, oranges, reds, blues, greens and purples were trampled into the dust by a simplistic culture of 'black and white' values."

This influence of the anti-color eventually reached past the aesthetic aspect of humanity and into the realm of natural inner gifts. I have read that women had a tremendous amount of intuition in pre-Christian days. It was common for women to have the second sight. They predicted important events, including their deaths, and even had feasts beforehand. But the officials of Christianity declared the practice of intuition demonic—thus putting ordinary people in fear of their own human nature.

I truly believe that color had a tremendous amount of power, strength, and acceptance in the past. Color and color vibrations were utilized by pre-Christian people in ways we may never recover. Then there was much more of a connection to the universe than we have now, and certainly more acceptance of vibrant colors in daily life, as well as the acceptance of bold colors symbolizing civility and expression, rather than garishness and immorality.

Our present fear of color, fear of clashing colors, fear of decorating with colors perceived as overstated, can be traced back to this transition in religious history.

This concept even overlaps into the basic senses. We aren't supposed to smell, for instance. We should have a scent, not a smell. We have invented toxic chemicals to make certain we don't smell, or that our earth doesn't smell. We frequently destroy natural earthiness and our animal side, to keep this "sinful" part of life under wraps.

Unfortunately, in restricting what colors are good and what colors are bad color police, both ancient and modern, have also restricted our humanness; what we could be, what we could express—if given permission to do so. Even in the world of new age spirituality there are subtle judgements; whereby in most contemporary metaphysical circles the colors purple, blue, and lavender are considered more beneficial and spiritual than oranges and reds.

Because of all this external pressure, people tend to shy away from, and to distrust, that natural urge in themselves. Instead, they worry about which color combinations would be most acceptable and safe rather than what colors they feel would be most exciting, vital, and nourishing.

As a designer, I strive to give color the influence and response that it deserves, and to guide my clients and students toward finding and using color in the most natural, positive, authentic way possible. I feel comfortable using a client's natural intuition. I try to expose them to as many color possibilities as I can, including color systems, healing techniques, and colors both in and out of fashion. Often, when I'm with people, I get a strong intuitive sense of what colors would be most beneficial for them. I freely share those feelings, they share theirs, and eventually, the best and right choices are clear.

Color can be your ally. I urge you to continually fight against puritan modes and the chants of the color police. Choose the colors and combinations of colors that please you—that you feel good being around.

So, do use colors freely, if that is your desire. Think of your color preferences as the flowering of your own personal color system, of your own personal culture—freely expressed. Your color system will be ever changing and growing like the qualities of light itself. Develop your own sense of color cadence and fly your magic carpet to new, exciting heights.

May the Force of Color be with you!

Chapter Eleven

PERSONAL SACRED SPACES

"Peace can vibrate when we are quiet."

—ROBIN LENNON

WHAT IS
A SACRED SPACE?

Every room, every nook and cranny, every large and small object in your home, has the potential to be *sacred*. A sacred space is anywhere your essential sense of self can be expressed. It is a private spot where you can be cocooned in objects that soothe or inspire; by colors, textures, sights, sounds, and aromas that nourish your soul and ease your mind. In essence, it is a deeply personalized area just for

DESIGNING

A HOME FOR

YOUR HEART

FROM THE

OUTSIDE IN

———

188

you. There are no set rules for a sacred space. You can create or design one in any way you want, for any purpose you want, in any size or location.

In my own life, I have devoted much time and energy toward making my entire apartment a sacred space. I live in a renovated railroad flat on the Upper East Side of Manhattan, a structure with interesting (some would say, challenging) angles and architectural details. Since at this point in my life I am willing to admit to having several different sides to my personality, and to show (even celebrate) these parts of myself to others, my environment reflects this willingness. Sections of my apartment are quite wild, actually. I've used a lot of different colors and color combinations throughout the rooms, including those which one might consider clashing schemes. For instance, I painted the walls of my home office in olive green, almost a moss green, while the adjoining hallway is a vivid blue-green. And recently, during a particularly strong growth phase in my life, when I was feeling quite jubilant, I painted salmon and orange and pink egg shapes all over my bathroom walls. There are also spots, such as my meditation area, that are rather subdued in tone, the objects in that space are more spiritual and serious than the 1950s memorabilia that top my hall table.

My bedroom is a sultry sanctuary. The bed itself is covered with soft quilts and plenty of lace and linen pillows. Clusters of pearls, tinsel, and gauze adorn my walls. Carefully arranged flowers (dried and fresh), scented candles, and incense burners enhance the soothing quality of this room, the place where I rest my head at night, the place where I dream and replenish.

My kitchen is especially important to me, as this is the room where I seem to spend so much of my time. If you were to visit me for a cup of herbal tea and a slice of homemade bread, you would find yourself in a room with rose-colored walls, and see cabinets painted alternately in tones of soft oranges and melons, touches of periwinkle blue and sea-foam green. You would not sit on a kitchen chair, because I have no chairs in my kitchen. I have a soft, comfortable, upholstered banquette. On the table, you would see, and touch, the glittery Indian fabric of my tablecloth and perhaps smile at the sight of my windowsill, which is bedecked with a whimsical angel holding an urn in his arms, and various dinosaurs guarding the window ledge.

I have been told that there is an other-worldly, childlike, playful quality to my home, as well as a subtle, aesthetically sophisticated feeling. All are parts of my personality, my inner and outer self. To me, all of what I have created at home is sacred. And I love being here, entertaining here, working here.

Yet even if you do not have the resources to make your entire home as sacred, as personalized as you would like, it does not follow that you cannot have a personal, sacred space at all. *You can have such a space, and you should.*

One of the nicest things about a sacred space is that you don't need a lot of room to create one. As you will see later in this section, a sacred space can be a quiet niche carved out of the family living room; a desk in your kitchen; a window seat in the den; or a corner of your bedroom. All of these places can be easily adapted into your personal retreat.

A sacred space, whether large or small, is still, in the purest sense, a manifestation of your spirit in the material world; a visible, viable, representation of the essence of your spirit. In your special space, you can safely put aside, heal, or release excess baggage. You can be alone, but not feel lonely. You can use the time you spend there to better deal with all the weightier parts of human-ness that keep you from being all you can be, or that are keeping you from achieving more fulfillment at this point in your life. Or, you can sit back, in sweet repose, revel in your success and spiritual bounty, and feel grateful for all that you do now have.

Even if you enjoy sharing your living environment, there are times when you *need to be alone with yourself,* to celebrate your oneness. That is why it's so important to include a personal, sacred space into your home for your heart project. In this chapter, I will show you how to find, envision, prepare, and design that space.

ALLOWING YOURSELF TO BE SELFISH

In your place, you should have the freedom to feel and be self-indulgent and somewhat self-consumed. Getting adjusted to this mode of thinking is not always easy, but to do so is an important step toward creating a truly intimate and personalized sacred space.

In the past, several of my clients have expressed feelings of surprise, even shades of guilt, when I mentioned the idea of creating a sacred space for themselves. Their reactions varied, but most often they were expressed in one of the following ways:

- We are already lacking space for our family, and you want me to take a piece of that space just for myself?
- We really can't afford to decorate another area, it's impractical.
- I don't deserve such a luxury! It sounds so terribly selfish to create a space just to satisfy my own needs!
- I wouldn't know where to begin.

DESIGNING
A HOME FOR
YOUR HEART
FROM THE
OUTSIDE IN
—
190

Allow me to address each of these concerns separately. First of all, as I already explained, a sacred space does not have to be large, nor must it significantly take away from communal family areas of your home. To further ease this concern, I have included (in the following sections of this chapter), several tips for designing personal areas in small quarters.

Second, a sacred space does not require an outlay of thousands, or even hundreds of dollars. It can be created to accommodate any budget.

Third, it is important, and necessary, to be a little selfish and self-indulgent once in a while. In this case, the word "selfish" has only good connotations. It means caring for yourself enough to make a special place where you can be yourself, pray to your god, love yourself, and thank yourself for all the hard work you put into overcoming countless life challenges each day. It means acknowledging that you need to relax sometimes, and that you would be most relaxed in an environment that is in total sync with your internal self. By taking the time and energy to design your own sacred space, you are also proving to yourself that you know (and acknowledge) what you need to feel content and at ease with yourself. Your private space then becomes a symbol of just how important it is to be true to yourself, and to what you love. It gives you a tangible material base to latch onto in this often chaotic and challenging world.

If you have such a place, you will also have an opportunity to emerge from your hideaway refreshed, replenished, renewed, and better prepared for the next series of challenges, or celebrations. Quite frankly, your family, and your friends, can benefit greatly from your sacred space, because in the long run, quiet moments of contemplation or personal creativity will make you calmer and happier.

Equally important, even if you are the primary home designer, it does not automatically follow that you are the only one who should have a personally sacred space! Any member of your family who needs and desires it could have a niche they can call their own. And, after reading this chapter, you can help them create one uniquely suited for their needs.

As to the last question, "Where shall I begin?" you can begin right now by deciding what type of sacred space would suit your individual needs and desires, and blend most harmoniously with your home for your heart.

FINDING A PLACE TO CELEBRATE YOUR ONENESS

Do you recall your great grandmother rocking gently back and forth in her special chair, or the over-stuffed recliner that your favorite uncle insisted was his spot to watch the football game? Is there a particular corner in your child's room where he always crouches to play a quiet game of blocks, or a stack of lumpy pillows near the bay windows where your preteen plops down and stares, dreaming, as most teens do, of her first love?

Or, in your own, personal experience, do you always seem to gravitate to one particular chair at the dining room table with a view of the sofa, one particular side of the porch swing, or one special room in your home to go to think or read? If you do, there is obviously something special about that space that makes you feel secure. The energy or objects there have a soothing effect on you, and although you may not have made a conscious decision to do so, you have already carved out a small but important sacred space for yourself.

Acknowledging this, I'd like you to ask yourself this question: *Is it possible for you to expand upon the spot, or room, that you already feel is special, and make it into an official sacred space?*

If the answer is yes, then you are well on your way. You need only place your personal mark on the area and start decorating. But if it is not realistic, for whatever reason, then you need to search through your home and find a place you can design for oneness. Even if ten other people share your home, there can be a spot in the house just for you. *You just have to find it.*

If space is limited, as it often is, then decide if any of the following alternatives can be freed up for your personal use:

- A corner of the living room, or any room, that can fit a chair, a lamp and/or a small table
- A little-used storage area, or a walk-in closet
- A spot in the kitchen where you can place a desk or bulletin board
- A spare bedroom that is now freed up, perhaps because your child has reached adulthood and moved away
- A guest room that is rarely used for guests
- Any room that is large enough to allow you to spare one wall
- The top of a table or dresser
- A portion of your outside garden or patio
- A basement or attic

DESIGNING
A HOME FOR
YOUR HEART
FROM THE
OUTSIDE IN

192

All of these are possible locations for your personal space. If you live alone, pick an area you don't mind changing at this point. (Yes! Even if you're solo, you should have a special spot which serves as a sacred, totally private space. A spot where visitors won't readily walk in, where you can keep parts of yourself private from the peering, curious eyes of the world.)

While searching for the ideal location, keep in mind that the actual site you decide on should be directly related to what you will be doing in your sacred space—and also to the type of environment, mood, atmosphere, or even the level of quiet, that you will need to become in tune with your self while you're there. If you long to create a comfortable corner you can relax in, read a good book, study for exams, or work on your monthly bills, then you can probably achieve this in a more communal area of your home then, say, a sacred space you will be using purely for meditation and prayer.

To feel completely spiritually refreshed, for instance, some people need to be surrounded by nature. If you share this need, then you might consider a sacred space located close to a window seat, or try stacking piles of floor cushions near your favorite window. This way, you can observe the life outside, whether it is the view of your garden or the birds frolicking atop the bird feeder in your yard.

A marvelous example of an external sacred space (and one can you easily borrow ideas from) is the John P. Humes Japanese Stroll Garden located in Mill Neck, New York. This Zen meditation garden was once part of an expansive private estate. It is designed entirely in shades of green, from the deep tones of moss to the translucent yellow-green of fern fronds. Margaret Roach (*New York Newsday,* April 17, 1994) describes this spot as "a garden (which) has a provocative asymmetry, so that rather than looking like man-dominated nature, the way most gardens tend to do, it looks as if nature is in charge." As you walk toward the garden on a symbolic uphill climb, you pass through bamboo gates. Then you are free to experience the array of stepping stones, uneven paths, waterfalls, and carefully chosen exotic trees, like the gnarled Japanese maple. Some spots have been left unplanted and natural. "What you don't see is as important as what you do; the one, by contrast, helps define the other."

You may choose to use small bamboo gates, wind chimes, stepping stones, and all green plants in your outside space, or you may choose to fill your garden with a visual riot of floral colors. An outside sacred space can become a wicker chair set in a rock garden or overlooking rose hedges and daylillies. It can even be a soft mat of grass nested between twin oak trees or pines (a spot where a hobbit might hide).

In my city home, my connection with nature is limited. But since I feel a powerful urge to have nature around me, I have tried to bring as much of it as possible to me. Along with the plants, flowers, and rocks that accessorize the various rooms, I also take care with my windowsills and windowboxes. In winter, I place moss, red berries, holly, miniature birdhouses, decorative kale, and crystals in the boxes, and the result is a magical winter garden. In spring and summer I plant fresh vegetables and herbs whenever possible. My neighbors have been amazed to see finches and bluebirds find their way to my mini bird feeders; nests of solitude and nourishment in a world of cement. Even in my bathroom I try to replicate the parts of nature I miss. With the right blend of bath oils, candles, incense, and sea salt, I can almost believe that I am in the ocean (not in my tub) on cool autumn nights. This experience is extremely nurturing to my Piscean soul.

If, after you have searched your home carefully, you still feel unsure about where that special place lies, then you can try the following discovery meditation, developed by Anthony Lawlor. According to Lawlor, you can use this meditation to search your unconscious for clues to your sacred space (where it is and what it looks like) and then take steps to bring it to consciousness, and finally, into physical form.

As you are preparing for this meditation, you should keep in mind the same things I mentioned to you while performing previous explorations. You should relax and allow your heart and mind to go where they will.

MEDITATION:
IN SEARCH OF MY
SACRED SPACE

Locate a calm, quiet spot where you can go through the following exploration without being disturbed. Have a friend read the sentences to you, pausing sufficiently between each one to allow your imagination time for a thorough experience. You can also read them into a tape recorder and play them back to yourself at a leisurely pace.

- Sit in a comfortable position and close your eyes. Allow your attention to settle into the rhythm of your breathing. Feel the easy flow of air, in and out, in and out.
- Allow your attention to go to your heart. Experience the feeling you find there. Let go of any thoughts you have about the feelings. Just settle into it. Experience its depths and subtle nuances.

DESIGNING

A HOME FOR

YOUR HEART

FROM THE

OUTSIDE IN

———

194

- Imagine a floor supporting this feeling. What are the qualities of this floor? Is it raised? Lowered? Level with its surroundings? What is its shape? What is the floor made of? Does it have a particular pattern?
- Imagine the walls that shelter this feeling. Are they solid or transparent? Are pillars used in place of walls? What are they made of? Do they have a specific color or pattern or shape?
- Imagine the roof that shelters this feeling. What is the shape of the roof? Is it domed, peaked, or flat? What is it made of? What color is it? Is it patterned?
- Imagine the doors and the windows that allow the feeling to flow out into the world. How many doors and windows are there? Where are they located? What are their sizes and shapes? What are they made of? What makes these windows special?
- Imagine the ornamentation that expresses this feeling. What is the treatment around the doors and windows? Are there paintings? Are there other forms of adornment on the walls, ceilings, or floors?
- Imagine the quality of light that reflects this feeling. What is the source of this light? Is it the sun, moon, stars, candles, fireplace, electric lights? Are there lights in special parts of the rooms? For special tasks?
- Imagine the sounds that echo this feeling. Envision the textures, colors, tastes, and aromas that have those qualities. How does the place that supports and shelters this feeling change from morning to afternoon to evening? In winter, spring, summer, and autumn?
- Sit quietly for a while, enjoying the sacred place you have created. Feel what it is like to inhabit a room or garden that cares for your soul. Imagine what you will do in your sacred space. Will you meditate? Will you read? Play music? Draw? Engage in a specific spiritual practice?

When you feel ready to leave this sacred place, open your eyes slowly and recall what you experienced. Draw and write about your impressions in your journal. Continue to let your imagination flow around the feeling in your heart, filling in any new details that come to you. Over the coming days, refer to these pictures and comments, adding or subtracting the qualities that feel right to you.

Lawlor then advises his students to translate their vision into what he calls a *seed conception*. A seed conception is a visual symbol that expresses the central feelings of your vision, a simple collection of lines that captures the essential qualities of the heart that you want to shelter and support. Ask yourself during this phase: My sacred space is a _____ place and is expressed by the shape of _____.

You should also seek to find one word, or one phrase, that sums up your feelings. This is the *seed concept* of your personal house. Seed concepts are as varied as the human personalities seeking them out: warm . . . safe . . . colorful . . . vivid . . . supportive . . . quiet . . . restful . . . responsive . . . enchanting . . . whimsical . . . inspiring . . . a place to be myself . . . a place to dream . . . These are all terms I've heard people use in defining their sacred spaces.

From the time of seed conception you can make a more detailed plan. There are many ways to bring your vision into a tangible form. In chapter three, your fantasy floor plan was one type of enactment, and you have done several others since then. The method you choose, or even the mode of expression (paints, pen, or crayons) is not nearly as important as the act of drawing itself. Freestyle. Thoughtfully. Based totally upon what you learned about yourself during meditation and without fear or reservation about what you are expressing. While drawing, recall any scents or sounds you experienced. What quality of light reflects the feeling in your heart? Windows, lamps, or both? What ornamentation did you see? What architectural details or window treatments?

On the following pages are two examples of sacred spaces that were rendered after the above exercise. As you can see, this meditation works wonderfully for children as well as adults.

This drawing of "My Sacred Space" was done by Jason, age nine. To Jason, sacred space means high-tech. This particular space clearly combines function with fantasy. Jason designed a floating bed, shiny red and green lights that suspend from the ceiling, and an electro-plant that not only sheds light, but also squirts out water in case he gets thirsty in the middle of the night. A floating computer, VCR, and video game center provides him with all the high-tech fun he could ever desire. A soft leather floor covering was chosen because it "felt good when he was walking around." When asked how he could reach his floating bed and equipment, Jason said that he simply uses the "Gravity Control" switch to turn off the gravity and allow him to float up—just like astronauts do.

DESIGNING
A HOME FOR
YOUR HEART
FROM THE
OUTSIDE IN

196

This drawing of "My Sacred Space" was done by D. H. Tews, who is the artist of most of the drawings in this book and a long-time student of mine. For Doug, sacred space means sensual fantasy and tropical relaxation—starlight; moonlight; sunbeams; candlelight; wind chimes; a rainbow-clean, waterfall smell; rustling palm fronds; strange, fun objects like the prism, radiometer, and aeolian harp; soft, cushiony earthy moss to walk barefoot on. There is a rich, otherworldly quality to his sacred space.

SELECTING OBJECTS FOR YOUR SACRED SPACE

Whatever its size, your sacred space should be decorated with objects and things that give you pleasure. A sacred object is one that reminds you deeply of who you are. "Sacred" doesn't necessarily mean religious, although it could.

Sacred objects are those things in your life, and space, that *are important to you.* One of my most cherished sacred objects is my grandmother Julia's prized curio cabinet. This was once used for storing her china and figurines, but it is now empty of tchotchkes, and I am using it in a very different way than she did. I have one solitary candle in a silver stand. It has taken on a new use with its new owner, but it is just as sacred to me as it was to my grandmother.

What objects mean to you can change over time. And, as we learned in chapter seven, Reclaiming Your Space, this is a natural transition. The wonderful thing about the objects in your sacred space is that if you awaken one morning and decide that these objects no longer seem right, you can simply change them. (Or, you can do what I often do, which is to give them away to my friends and loved ones.) In replacing or altering objects in your space, the entire mood, and look, of your space will change with you.

You should also take care as to exactly how you position these objects. The geomancy of objects is important. Therefore, you may choose, as I did, to learn how to place objects so that the energy is balanced and feels right. I have quartz crystals in a basket in my living room arranged so that the north-south and east-west are aligned in terms of Feng Shui principles. But most of the time if you experiment with the placement of objects, you will find the right and best place without referring to a manual or book. You will just *know* when the spot is right.

Once you do find the location for your sacred space, the next decision is one that I touched upon earlier in this chapter. *What you want to use your sacred space for most?* Do you plan on working, creating, meditating, thinking, or simply relaxing? Do you have no particular plans, or many plans?

Your answers will determine the type of functional and aesthetic objects you should place in your space. For example, if you long for a corner of the kitchen to do your bills, or organize your household records, you will need some basic stationary supplies, a good, sturdy, comfortable chair, and perhaps a bulletin board for memos. That's the functional part. But taking this a step further, you could think about what types of objects and things you can acquire to help you get into the proper mood while you're there. What colors inspire you most? Sounds? What small objects or mementos can you place on that bulletin board to stamp it as your own? Do you prefer a bright overhead lighting fixture, the glow of a small, ornate lamp, or candlelight?

You should start, right now if possible, to make lists of things you'll require. Go back to your "I love" lists and clipping files and see what caught your eye before. Perhaps, when you first started organizing those lists, you clipped out pictures of objects that you couldn't ever imagine really using, but now that you're thinking in terms of a personalized space, you might find a picture of just the thing you need.

Generally speaking, you are looking for objects that personalize your space—things that give you pleasure, make you feel relaxed, or have special meaning for you. If you want to get a round corner table for a spot in your living room, a place to sip coffee or tea and think (or to share a repast with someone special) then take the time to find the perfect tea cup and the most glorious placemats.

DESIGNING
A HOME FOR
YOUR HEART
FROM THE
OUTSIDE IN

————

198

Or, if you have the luxury of designing a space in your backyard, then consider something truly special, like a gazebo furnished with funky or natural wicker chairs.

Even if all you can allot is a small portion of a larger room, you can separate that area by using a decorative object, such as a hand-painted standing screen, or hang silk curtains from the ceiling. Behind that divider sits your favorite chair and a separate area rug, maybe a small table decorated with Irish linen, collectibles, or family heirlooms.

Whatever your design choices, I do suggest you make sure you incorporate your favorite colors into the room. Refer back to your journal and see which colors have continually been surfacing in your freestyle plans and meditations. According to the principles of Feng Shui, if you are using your sacred space primarily for reading or studying, for example, then light blue or pale green is favorable, as are shades of pink. If the nature of your reading is serious, then brown would be a good accent color as well. The many charts that are displayed on pages 174 and 175 can also give you ideas, allowing you to match the colors of your personal, sacred space to your personality, your astrology sign, or your desired mood.

From there you can add music, and surround yourself with visual or tactile memorabilia that helps you feel good about yourself . . . that evokes your soft strength.

Aromas are also important in your space. They can be brewed in a pots on the stove to fill the air with scent. They can be placed in baskets in your space, woven into natural fiber decorations, or tossed into your bath. Many of them can be ingested in the form of tea.

With so many herbs available in stores and through mail-order catalogs these days, not to mention those you plant yourself, your sacred space can become an aromatic heaven. Here are some suggestions to get you started.

To ease tired limbs, try *meadowsweet, rosemary,* or *hyssop.*

To calm your nerves try *pennyroyal, camomile, lemon balm,* and *lime flowers.*

To feel more energized, try *elder leaves* or *flowers, borage,* and *sage.*

Do all you can possibly do to make your sacred space a total sensory, even sensual experience. Also strive to make it uniquely yours. Your space should be stamped clearly, through its design, as yours. And, as you can see, thinking small does not necessarily mean thinking less in any way. When you use your imagination and tune into your needs, you will create a perfect sacred spot *for you.*

HOME ALTARS AND MEDITATION AREAS

When most people hear the term "altar," they often associate both term and purpose with religious structures such as churches, shrines, or mosques. From there, two images usually come to mind: a huge Gothic cathedral decorated with giant statues of saints and stained-glass windows with a forbidding plat-form from which the priest or minister conducts a high mass. The second im-age is of a dark, cavernous space with strange symbols on the walls, and in the center of it, a structure utilized for the sacrificial rites of satanic worship. Need-less to say, although these places could certainly be considered sacred, they are also *not* the kinds of altars I suggest you include in your home for your heart. As Anthony Lawlor pointed out in his article, "Om Sweet Om" (*Yoga Journal,* September/October 1994), "Since the sacred is the most intimate part of our-selves, we ought to find it close at hand, in the immediate circumstances of our daily existence. Spiritual architecture is not solely the province of religious structures dedicated to particular rituals and occasions. It can be created wher-ever the physical surroundings are shaped to give our lives depth and meaning."

It is highly unlikely that you have the capacity in your home for an altar of great magnitude, but you certainly have room within your sacred space for a small altar, meditation area, or even a magical circle. Historically, altars were

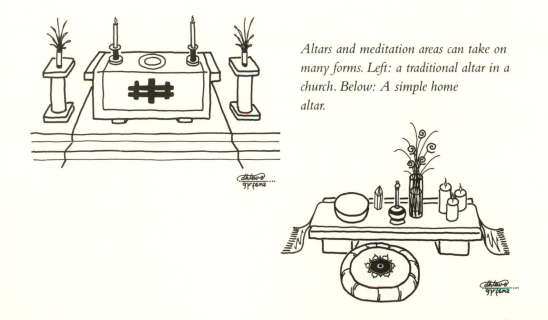

Altars and meditation areas can take on many forms. Left: a traditional altar in a church. Below: A simple home altar.

DESIGNING
A HOME FOR
YOUR HEART
FROM THE
OUTSIDE IN

200

(and still are) connected to religious or cultural beliefs. Many of my clients perform specific rites and prayer routines near their altars. They have found, like I have, that personal or religious ceremonies, either borrowed or self-created, further enhance the time spent in their sacred space.

When describing sacred spaces that are designed exclusively for cultural or religious ceremonies, there are often rules that apply to size, site, and care. These rules vary widely with each culture. For example, some ancient Eastern philosophies that have carried over into contemporary times believe that an altar must be located in the specific part of the home that represents the invisible point in the heavens where the sky and earth come together. Since allegedly it is only there where spirit and matter meld, practitioners take great pains to determine which exact spot in the home meets that requirement. I also know several Spanish women with strong Catholic beliefs who make certain that their home shrines, or altars, are visible and prominent in their homes. These structures are usually built into a concave part of the wall, and each and every saint icon, including the Blessed Mary, is adorned with a special flower or a special blessed cloth. It is also important to many Catholics to have holy water in a bowl nearby and a bead rosary suspended from above.

Not everyone, however, relates the term, nor the need for an altar to a specific religious or cultural sect. An altar in the most general eclectic sense can best be described as *a place set aside for quiet thoughts and reflection,* or simply a quiet place to perform personal ceremonies.

One of the more insightful descriptions of a sacred space can be found in *Llewellyn's Magickal Almanac.* In his treatment, "On Creating a Magic Space," Amber Wolfe says: "The creation of a magical space is a sacred art. It is a craft . . . The Craft of the Wise. When we create magical places, we are drawing energies into form. We are receiving, connecting, and activating all the elements of Nature, all the elements of our Self, and the indivisible unit of Spirit." Wolfe then discusses the fact that from nature we have the four elements of fire, water, earth, and air, and that these manifest in the self as faith, intuition, wisdom, and illumination. "Only with a true understanding of this relationship between Nature and Humankind can we begin to create the magical spaces in which to activate spirit . . . We create effective magical spaces by being in a personal place of harmonious, flowing, evolving connection to Self, to Nature and to Spirit."

It is evident, then, through the writings of Wolfe, Lin Yun, and others I've mentioned, that our sacred space, especially if part of this space is to be used to get in touch with ourselves and our god, should be designed from our knowledge of our inner self. The meditation you did brought you even closer to that place in yourself, perhaps you knew where it was already, and now you are preparing to bring it to life in physical form.

Just like any other personal space, altars and meditation areas can be carved out of a relatively small area of your home. You can set up an altar in the corner of one room, on top of a dresser, inside an empty closet, or even in a free space of your garden. *But wherever you choose, I feel it is highly desirable to locate this particular space, this spiritual space, separate from any other personally sacred space you use for general relaxation, such as watching television or reading the newspaper.*

Your home altar doesn't have to be elaborate, although it can be. You might prefer simplicity in this type of sacred space. If so, then your altar may consist of a plain table topped with a crisp cotton cloth. The table can hold incense, candles, a cassette for listening to relaxing music or inspirational songs, a holy book, a diary or day book, or an icon. Behind the table, framed inspirational phrases can be mounted on the walls. You could even place a silk pillow or a natural fiber mat in front of the table to accommodate your daily exercises, like yoga.

The actual objects you place in your sacred space can be thought of as tools to allow you a deeper, more tangible connection between your body, mind, and soul. Such tools should be chosen with the knowledge that they are there because they are special. They are outward signs of our inner, invisible spiritual state, tangible proof that we love ourselves, or our god. *They should be treated with care and respect, and ideally, they should be blessed.* One of my friends, a student of the Buddhist practice of mindfulness, encourages her clients not only to place objects they truly love into their sacred spaces, but to also place objects that represent who or what *they want to become* either in this life or in an afterlife.

Additionally, objects can serve to nurture a weary soul or inspire hope at times when everything seems to be going wrong. For example, another client, named Leah, keeps a small box (that once belonged to her great grandmother) on her personal altar. Whenever Leah needs something very badly for herself or her loved ones, she writes the request down on a small piece of paper and places it in the box. She believes that the act of writing down (in positive terminology) her needs helps bring them closer to being met, and helps her communicate with her god. When Leah says her prayers, she keeps the needs in her hope box nearby and in mind.

As you can see, a home altar can take on countless forms, moods, and meanings. How you decorate it is totally up to you. However, I would like to make one more suggestion. Once you set up your sacred space, you should go one

DESIGNING
A HOME FOR
YOUR HEART
FROM THE
OUTSIDE IN

202

step further and make certain everyone else in your home knows that it is *all yours*. Brand it as your own, and make it clear that no one is allowed to redecorate it, move your things around, or otherwise change its appearance. It may take a little time for your family to understand and respect the importance of this request, but eventually they will abide by your wishes.

In closing, I want you to keep in mind that the most important aspect of a home altar (or any type of sacred space) is to provide a special site for you to have uninterrupted access to your inner spirit. A spot that promotes a feeling of peace and safety—or acts as a temporary refuge from a complicated, stressful world. A place for hope. A place where you can feel whole.

On the off chance you are still experiencing uncertainty about how to actually begin designing your sacred space, in particular, an altar, I have included the following essay, written by spiritual healer and channeler, Christina Whited. Christina encourages her clients to create a *Personal Point of Attunement* (PPI) in their home, and she offers guidelines on how to accomplish this in what, she feels, is the most satisfying way. You might find her idea works as an inspirational jump start in creating, or enhancing, your own sacred space.

YOUR PERSONAL POINT OF ATTUNEMENT

A Personal Point of Attunement (PPA) is a very unique thing. It is generally composed of three elements: something sacred, something of beauty, and something which reminds one of *light*.

When three such objects are placed together, in the fashion which I will soon describe, they will usually vibrate in harmony with the universe. It is this harmony which we all seek, consciously or unconsciously, and by having a PPA (or several) in your home or office, you can bring more, and better, harmony to you, your life, and to those who are associated with you.

Something "sacred" can be a representation of anything which you hold to be the essence of God. As a healer, I know it to be a hand; as a mother, it is the image of the Holy Mother and child; and for "myself," it can be anything from a postcard of an angel, to a statue of the Madonna which once graced a church near my home.

Behind the sacred image should always be placed first, the symbol of light. A picture of the sun, a quartz crystal, the image of a rainbow. And behind that, you can place a natural object of beauty. For this, I usually employ flowers. Most often, I use dried flowers, as this is a bit easier in terms of maintenance, but I make sure they always look fresh.

When I travel, I often use simple images on postcards, or ones I have cut from magazines, which work just as well.

The point of PPA is to remind each of us of our connection with the infinite, with God, and with the forces which shape the universe. Each time I pass by my PPA, I say a quick prayer or acknowledgment, and thank God for the good life I know. The PPA can also be used as a focal point for meditations, or other acts of devotions, such as saying prayers.

Your PPA should help extend and clarify your relationship with God, while bringing peace and harmony to your home and life.

May the peace and grace of God, and the most Holy Mother, be with you.

—CHRISTINA WHITED, 1996

Chapter Twelve

THE RELATIONSHIP ELEMENT: DESIGNING FOR TWO HEARTS

"When we hold on to what is no longer right for us, we are unconsciously saying that we believe our past is more important than our future."

—ROBIN LENNON

The process you set in motion when you set out to create a home for your heart reverberates throughout your life. Like a pebble tossed into a pond sending concentric ripples toward the shoreline, it affects every aspect of your reality—your spiritual and mental planes, your aesthetic enjoyment, your physical comfort, and your emotional heartstrings. What's more, if you choose to, you can use that

DESIGNING
A HOME FOR
YOUR HEART
FROM THE
OUTSIDE IN

206

process to bring intimacy and romantic love into your life. Even if you are already in a relationship, there is much you can do to strengthen this relationship by enhancing the parts of your home that directly affect "two hearts."

ATTRACTING A NEW RELATIONSHIP

The need for love with a significant other is so universal that most of my clients are experiencing some time of significant romantic transition at the same time they are redecorating their space. Even if they haven't as yet made a conscious connection between romance and interior design, they have unconsciously designed their space in such a way to send out specific emotional signals to others.

These signals are not always conducive to encouraging intimacy and open communication. Nor do all chosen design schemes generate the type of positive energy that would attract a new compatible mate. But once I make them more aware of the direct connection between love and home, they are able to make meaningful relative changes to their space.

Soon, wonderful things started to happen! Before I expound upon these "wonderful things," and start giving you suggestions and tips about how you, too, can improve your love life via your living space, I want you to answer two essential questions.

Do you really want to be in a serious or more intimate relationship, right now? And, if so, is that longing powerful enough for you to make changes in your home that are directly related to achieving that intimacy?

If you aren't genuinely interested in getting seriously involved with someone to the point where they will share your space (at least a good portion of the time), if that desire is currently a low priority in your life, or even if the topic itself seems too hot to handle, then so be it. That's just fine; that's where you are now, and you should continue to focus on a home for *your* heart, not a home for two hearts.

Still, I encourage you to at least read through this chapter, just in case the day arrives when you do want to make your home more conducive to nurturing a new relationship. This advice also applies to those of you who've decided that, when you finally meet your soul mate, you two will simply move somewhere else—sparing you the need to adjust in your present environment; or even if you feel that since you've shared space your entire life (with a brother, sister, or roommate, for example), there's no big difference sharing it with someone new.

Regardless of these variables, you might still find some valuable insights in this chapter! Somewhere along the line, your need for compromise, sharing, or strengthening a romantic interest will come into play. And, a relationship with a lover or spouse requires a different type of shared intimacy than with a sibling, parent, or college roommate. The emotional connection is different, and most often more challenging. But in all of these cases, an emotional connection needs to be acknowledged, respected, and nurtured to establish a healthy, solid foundation for a long-lasting relationship. And your home can help you achieve it.

Your dissatisfaction with the quality of your present relationship, or any tendencies to be involved continually in no win romantic situations, stem from a variety of sources. You cannot solve all your romantic problems by redesigning your kitchen, bedroom, or living room, but you can take steps to make certain you are capitalizing on the strengths already in place. And certainly, if at this point a romantic, cohabitational relationship is definitely something you want, then this chapter is tailor-made for you.

To achieve your goal, you'll need to learn how to blend your surroundings in such a way as to reflect your personal taste, as well as to illustrate your openness and willingness to share that space. You'll need to become more aware of the importance of showing clearly in your decorating scheme that the other person in your life matters.

DEFINING YOUR ULTIMATE ROMANTIC DREAM

The premise of sharing space is not new, yet today it can involve a major transition, and a major change in lifestyle for many of us. This transition can be much easier, and much more enjoyable, if you prepare ahead, before you dash out and bring another human into your home!

And, as you will see in a moment, the first step involves your personal vision of *what you want most in, and for, your heart!*

In chapter three I asked you to design a fantasy floor plan, free from thoughts about financial restraints and other external obstacles. Now I want you to think about your fantasy love life, without worrying about what is realistic or unrealistic, what emotional obstacles are in your way, or what has worked (or not worked) for you in the past. I want you to define your ultimate romantic dream.

You can achieve this in a number of ways. Start by using your design journal to record all of the ideal characteristics of your dream man or woman. What does he look like? What color hair and eyes does she have? What kind of speak-

DESIGNING
A HOME FOR
YOUR HEART
FROM THE
OUTSIDE IN

208

ing voice does he have? How does she laugh or cry? How does he dress? Equally important, how do you look and feel together?

If you've already met someone you would like to get to know better, then envision that person with you at this very moment. Recall visually all the details you can, and even try to hear him or her actually talking to you. Laughing with you. Whispering sweet thoughts to you . . .

As you are conjuring your ideal mate, also think about the types of things you are doing together in your home. Do you envision quiet evenings reading or watching television, or sharing a meal by candlelight? Do you envision the two of you making love in your bedroom, decorating a Christmas tree, planting a garden in your backyard?

Continue the envisioning process until you feel your vision has crystallized. Then, in order to further affirm your desires, you can draw another version (or an enhanced version) of your fantasy floor plan, for example. But this time, design a floor plan for two. If you enjoyed the Angel Meditation in chapter one, then perform it again, meditating on the experience of sharing your angel home with another special person.

What does your angel home look like now?

How is it different from your present home?

How is it the same?

What colors are used on the walls and floors?

What sounds do you hear in the background?

Record (or draw) in as much detail as possible, everything that comes to mind.

At all times, picture yourself already in a healthy, gratifying relationship. Forget about any unsuccessful relationships you have had in your past. Do not allow any negative thoughts or images to enter your mind! Just have fun and enjoy the experience of dreaming.

A LOOK THROUGH YOUR MAGICAL GLASSES

With a vision of your ideal mate fresh in your mind, and a good idea of how the two of you will appear together in your home, you are ready to move into the next stage.

It is probably clear by now that to attract intimacy into your home, your external surroundings and decor must match up with your internal romantic desires. But since intimacy also involves someone other than yourself, you must now begin to combine your romantic fantasy and vision of intimate surroundings, with that of the other person. In designing a home for two hearts, it is important to take an *objective* look at your present surroundings to determine what they are saying about you right now.

Imagine that you have just been handed a pair of magical eyeglasses. You can see the world through the eyes of another. Now, focus on the person who interests you romantically, or your conjured ideal mate, someone you have not yet met.

Put on your magical glasses and look at your living space through his or her eyes.

Moving from room to room, tune into what the other person would see and feel. Consider the type of responses that each individual space would trigger the very first time a potential lover strolled through your home.

- What sort of overall impression does your home make? Warm, inviting, cluttered?
- What type of information does it convey to others? Is your past evident in every nook and cranny? Or are your future dreams more evident in the design?
- If the rooms could talk, what would they be saying? "Come in. Stay as long as you like. There's plenty of room." Or are they saying, "Go away. Don't get too close. I have no room in my home or life for another person."
- Generally speaking, do you see any extra room in your present space that can accommodate another person?

Now, take off your magical glasses and once again view the room through your own eyes. Is what you saw through the other person's eyes the type of vision that matches what you really want to portray? How close is it to the vision you had when you were perceiving intimate moments through your own eyes?

By doing even this simple exploratory exercise, you can further learn to understand the direct link between your living space and your love life and how to begin blending your personal taste with that of another.

The
RELATIONSHIP
ELEMENT:
DESIGNING
FOR TWO
HEARTS

———

209

$\mathcal{D}$ESIGNING
A HOME FOR
YOUR HEART
FROM THE
OUTSIDE IN

210

$\mathcal{T}$HE CONNECTION BETWEEN YOUR LIVING SPACE AND YOUR SELF-IMAGE

Until this point, I have urged you to explore and visualize from the outside in, concentrating on physical, tangible characteristics of your potential mate, and the space you will reside in together. Now I want you to focus on the connection between your living space and your own self-image.

Whether it's a meticulously organized apartment that doubles as a home office, or a rambling house in the process of renovation, your space and what you've done with it shows who you are and what you are striving for. It tells much about your self-image, your emotional state and aspirations, and your willingness to be part of a relationship that involves not only sharing quarters, but sharing of yourself. Therefore, you need to continue surveying your surroundings:

The way it is now, can you really accommodate another person in your home?

What is your home saying about you, right now?

If your home is always a mess, for instance, and looks as if it has been haphazardly thrown together, or in some other state that makes you feel a need to apologize for it, then you are, in essence, *apologizing for yourself.* If the person you are apologizing to happens to be a person you want to build a relationship with, then you are telling that person that "yourself" is not priority enough to make sure that your living space is comfortable, clean, and pleasing to the eye.

To help you determine the type of signals you are sending out to others, I suggest you carefully examine all your belongings, your closets and medicine chest, the contents of your bookshelves, cabinets, and refrigerator, and ask yourself:

- What do these say about my capacity to let another person inside?
- Can I entertain, cook with, cuddle up to, offer a sensuous environment to another person?
- Is there space for another person's belongings?

If you are obviously short on space in your home, this will be transmitted to another person. Sometimes, this simply requires you to make space, to perform the inventory exercises from chapter seven and clear away what you no longer need, thereby automatically creating space for someone else.

A cluttered, messy home may be interpreted as an unwelcoming message. A potential mate may get the impression that you don't care that there is no room for two people to even walk in the apartment—you are a single person and will live exactly as you choose. In the same way, if you are a highly organized, obsessively meticulous, or inflexible housekeeper, you may be giving out a signal that you can't stand the thought of someone else sharing your space.

None of these messages is particularly attractive. And certainly, none of these messages encourages someone to walk in, hold you in their arms, and bask in the intimate, harmonious aura of the room!

Tina, one of my past students, admitted that her home was an "absolute mess," but she also knew she would have to clean up her act to attract the man of her dreams: an organized man who could counter her scattered tendencies. Tina was an absolute delight to teach and work with; she was forever bubbling over with enthusiasm and energy. She loved the thought of romance, of intimate dinners, of being together with another person in her space. Even though she'd had a few mismatches in the past, this didn't faze her enthusiasm. She felt there was someone perfect out there for her—she just had to find him. She'd been raised with six brothers and sisters and was accustomed to sharing space. Her only problem was that she was really disorganized. Using many of the methods and meditations from the "Reclaiming Your Space" chapter (along with most of the ideas you will read later in this section), Tina was able to redo her apartment in a relatively short amount of time. Soon she had not one, but three, potentially wonderful people in her life. She is still struggling with the actual process of maintaining her apartment, but she is working on it, every single day, one step at a time.

Not everyone, however, has a problem, or dream as clear-cut and as easy to overcome as Tina. At this stage of the creative process, you might feel that you do realize you have to change, but either you don't know where to begin or you just can't seem to muster the energy to start making major changes in your home—changes specifically geared to attracting a new relationship. Even though you have decided that you do indeed want a new or better relationship, and that you are willing to alter your living space to accommodate that desire, you might still feel hesitant about actually plunging in and doing something about it.

If this is happening to you, then it is probably an indication that more is involved here than a lack of physical energy or time. Part of you is not quite ready to make a total commitment. Some type of internal, psychological, or emotional barrier is in the way. This barrier must be overcome in order to establish the best mood and message for an intimate, loving relationship.

In the following section, I am going to expand upon some of the common blocks and signals that I've seen manifested through people's living spaces.

DESIGNING

A HOME FOR

YOUR HEART

FROM THE

OUTSIDE IN

———

212

THE FEAR OF LOSING PRIVACY

How do you feel about actually sharing your most intimate space? Are you ready to welcome a lover into your home, right now, and make them comfortable? Would you be willing to have someone stay overnight, for a weekend, or indefinitely?

If you have been living alone for a substantial length of time, these questions may stir up a cauldron of mixed feelings: delicious anticipation, confusion, doubt, even fear. You needn't feel alarmed by these feelings. These are natural responses, because although sharing your life and space can be a satisfying, intimate experience, it also affects something we cherish strongly—*our privacy.*

Living with a significant other, whether you are married or not, means that you will be expected to alter (at least to a degree) your daily routines and rituals. When you live alone, you can choose to be neat or sloppy at will. You can eat ice cream for breakfast, invite friends over for dinner on the spur of the moment, or take the phone off the hook and spend an entire Sunday afternoon in your pajamas watching cartoons. When you are living alone, *the only person you are accountable to is yourself.*

Carole, one of my students at the Open Center in New York, expressed this very sentiment:

I've been thinking about home lately, and wondering why I am so terrified of it. I believe it was living together that was the death knell of my relationship with Ian. I have been feeling blissfully free since the split three weeks ago. I sprawl horizontal across my queen-sized futon in my white satin pajamas and I read until all hours. I break all the rules of proper housekeeping and eating habits. (Healthy vegetarian, of course, but granola for dinner, a carrot for lunch, however I feel.) Once a romance moves to the live-in category I want to get out. So, living with Ian was not a path with a heart. Not for me. He has a heart, yes. But my soul was not free when I lived with him.

Carole was not ready for a new relationship, and through her explorations during the Home for Your Heart course, she was better able to define why. One day, she will be ready to share her space. But at that time, in spite of outside pressure to get into a new relationship immediately, Carole decided she did not want to compromise her space, her creative time, her aesthetics, or her heart. This was an important discovery process for Carole, and if you can relate to her feelings, it would be just as important a discovery for you. Sometimes some precious alone time is what we need to get ready for another heart.

Sharing your space with another person, even one you love dearly, will change your lifestyle, and can limit your freedom. In most cases, you'll be expected to compromise, to consider another person's feelings, consult them before making major decisions, or even forego spur of the moment plans. You will need to share closets and shelves, the bathroom, the bed, television . . . the list goes on and on. I had one client who absolutely couldn't imagine sharing her sock drawer! This really bothered her; the thought of a man's socks mixed with her carefully rolled, color-organized, lines of socks unsettled her! This happens not to be an earth shattering problem, but the point is, when you make a commitment to sharing space, it means sharing your most intimate spaces as well.

If your barriers to change involve storage problems, they can be remedied. As you will see in chapter thirteen there are many products out there to accommodate extra belongings, and many tools and tricks to accomplish this in a relatively pain-free manner.

However, some people are extremely private by nature. They cherish and guard their privacy with great passion. If you are such a person, then you'll need to do a little more up-front planning.

Ellen, a forty-year-old account executive, had been living alone for all of her adult years until, one spring, she met Mark, and actually considered living with him. Ellen didn't mind sharing closets and other neutral space, and since she and her lover shared the same decorating tastes, she knew they would be able to create a cozy nest for two. But when it came to her personal possessions, she went into a panic. "I love this man and want to be with him all the time, but I am not ready to share all of my past. I feel that is private," Ellen told me. "I have all these diaries and journals from my childhood, all these old love letters and things I just want to keep to myself. But if he moves in, I won't have any private spaces."

The entire situation bothered Ellen to the point that she was going to cancel their plans to move in together. Instead, I suggested she talk about this with her lover. I also suggested that they establish "private, hands-off" spots in their apartment. In these areas, the items that each of them felt were only theirs, would be stored.

In the end, he agreed wholeheartedly with this idea, and thankfully, they were both the type of people to respect each other's personal places. When Ellen realized that she didn't have to give up all her privacy, that she was allowed some boundary to her individuality, and that she could develop alternatives, the most frightening parts melted away.

DESIGNING

A HOME FOR

YOUR HEART

FROM THE

OUTSIDE IN

———

214

If your fears of losing your privacy are based in deeper emotional waters, you will need to confront, and hopefully overcome them, before another person shares your space. You may view your present home as a fortress that walls you off from intimacy and worry about what will happen when someone else enters those walls. You may fear the prospect of sharing your space because you feel that to open your home (and heart) to another is just asking for heartache and rejection. The prospect of giving up your freedom and exposing the daily aspects of your life and emotions makes you vulnerable. These feelings may surface even if your heart truly longs to share your life with another person, and you do need to face them, as well as to communicate these concerns to the other person. Strive to deal with them, as best as you can, *before* the other person moves in.

SHADOWS OF YOUR PAST

Another type of personality block I have encountered in my work has to do with *past relationships.*

I have worked with several clients who really longed to attract a new relationship, but surrounded themselves with remnants of their past relationships—thus turning off prospective mates. Sometimes this was a conscious and obvious process, such as the practice of displaying an abundance of photos of past lovers or mates; in other cases the signals given off in a person's interior design scheme are more subtle, more unconscious, but equally obstructive to attracting a new relationship.

I recall one person in particular who was unconsciously sending out this particular type of unavailable message. Millie was in her mid-thirties and employed as a copy editor for a large advertising firm. I met Millie two years after she had broken off with her boyfriend of five years. Al was a wealthy, sophisticated businessman who loved to lavish Millie with gifts, clothes, and expensive furnishings. They never lived together, but they did spend a lot of time together in her home. And because Al liked to live in luxurious surroundings, he readily transformed Millie's simple apartment into a reflection of his own upscale lifestyle.

Millie didn't mind. She adored Al, and his decorating taste, and looked forward to the time when they would live together full time. Unfortunately, although Al did eventually break up with his wife, he also decided to return to her. After much heartache and disappointment, Millie finally ended the relationship, realizing that she had to get on with her own life.

THE
RELATIONSHIP
ELEMENT:
DESIGNING
FOR TWO
HEARTS

215

By then, there was little in her spacious apartment that wasn't a gift from Al, or something they had purchased together during one of their many exotic vacations or romantic afternoons roaming the New England countryside. Millie didn't even consider removing these pieces, although she did occasionally rearrange them.

"I told myself I loved those things," Millie confided, "and, in an odd way I felt I earned them. Every painting, every expensive figurine, every oriental carpet, was 'compensation' for a lie told or a promise broken." Her possessions were what she had to show for the past five years of her life, and to dispose of them might seem that she had truly wasted every moment of those years.

Millie began dating again, and acknowledged that she did meet some very nice men. Yet she couldn't quite click with them, and whenever she entertained them in her home she felt uncomfortable. One man in particular was especially wonderful and they actually discussed living together. But still, whenever she pictured his clothes in her closets, his shoes under her bed, or him reading the newspaper sprawled across her sofa, she backed off emotionally. Eventually, she ended that relationship as well.

Although it was obvious to her friends and family, Millie didn't realize that the reason she couldn't open her heart to a new relationship was because the ghost of Al was consuming her space. I asked Millie to really look around her apartment one day, and decide if her surroundings reflected her personal taste, the person she was now.

At first she said, "Of course!" But after a while, she confided in me that objects she had loved before no longer appealed to her, that underneath it all she would have chosen a different dining room set than Al had chosen, that perhaps she would have also preferred blue tones in her bedroom, as opposed to the somber greens Al had selected for their love nest. Together, Millie and I designed a new look for her apartment, keeping only those objects and furnishings that she felt still reflected her now. Millie held a home sale, selling her castoffs to a steady stream of collectors and bargain hunters.

Late in the day after most of the furnishings were gone, a handsome, soft-spoken man arrived and wandered among the remaining items without showing any real interest in them. Still, he stayed around for at least a half hour. "He was just trying to get up the nerve to talk to me," Millie recalled with a smile. He finally did, and today, they are involved in a deeply satisfying relationship. They aren't yet sharing quarters, but according to Millie she no longer resists that idea, nor feels uncomfortable entertaining him in her newly decorated apartment. "When the time is right, we'll get married," she said. "And we'll be able to move into my place without the ghost of Al staring at us from every corner!"

DESIGNING

A HOME FOR

YOUR HEART

FROM THE

OUTSIDE IN

216

Holding garage sales, or eliminating remnants from a past relationship, aren't foolproof methods for attracting a potential lover or spouse, but they are steps in the right direction. You have heard many times in this book that if positive energy is being given off in an environment, positive events start to happen in that environment. The same concept applies to attracting a mate. If you are open to it, and if your home environment supports this openness, then you will attract someone into your life. Therefore, you, like Millie, should take a good look around your home and decide if the ghosts of past relationships are stifling your ability to establish a new one.

In essence, I am asking you to clear house, to cleanse your environment from shadows of your past that are haunting you in a negative way. If you eliminate these ghosts, you will find yourself much more comfortable with the idea of beginning a new relationship, and certainly create an environment less daunting to a prospective mate. For example, objects and furnishings that represent memories of extremely intimate moments with a past love should be stored or given away. The meaning of "intimate moments" varies greatly from relationship to relationship, but generally items such as bedsheets, pillow cases, lingerie, bathroom towels (especially those with shared monograms!), and any items associated with the lovemaking should definitely be replaced.

Just as importantly, the more of your personal taste that can be seen in your home, the more opportunities there are for someone to see that and discover things you might have in common. Display your favorite collectibles, your favorite books, your coveted china. Display your Hummel figurines, a neat pile of vintage comic books, or theater posters on the walls. Such decorating touches can spark conversation, show off the interesting person you are, and add warmth to your environment. Give the person who walks into your home a chance to see all that is the *present you*.

As you are deciding which objects to display, and which objects reflect the new you, I also suggest you leave some room for another person's belongings. Clear away a portion of your kitchen shelf space, your bedroom closet, or even your bathroom cabinet, leaving sections of these empty. Make it obvious to all that there is indeed enough room for a new person in your life.

I often tell the story of a friend of mine, a library administrator named Paul, who wanted to attract a very specific kind of woman into his life—a woman who loved to read as much as he did. In order to draw this person into his life, he had, in part, done the right thing by making bookshelves and books a major focal point in his living room. He constructed elaborate shelving and displayed

THE
RELATIONSHIP
ELEMENT:
DESIGNING
FOR TWO
HEARTS

247

both collectibles and personal favorites for all to see, complete with wonderful lighting effects. The living room was beautiful. It looked like an English estate library from the late 1800s. Paul reasoned that if a woman loved the written word as much as he did, she would immediately respond to these shelves in a positive way. But Paul made one error in his master plan: He did not leave room for another person's books on his shelves! If a potential mate shared his love of reading then she would surely have her own collection. But where would they go?

I helped Paul reorganize his living room, making certain that there were empty bookshelves as well. The statement of the redecorated space was "I love reading, share yours with me. I have room in here for both of us." Within two months, Paul had met a terrific woman who was an antique book dealer. The last I heard, they were getting very serious indeed, making plans for sharing their love of reading, and their love of each other, in a permanent arrangement.

The home that is overwhelmed by self

Another extremely common barrier to encouraging a new relationship lies in the home that is so blatantly overwhelmed with the personality, feelings, or habits of the self who resides there, that there is no possible way another person would feel comfortable moving in, sometimes not even with visiting!

This manifests itself in two major ways. The first is with the type of person who is so obsessed with doing things a certain way, they absolutely refuse to change their surroundings one iota, fearing this will mean they are giving up either their organized lifestyle, their individuality, their identity, or their freedom. This is the residence that shouts, "Go away! I have my own organized, completely self-sufficient, lifestyle that I do not want disrupted." Homes like this have "mine, mine, mine" stamped all over it. They are uncomfortable to visit, and daunting to imagine staying in for any length of time.

The analogy that always comes to my mind when I enter a home like this, is the old television series, *The Odd Couple*. Meticulous Felix was forever obsessed with keeping things neat, keeping this clean, keeping things his way—which he felt was the only way to live. Although this was a comedy series, in real life it would be (and often is) an uncomfortable, tense situation that would do anything but encourage harmony.

How do you know if you are sending out "mine, mine, mine" messages?

DESIGNING
A HOME FOR
YOUR HEART
FROM THE
OUTSIDE IN
——
218

Well, think about the way you feel when you entertain guests. Do you spend hours and hours cleaning and scrubbing your home, and preparing a meal, anticipating the event? But then, when your guests arrive, are you happy to see them, but also find yourself wondering what type of mess they will make before they leave? Or, when you and another person are standing in your kitchen, for example, and they suggest an alternative, easier way to perform a task (like mashing potatoes), do you automatically shake your head and say, "No. I've done this for years and it's the only way." Do you have the same response to suggestions concerning your home?

Do you visibly tense up when your date, or other visitor, is about to touch items in your home? Do you immediately replace something they move an inch to the left of its original position? If so, you must realize that you can expect a major emotional and mental transition period before you are comfortable living with someone else. Unless you find a person as neat and meticulous as you are, and unless they also like to do things your way (or will give in to you), you will eventually have problems maintaining harmony.

You'll need to become more flexible, more receptive to the prospect of sharing your space, and lifestyle.

Fortunately, for most people, the most extreme side of behaviors such as neatness, privacy, "clutter-bugging," and selfishness, usually dwindle substantially when one enters a loving, stable relationship. Over time, much of what they feared dissipates because of the harmony and understanding that comes along with a good relationship.

Of course, much of what happens after a person moves in with you is determined by the type of person you allow in to begin with!

ACTING AS IF YOUR RELATIONSHIP IS ALREADY HERE

In attracting someone wonderful into your home, one of the best things you can do for yourself is to "act as if . . ." that person is already there.

This means having faith in your vision and taking specific steps to make your living space one that would accommodate the person, and the type of relationship, you want in your life.

I want you to look around your present space and decide what you would do, right away, if someone were moving in to your home tomorrow.

Would you clear out a closet space?

Redecorate the bedroom?

Stock up on food to fill the kitchen cabinets?

Scrub your floors and walls?

Make the mood of your home more intimate?

All of your answers are clues to how you perceive a shared, intimate relationship. And the steps you take to change these answers into tangible realities act as both mental and physical affirmations that it can, indeed, come true. If you've imagined yourself cooking dinner or breakfast for a lover, but you don't have the pots, pans, or dishes that were in your vision, then go out and buy them. (Remember Elliot, the man who designed his entire kitchen to attract a woman who loved him and loved to cook?) If you want to attract an earthy person who loves nature, then fill your home with plants and flowers. If you want to attract a person who loves art museums and modern art, then place attractive prints or originals in your entryway and living room in highly visible spots. If someone special arrives, he or she will no doubt notice them, opening the floodgates for a conversation based on a common ground, and more. If that person is the right person, then you will both feel good about the fact you share the same interest. After that? Well, it is entirely up to you!

And don't forget the romance. By making your living space more conducive to intimacy you can change the vibration to one that is more likely to attract a suitable mate. Redo your bedroom with a romantic theme . . . go out and get new, soft bed linens . . . buy twin recliners for the living room . . . start using the fireplace that you haven't fired up in years—and place a thick, soft throw rug in front of it—just in case.

Establish a section of your home that is especially conducive to relaxing, open conversation. For example, you can put a wicker loveseat on your back porch; place big, fluffy pillows in front of your fireplace; place "his and her" chairs in the living room or an alcove; and make certain your kitchen chairs are comfortable enough to encourage long conversations after a specially prepared meal. It also helps to keep the lighting in such areas soft and low key. The walls could be done perhaps in shades of blue (which stimulates self-expression) or in soft pinks and greens, which are the colors of the heart.

If you invite someone special over for lunch or dinner, you can make the setting just as special as the meal. Time honored romantic highlights such as candlelight, water goblets, cloth napkins, and soft, sensual music, rarely fail in making the event romantic. And don't forget wonderful smells! You can even create a thematic meal, perhaps a theme connected to a particular hobby or interest that you and your date share. Imagine the delight if a miniature train en-

DESIGNING
A HOME FOR
YOUR HEART
FROM THE
OUTSIDE IN

———

220

thusiast finds a table bedecked with centerpieces relaying that theme . . . or a history buff finds a meal prepared from an nineteenth-century cookbook in your living room.

Most of all, always be prepared. You never know when that special someone might walk into your life, or home. These magic moments can happen in unexpected ways. You might just meet someone new at a friend's home and find yourself asking him or her back for a drink. To be comfortable with that possibility, you should always keep your home as "ready" as possible. Keep it organized and neat, keep an extra bottle of wine in the refrigerator, cookies in the cabinet, or a container of exotic teas in your kitchen. I have seen this seemingly magical process work countless times in my work with people. And it can happen to you too, if you believe in yourself and your vision.

When designing a home to attract a new relationship into your home, and life, the decorating possibilities are endlessly exciting.

But what happens after that someone special is in your life? What can you do to help sustain, and nurture that relationship?

Let's find out.

SHARED SPACES

When you move from the stage of attracting someone new into your life, into the stage where that person actually moves in with you (or you with him or her), then you will want to continue using your surroundings to nurture and strengthen the relationship. As I mentioned earlier in this chapter, living together involves sharing almost all the rooms and spaces in your home. But not surprisingly, the room that most people want to concentrate on first (in terms of home and life design) is the bedroom.

The bedroom is the place where you and your loved one enter to regenerate and revitalize your bodies for the daily challenges of life. It is a place in which to make love, to share secrets and sorrows, to embark on fantasies, to feel warm, close, and relaxed. You will also spend a good deal of time sleeping in the bedroom. And since sleeping is an integral part of your spiritual realm, the conditions and place where you sleep should be given great care and consideration.

I feel strongly that shared bedrooms need to reflect a sense of style unique to each user of that room. The bedroom should incorporate objects, colors, and things that reflect the uniqueness of the individuals that share that space, as well as their relationship. In creating a harmonious space, you will need to talk about

THE
RELATIONSHIP
ELEMENT:
DESIGNING
FOR TWO
HEARTS

———

221

your needs and desires with your mate to learn about the type of ambiance you want your bedroom to reflect. Some couples want to create a strong mood of sensuality in their bedroom, others want quiet serenity. I even know several couples who practically live in their bedroom. They come home from work and go right inside the room (with a short trip to the kitchen to prepare a meal) and then spend the entire evening together. In such cases, the bedroom will serve many functions and will take even more planning.

Other couples want their bedroom to be a fantasy world. I am now designing a bedroom that looks like a room in a medieval castle. The couple in this case wants to combine fantasy, drama, and whimsy, as they are almost always laughing and making big plans together. In my own life, I have always dreamed of sharing a fantasy bedroom that resembled a bedouin tent home, with a tall, ornate, pedestal-styled bed surrounded by masses of flowing iridescent silks. You should encourage this type of fantasy in yourself and your loved one. Even if you cannot re-create an entire castle in your home, you can find many accents and pieces of furniture to help provide whatever illusion you might fancy.

Compromise will be called for in designing a bedroom, or any room for two, but often small changes can go a long way. For instance, each of you can have your own storage area, own dresser, a niche you can call your own. Color combinations can be chosen with both preferences in mind, as can furniture accessories. Find the common denominators.

The color of bed sheets can create or enhance a mood. Sleeping on pink sheets will increase your love prospects (if you have no one special in your life) while yellow can reinforce understanding and longevity in a relationship. Blues and greens, lavenders and whites, all promote a feeling of serenity. Orange, salmon, or apricot, along with fuchsia and deep purples, are all good colors to stimulate sensuality. I cannot stress enough that you should be open with your mate, and ask him or her what mood he or she wants to create in the bedroom. Then you can take whatever steps are necessary to make it a haven suite for two hearts. This extends past color and design into areas like lighting and media habits. If you like to read before falling asleep, for instance, while your mate prefers watching television, then perhaps a small targeted lamp could be added on the reader's side, along with headphones that allow the viewer to watch television without disturbing the reader.

If you and yours like cozy chats in bed, then make certain the pillows and comforters are those you can truly snuggle into. If you like to have coffee in your bedroom in the morning, then add a small round table and two chairs to enjoy a quiet repast before your busy day begins. If you do your best communicating simply by lying side by side listening to music, then invest in a built-in sound system.

DESIGNING
A HOME FOR
YOUR HEART
FROM THE
OUTSIDE IN

222

You can also call upon your own mutually shared needs and desires to incorporate meaningful (and purposeful) objects in your bedroom. The music you play while talking, while trying to sleep, while dreaming, also influences your feelings while in the bedroom. The pictures you choose should have special meaning for both of you, and you can certainly choose photos or art work that you both like to gaze at for long periods, or those that evoke warm (preferably shared) memories. When choosing such room accessories, don't forget the ceiling. You will both spend a lot of time staring up in the bedroom, and the ceiling could be an integral part of the overall experience. The possibilities, and potentials in this room, are truly endless.

Nurturing the Dream State in the Bedroom

It is true that you may not lie alone in your bedroom, but you do sleep alone—and you dream alone. Your shared bedroom, or your solo bedroom for that matter, should encourage peaceful repose. For many people, the time they spend dreaming is just as important as the time they spend consciously, physically relaxing in their bedrooms. In discussing the dream state, I am not only referring to the deepest dream period, the REM (rapid eye movement) stage, but also of the twilight state, those previous moments directly before we nod off, the point where our creative energies are highest. The dream state can also be extended to meditation time.

In chapter nine, I discussed Feng Shui, or geomancy, and the specific types of home design that practitioners feel should be included to promote positive energy and harmony in particular rooms. Understandably, the bedroom is always a primary concern, both in terms of conscious activity, such as spending active time in the room and during moments of communication, and during your unconscious dream state.

Although many geomancers consult an individual's horoscope to make final depictions pertaining to bed placement and design, there are certain universal laws that you can apply, right now, to help ensure your bedroom (and its *ch'i* energy) is in harmony with nature, your other rooms, and of course, your *inner self.*

Ideally, bedrooms should be located off your sitting room, and on an upper level of your home. And, since you spend about one-third of your life either sleeping or reclining, the actual placement of the bed is extremely important. The bed should be oriented in a north-south position, with the headboard facing the magnetic north, to eliminate glare in the morning and to achieve the most energetic balance. Geomancers believe that it is unlucky to place your bed toward the door because in ancient China the dead were placed with their feet toward the front door of the death house. If possible, you should also avoid placing your bed beneath a sloped ceiling.

The bed should not be placed facing a mirror because the Chinese believe that the soul leaves the body when a person sleeps. By placing a mirror opposite your bed, you risk the chance of your roving soul getting a shock when it sees its image. To circulate the good ch'i in your bedroom, you can also place wind chimes outside the window or install a ceiling fan. All of these steps can help promote harmony in the bedroom while you are in the dream state, as well as while you are awake.

The
RELATIONSHIP
ELEMENT:
DESIGNING
FOR TWO
HEARTS

223

A HAVEN FOR LOVE AND TOGETHERNESS

In addition to Eastern arts like Feng Shui, I also urge you to take simpler, but equally meaningful steps to make your shared bedroom special. For example, you can take advantage of those wonderful thoughts that fill your mind when you first awaken in the morning by keeping a notepad (one for each of you) near your bedside to record all you have learned while asleep. I also suggest keeping the bedroom organized and uncluttered, and to avoid jamming the area beneath your bed with all matter of dust-catching and environmentally static objects.

Sleeping atop clutter unconsciously affects us, and usually not in a good way. Since we are more vulnerable in our dream state, it seems logical that the area surrounding us should promote safety and sanctuary, openness, and harmony. Sometimes this will challenge you to change long standing habits. When you placed piles of work, papers, and books beside (and beneath) your bed when you were alone, the effects of all that excess may now actually change your relationship. If your mate has to literally crawl over, or otherwise maneuver around a pile of objects when he or she rises in the morning, it may not be the best way to begin anyone's day.

On a deeper level, we all do a lot of processing while dreaming and if the bedroom supports that state, if it nurtures it, it can only make the process more meaningful and healing. Looking at the bed as the foundation we sleep on during this state, it follows that the more space under or beside the bed that is clear, the clearer our foundation for our nightly discoveries.

DESIGNING
A HOME FOR
YOUR HEART
FROM THE
OUTSIDE IN

224

To create a home for two hearts you should take as many of these these steps as possible, and begin merging your tastes with your mate's, *from the very beginning.* I am not talking about merging your tastes to the extreme, of course! You don't want to merge at the expense of individuality or obliterate the natural tastes of either of you. What you need to do is find common denominators. Not only in the bedroom, but in all the communal areas of your home. Of course, this process will be hard for some couples and easier for others. If you and your mate share a similar decorating taste, furniture preferences, feelings about how much to spend, and other design variables, your bedroom, and other communal areas, will soon become havens for your mutual lifestyle. Unfortunately, this is not always the case. Even in the best of circumstances, the task of pleasing everyone in a home isn't easy, and if you are in a relationship that is less than stable, your well-meaning efforts to decorate together can turn your humble abode into a war zone.

There are ways to avoid this problem, though—by planning ahead, by approaching the process as a way to learn about each other and grow through it, and by utilizing the best each of you has to offer, you can indeed create a wonderful harmonious nest for two. It is important to anticipate problems ahead of time before emotional discord strikes home.

And if emotional discord develops, it is possible that it was meant to develop. Swami Satchidananda once said that people in relationships are like two rough stones rubbing up against each other to make each other smooth. When certain issues or disagreements come up between people during the home design process, it sometime means that this issue was meant to come up––meant to be there to allow the couple to get to know the other person (or themselves) better.

To achieve true comfort in your bedroom, you'll need to move beyond function and form. Although the actual type of mattress you select, whether firm or semi-firm, is extremely important for your physical well-being, you probably realize at this point that the overall effect of your bedroom design should promote *peace and togetherness.* To determine how to best achieve this often requires both of you to take time out for an honest appraisal of your past lifestyles alone, and then further soul-searching into what exactly you want your shared spaces to mean to both of you, now and in the future. You can make all your shared spaces living symbols of your love, and a safe peaceful hideaway from the everyday world.

Chapter Thirteen

BRINGING LOVE HOME:
FAMILY HARMONY CENTERS

*"Creativity is a process, not an idea. The most successful people can deal
with the most ambiguity."*

—ROBIN LENNON

I magine for a moment, an idyllic family design structure: You walk into a home where all the individuals sharing that space bask in surroundings reflecting
similar interests and decorating preferences. They enjoy the
same styles and period of furniture; migrate to the same colors;
agree on window treatments; perhaps even prefer the same type
of music, which fills the air with pleasant, inspiring rhythms. No
fuss. No muss. Just pure harmony. Twenty-four hours a day.

Designing
a home for
your heart
from the
outside in

226

Now picture another more chaotic scene: a home where the air isn't filled with Beethoven's "Moonlight Sonata," but rather the sounds of pots clanking, telephones ringing, rock music blaring, siblings squabbling, and doors slamming. A home whose inhabitants have differing opinions about what is beautiful and ugly; soothing or stimulating; spacious or confining. One or two may not seem to care either way about their living space.

Although we are certainly led to think otherwise, the daily lifestyle of the average family cannot be limited to such contrasting descriptions as chaotic or idyllic. There is a steady stream of television sitcoms and movies highlighting one of these extremes for the purpose of entertainment. We watch reruns of *Leave It to Beaver* or its antithesis, the movie *Home Alone,* and wonder: What we are we *supposed* to be doing here? What way can we be together? What is the real meaning of an *average* family?

Well, serious internal problems aside, the average American home, and your home, is a complex, ever-changing network that requires work and effort from its members to maintain what harmony does exist. It then requires more work to build upon that harmony as a means to create a comfortable, welcoming, practical (and certainly, durable) living space. And although the less than idyllic family frequently gathers in shared spaces to disagree about everything from where to spend summer vacation to brands of soap, the aura of those same rooms can soothe a child's wounded ego at the end of a harsh school day; or evoke humorous tales from a grandmother about her youth; or provide a group to prepare homemade dishes that fill the air with mouth-watering (and memorable) aromas.

If you are reading this chapter, then you are probably the family member spearheading your home design project. Since you have chosen to pick up that gauntlet (or the situation has chosen you!), you are also faced with the prospect of designing a space with everyone who lives there in mind.

You will be relieved to know that all of the principles you've learned, and the exercises you've already completed, can be brought forth and used to balance individual and collective needs. The only difference is that you will be gathering more information from those who share your space. How much your family becomes involved is based, in part, on how much you want them to be involved, and also on how much they want to share. Since I am not with you, only you and your family know the answers to these questions. Whatever the answers, you will continue with the creative design process, but now the term *home for your heart* will take on a new, multidimensional quality in both meaning and form.

In this chapter, I am going to introduce you to a series of techniques and thought processes that will help you begin to think more *collectively*. I have even designed a special information gathering exercise you can use to capture the essence of your family to form a *collective floor plan*. From that point, I will give you a sampling of design strategies you can use to begin decorating the communal rooms in your home, as well as information about how to make such spaces both emotionally and environmentally safe.

A shared space, if designed from the heart, can become a shared sanctuary, a *family harmony center,* where everyone can relax at twilight and think: "We truly feel like a family. We love each other and our home." Perhaps it is through this sharing, this feeling of togetherness, that the true meaning of "idyllic" comes into play. Just as you have used the design of your home as a means to know yourself, you can now use it as a journey to learn more about, really appreciate, and enjoy, your entire family.

Indeed, it is a major challenge to create a home that pleases the eye and nourishes the soul when many souls share the same roof. But it can also be an enlightening, healing experience which brings very satisfying results.

Using Design to Bring Your Family Closer Together

In the most general and realistic sense, today's American family can best be described as a conglomerate of souls who end up living in the same house together. And in designing a home for these multiple hearts, I feel that the most important thing for you is to *know, accept, and deal with* your family's dynamics, regardless of how many people share your space. Realistic collective knowledge is paramount to a successful interior design plan, and to learn more about your family's dynamics is the best way to begin designing for harmony.

As the primary designer of your home, if you choose to, you can promote and nurture this harmony. You use the design process to create an environment that brings your family even closer together, or you can help draw your isolated family toward becoming a more unified whole. To achieve this, you will need to do more than select kitchen wallpaper that everyone seems to enjoy. Although that would certainly be a positive influence, the collective design process goes much deeper.

Shared interiors that foster long-term, positive results are rooted in a knowledge and understanding of your family's needs and preferences. And how you

DESIGNING

A HOME FOR

YOUR HEART

FROM THE

OUTSIDE IN

_____

228

actually seek out these responses; how you encourage honest communication and expression; how you use that information to meet collective needs in a practical way, also influences the result.

I vividly recall a client named Lacy who consulted with me on the addition of a large recreation center for her Maryland split level home. She had defined her needs. Outlined her ideas. Chosen a color scheme. But she felt she needed professional help pulling her ideas together and making her vision more "cozy and inviting." Lacy had the insight to realize that since the one thing her entire family loved was high-tech equipment, that to incorporate a room just for that purpose would probably lure her children out of their rooms, get her husband away from his research books, and provide additional entertainment space for visitors. Lacy had thought of everything—well, almost everything. When I asked how the other family members felt about her design, she merely smiled. "They don't feel anything either way. As long as the television is a large screen model and the sofa is comfortable they'll be happy. I am the only one who cares about the actual design."

Instinctively, I felt Lacy was wrong about her family's apathy. Using gentle persuasion, I asked her to gather the family inside the present recreation room for an informal brainstorming session. After a discussion of the high-tech dream objects (video and pinball machines, quadrophonic sound systems, etc.) I led the topic toward colors and furniture and division of space. Within an hour we had learned that her preteen daughter resented the fact that Dad always got the comfortable recliner. She wanted her own. Lacy's seven-year-old son was frustrated because he couldn't reach the tapes piled on shelves high above his head. Lacy's husband wanted an intimate area where he could read—and complained the present lighting was so dim it bothered his eyes. In the end, Lacy used ninety percent of her original ideas, but we added special chairs for each family member (that they each selected from magazines), reorganized and lowered the shelving units, and set up a well-illuminated reading area. The result was a shared family space that captured everyone's needs and satisfied them all.

Of course, not every collective decorating task will be this easy. It takes more time to involve others in the design of your home, and the more people living together the more responses you will have to deal with. Still, because the tone of your household, the vibes, energy, how your family members meld and communicate, has so much to do with its external appearance, you should start out with the goal of nurturing harmony. Don't add to any existing chaos—attempt to disarm it by building up, focusing on, and enhancing those areas that, for whatever reason, are already harmonious.

As Lacy discovered, designing cooperatively not only gives you additional decorating ideas, but also allows the entire family to experience the satisfaction of participating in a joint effort, and then watching with delight as a space meta-morphosis takes place before their very eyes.

This idea naturally appeals to those of you residing in a lively household full of open communication and action-oriented family members. You may even be smiling broadly: "What a terrific idea. I'll gather everyone around the fireplace tonight and get feedback."

Yet, others among you might be frowning. "A team effort? Shared ideas? I can't even get my teenage son to talk about his Saturday night date let alone share his preferences for carpeting in the living room. And my spouse works so many hours that by the time s/he arrives home the last thing on the agenda is choosing a tile backsplash for the kitchen."

For those of you in the latter group, I would like to offer you a bit of inspirational advice: Take some time to re-evaluate your assumptions and open your mind to the notion that, *it is important to make a differentiation between what seems to be and what is.* Your family members may appear to be oblivious to their surroundings, but they respond to them as much as you do. They may appear not to care (or know) much about draperies and antiques, but they respond to the visual and physical presence of such objects in the house. They may seem to have no interior design preferences, but they certainly have opinions. To pave the way for collective designing, you need to block out negative perceptions and make a decision to at least ask for help. Another reason to solicit family members to participate in the design process is because it is yet another way of communicating. If you do not usually easily communicate as a family, the home design process is a good way to start. If you are accustomed to doing all such projects yourself, it might not be easy to ask for help. But in the long run, everyone will probably benefit from sharing the process. This will require you to give up some of your control to other family members, but it might be just what is needed.

After you have asked, you will take the creative process to the next level and find collective solutions, in the same way you made decisions while designing for two, or designing your sacred space. I have no doubt that you will find solutions, but you should be prepared for the fact that these solutions might not always seem logical to the outside world. Let me give you an example.

One of my favorite stories about meeting collective family needs also happens to illustrate one mother's determination and ingenuity. About five years ago, an acquaintance of mine decided to redecorate her living room to meet a rather specific, albeit unusual, need. At the time, her fifteen-year-old daughter was heavily involved in gymnastics, to the point where she was headed for Olympic status. It was winter, and her mother decided she had to find a warm inside area for her daughter to practice. She considered adding an addition to

DESIGNING
A HOME FOR
YOUR HEART
FROM THE
OUTSIDE IN
————
230

the home for this purpose, but in assessing the situation she saw that the family living room was spacious and large, and well suited to use as a practice area. Since that space was hardly ever used (they had an equally large recreation room), she, her husband, and her daughter all agreed that the best strategy would be to place the living room furniture in a storage unit and make a temporary, professionally equipped workout area—one that could include extra storage and seating as well.

Excited about this way of using the family's space in support of her daughter, the mother headed to the local upscale store and asked the decorator on duty for advice. The decorator was appalled. "You want to use your living room as a practice room?" she asked my friend. "That is ridiculous. It just isn't done. I am sorry, I just will not help you design a space like that."

My friend quickly left the store feeling rather frustrated and disenchanted. But, in the end, she stuck to her guns and chose the most appropriate design and objects *by herself.* Both she and her daughter were more than pleased with the results! For the next two years, their living room served the purpose for which it was needed. Then she changed it back into a living room. (By the way, her daughter never made it to the Olympics, but did become a successful gymnastics teacher.)

This story also illustrates the importance of a point that I have stressed since the beginning of *Home Design from the Inside Out:* Good taste is whatever addresses your real needs and uniqueness. Only by experimenting, by taking chances, by trusting your sixth sense of what is right and good for you and your family, will you be able to commit yourself to a choice and then turn your internal dream into an external reality.

As you are shopping for objects for your family home out there in the commercial world of retail, you should prepare yourself for a flurry of opinionists who will attempt to shape your taste to their own. If you are in a specialty furniture store, expect to be told (sometimes in an intimidating way) which sofa colors match which draperies, that purple and green do not mix, that the latest craze is bedding decorated with rhinestones, and that you simply must follow these directions to keep up with the current design trend.

Although many of these people will have sound, useful advice, you should only take advice that you feel, in your heart, is in keeping with your personal or collective needs. With that thought in mind, it is time to move on to the first family exercise.

Capturing Your Family's Collective Essence

Bringing
Love Home:
Family
Harmony
Centers

——

231

In chapter one you visualized your own angel house and began to manifest it on Earth. One way to involve your cohabitants in the design process is to let them tell you what their angel houses look like. If possible, sit down with each member of your family and lead them through this or some of the other guided meditations. Some meditations are more amenable to certain personalities. If they are reluctant to participate, then just review your ideas and thoughts and ask for random opinions. Lead them through the "I love" list activities and schedule family brainstorming sessions. Make it a fun event, a special occasion.

What you are looking for now are honest responses to objects, furniture, color, space, and floor treatments, etc. Therefore, do not dismiss any idea as ridiculous, too costly, or bizarre. Hold back on your tendencies to lecture or point out negatives during the capturing process. You may not agree with the opinions you receive but allow them to be expressed. You can work on a system of compromise later. Right now, you want to get as much feedback as possible. Listen, heed, and *write everything down*. And, let your family see you are doing this! Let everyone dream . . . explore . . . wish . . . and plan along with you. Let it get fun and exciting.

With the very young children in your environment, you can use visual stimulation, such as color charts, fabric swatches, and the photos you have already clipped out of magazines to determine how they respond to them. Children are natural born artisans and have strong feelings about their environments that can be tapped into at this point. Make it a game, or lead them through a toned-down version of the angel exercise.

With teenagers, be receptive to the many comparative responses they're naturally inclined to give you. You may hear: "My friend has this in his living room" or "The guys think green carpeting is the best because . . ." Teenagers feel what others think and do and feel is best, so allow them the freedom to state these feelings, and then try to pin them down to stating their own feelings, needs, and preferences. Sometimes, in their hearts, they do feel the same as their peers, sometimes they do not.

Another thing to capture is something I have coined "a family cadence." If you think about your family in a historical sense, particularly from what country or part of the world the family's ancestors lived, you might uncover shared tendencies in your present life that you can now use. For example, I am part

DESIGNING
A HOME FOR
YOUR HEART
FROM THE
OUTSIDE IN

———

232

Mediterranean and have a strong propensity toward garlic and the other flavors of Mediterranean cooking. I have strong sensual tendencies as well. Capturing these historical and cultural tendencies is inspiring—you can almost pick up each family's own musical key.

When you are finished with your capturing process you will have numerous notes and answers, some of which may surprise you. Write their responses down in your journal as you will need this information later.

BLENDING YOUR FAMILY'S ESSENCE WITH YOUR OWN FEELINGS AND IDEAS

At this point, fresh from your interviews with your family, I'd like you to try to view the communal areas of your home as outsider looking in. You are watching a movie unfold and your family members are the stars. Keeping an objective, open mind, answer the following questions:

- Which area of what room do the adult members of your family seem to migrate to and why? What about the children?
- When your family is gathered at the table during mealtimes, what do you see? Hear? Smell? Equally important, what do you feel about what you are watching?
- Are there any problems that seem to recur at mealtime? Do each of your family members have a particular seat they prefer? Does the space seem cramped? Is there enough room on the table for the food dishes?
- What area of your home seems to evoke the most pleasant family meetings? Is there a special place or room (inside or outside) that naturally promotes communication? A setting where your family seems particularly calm and happy?
- Which shared space in your home seems to evoke the most poignant happy memories? Unhappy memories?
- On a daily basis, what shared space in your home causes the most trouble and chaos?
- What is the best thing about your living room? What is the thing about that room that bothers your family most?
- What is the best thing about the bathrooms? In what ways do you feel they could be better organized?

- Think about each member of your family individually. Where is their favorite spot to think? Read? Work?
- What rooms or spaces do they complain about most? Which spots make your children feel most secure. Why?

Once you begin answering these questions you will uncover patterns in your family's interaction. You will notice that one room or space promotes more harmony than another. And you will also pinpoint the biggest problem area in your home. It may be that everyone has to use the bathroom at once in the morning and arguments frequently erupt over lack of space, clutter, or time spent there. The kitchen may be the spot where your own frustration seeps through simply because it lacks counter space. Your twins may constantly complain that they have no privacy in their shared bedroom quarters. Patterns of behavior signal positive or negative environmental needs as well as emotional needs. You cannot possibly solve all the problems in your home through decorating, nor can you use decorating to make certain a happy home remains so, but you can use the objects and space around you to capitalize on the positive. To reach compromises. To show you care. To nurture and focus on your family.

BRINGING
LOVE HOME:
FAMILY
HARMONY
CENTERS

233

ORGANIZING FOR ACTION

Much information is coming your way now and you need to start organizing it before it becomes overwhelming. As you organize and focus this information, you will also begin to see just why I asked the questions I did, and how your answers and feelings will become concrete tools in designing your home for your heart.

One of the easiest ways to proceed at this point is to assemble (and label) one folder for each room (or major space) of your home. Inside each folder, place the appropriate clippings and photos for that room; along with the sections of your "I love" lists that apply to each room; and any other type of stimuli you have gathered until this point. Also, go back to your design journal and look for the responses you captured (during chapter thirteen) concerning the ways you felt your family was responding to your space. Were you right, for example, in your belief that your son wanted more privacy in his room? That your spouse hated the kitchen table? That your daughter longed for a garden of her own? No doubt, you touched upon some of these areas during the capturing process. You should continue to blend, bring forth, and blend again, fine-tune, and scale

DESIGNING
A HOME FOR
YOUR HEART
FROM THE
OUTSIDE IN

234

down information until only the most important immediately useful information is at your fingertips, and in your folders.

PUTTING IT ALL TOGETHER: THE FAMILY DESIGN GRID FOR SHARED SPACES

I have developed a system for further organizing the information my clients accumulate during the capturing process. On page 235 you'll see an example of a collective grid used by a family in Manhattan who pooled their ideas for the design of their kitchen. You can use a grid similar to this for your own family, but realize that every grid for every family is going to be unique and different. Your family's list of preferences and ideas (the column at the far left) will be different than the example purely because every kitchen project varies. Certainly the number of categories and the length of the columns will change in accordance with your family's size, communication abilities, and present budget.

Take out your folders and transfer data onto the appropriate grid. You should complete one such chart for each shared space of your home. List the room, major headings, and the names of all family members who gave you their feelings and ideas.

When you have completed your grid you will see areas everyone agrees on. *Circle those areas and take note!* Those are the objects or styles that are the common denominators and will provide a harmonious foundation for your design.

Now look at the areas that some members of the household agree on. Underline those and think of these areas as possibilities for decorating accents. If the majority of your family prefers orange and yellow wallpaper but the remainder are partial to a shade of blue, perhaps you can choose accessories, wall art, or even lamp shades to bring in this color preference.

The remainder of the grid will involve objects and styles that no one seems to agree on. In such cases you must measure the depth of the internal feelings of yourself and your family for each area. If you feel strongly that you want and need a sofa that pulls out to a bed to accommodate guests, but your spouse resists the idea because sofa beds are sometimes less comfortable, then you need to decide which would serve the most practical purpose in the overall design of the room. Or, add another chair that your spouse does feel is comfortable in the room and use both in the design. In cases where children dream up objects they want that you just cannot afford, place them on a separate list for the future.

If the living room is too cramped for everyone to sit in comfortably, then it follows that your new design needs to accommodate that need. If you feel sure that your present kitchen is designed in a color scheme that seems to block communication, then go back to the color chapter and find a color (like green) that promotes communication. At times, the deciding factor of what works best for your family will come down to matters of physical or environmental safety. Your son may think it would be a terrific idea to place a wooden hall tree in the foyer (one just his size) to hang up his clothes, but if everyone else is going to trip over it, then that object needs to go elsewhere.

FAMILY GRID FOR A KITCHEN				
Preferences/Ideas	Mom	Dad	Linda (age 5)	John (age 9)
Paint or paper?	_____	_____	_____	_____
Favorite color?	_____	_____	_____	_____
Second favorite?	_____	_____	_____	_____
Shape of table?	_____	_____	_____	_____
Cabinets or types of storage?	_____	_____	_____	_____
	_____	_____	_____	_____
Accessories?	_____	_____	_____	_____
	_____	_____	_____	_____
Window treatments?	_____	_____	_____	_____
	_____	_____	_____	_____
Appliances?	_____	_____	_____	_____
	_____	_____	_____	_____
Lighting?	_____	_____	_____	_____
	_____	_____	_____	_____

Other family concerns and ideas: _____

_____

DESIGNING
A HOME FOR
YOUR HEART
FROM THE
OUTSIDE IN

236

Again, take this step by step. Pick one room at a time, complete the grid for that room, and only then move on.

Some of you may decide to tackle the least harmonious shared spaces; others may prefer to begin with a room or space that only needs a minor facelift or limited changes to feel success quickly and easily. Once your grids are completed, put them away for a day or two. Then, gather the grids, remaining folders and lists, along with your design journals, and look through everything again. This time around, you will add any additional areas you feel are important and delete those you realize are not. You can begin to get more specific as well, starting lists dealing with decorating costs, for example. Determine what costs are required to redecorate and set up a schedule for achieving the job.

If you really want to get organized, take out your floor plans and make them even more specific, making certain you have one that corresponds to each individual grid. Draw in (or paste) the objects you want in the space. Along the side of the floor plan write notes about the colors, fabrics, or wall treatments you have decided are best. Remember, this can (and probably will) change slightly as you go along but it is a solid foundation.

Other master lists to consider at this point:

- Stores you know have the objects you need
- Specific catalogs that you'll need to refer to
- Decisions as to whether or not you need a architect or professional designer to help you
- Time tables and schedules

At this point, I'd like to take the time to talk more about the very special needs of that very special group of people—*children.*

CHILDREN'S BEDROOMS

Even the most well-meaning parent will sometimes experience resistance from the younger members of their family during the design process. In my classes I frequently hear from students who are frustrated because they just cannot seem to get their children, especially their teenagers, actively involved in the home for your heart process.

If you share this challenge, I have a few suggestions to help you move past this hurdle. I have found that children, even the most contrary, become extremely interested and excited about home design when that design focuses on their own personal home, their bedroom. You might be better off concentrating on this area first when you are capturing information for your grids and shopping lists. It also helps to lead your children through the sacred space meditation in chapter eleven or the Angel Meditation in chapter one. If they will not sit still for all of the meditation, even part of it will be helpful to you, giving you much insight about your child's needs and desires.

While gathering information, set at least one quiet hour aside and really *talk* with your children about what you are trying to accomplish. Let them know you understand how important their space is to them, and that you want to help them create their own sacred space.

Open up a lighthearted but nurturing dialogue. Ask them to talk about how they like to use their space, whether to relax or watch television . . . to read and study . . . to explore new ideas . . . to entertain friends . . . or even (at times!) to sleep. Let them know that you know that the bedroom is a magical world where one can find privacy or peace in a sometimes hectic house, or lie on the bed facing the ceiling trying to figure out the way the world outside works, and how one fits into it. Share stories of your own childhood bedroom, if you feel that would help.

As I mentioned before, you could show your child color charts, fabric swatches, and magazines, and then brainstorm room ideas and preferences. When you show your child fabric swatches or color samples, how does he or she respond? Notice your child's eyes at the moment they see a color or pattern. Tune into emotion, not just aesthetics.

You could also refer back to the color chapter, and see which colors might meet your child's special needs. For example, it has been found that a hyperactive child is soothed by blues and greens, a quiet solemn child can be perked up with reds or oranges, and creative children become even more inspired when they are amidst yellows. Green promotes healing in the handicapped child. Colors included in a design scheme for a specific purpose, such as to encourage calmness, do not have to be the primary color painted on the walls or in the wallpaper design, they also work effectively when they appear in curtains, rugs, and bedding.

While planning your child's sanctuary, do not forget the size of your offspring! Remember the story of *Alice in Wonderland*? At times she was so small she couldn't reach a thing . . . couldn't climb onto the big chair . . . couldn't reach a window to peek through? At other times she was so large she broke those same chairs or had a terrible time moving freely from place to place? Now relate this to your own child—especially the toddlers.

- Do you still have that first finger painting from your child's preschool? If so, place it into a colorful frame. If it is small, then enlarge the art with a color copy. Through this process, you can inexpensively transform a small item into a masterpiece of poster-sized artwork.

- If your child lives with only one parent, consider displaying photos representing happy memories with the "out-of-home" parent. This adds warmth to the room and evokes a deeper connection with that parent. You can even set aside an area for photos of cousins or other family members that your child rarely sees, just so your child can be reminded of his or her extended family.

- If your child loves dinosaurs or offbeat action figures, but you just can't bring yourself to purchase curtains or bedcovers designed entirely with these characters, then use thematic wallpaper borders in that design, or set up a small table where your child can place his or her collections. That same table or space can be used all over again when the next fad or phase arrives.

- If you are always worrying that the good bedding on your child's bed is going to get ruined from constant jumping, dripping, or activity, then consider purchasing two sets of bedding, one expensive, one inexpensive. Put the expensive bedding on only during special occasions or when company is coming.

- Think three-dimensional. A picture of a galaxy or sky looks nice, but imagine the impact of a 3-D sky! Cut out the cloud patterns from sheets, and stuff them with natural fiber materials. Set the completed objects behind your child's bed or run a chain of stars (or mobile) in one corner. Hang kites from the ceiling. Have fun!

- If dirty sneakers continually cause marks on the carpeting, then use rubber backed or fluffy, bright-colored bath mats in problem areas, or use patterned carpeting in darker colors.

- Use soft fold-up furniture futons for extremely active kids. These durable and inexpensive child-sized furniture pieces transform from chair to play mat to extra bedding in a minute! They are safe and comfortable.

When selecting chairs and beds, and designing closets, do so with their special miniature size in mind. They need to be able to reach something to use it. Otherwise they will call on you at every given moment to do it for them. If you want to encourage a child to hang up clothes then make sure those hangers are small and the hanging bar is reachable. If you are afraid your preschooler will fall out of a bed then purchase a bed that can grow with them—beginning with the lowest of sizes.

If you have more than one child sharing a given space, then you'll need to apply the same concepts as you did with shared adult bedrooms. A sense of each individual should be evident in the room. Allow each child one wall of his or her own to decorate. Allow for separate storage bins, perhaps in different colors, and concentrate on creating small distinct niches while keeping an overall color scheme that is harmonious. Design for some privacy if possible.

In designing your child's room, I must caution you to be very careful that you do not begin to re-create the room you never had. You should strive to accommodate your child's tastes, talents and needs, not your own latent interests. I have seen parents who still imagine that little girls love to sit idly on their beds for hours drawing pictures of fairy queens, and then, when their child shows a preference for collecting baseball cards or jumping madly on the bed fighting imaginary super-rivals, they are shocked or disillusioned.

Consequently, one of your most important goals is to *accept your child's uniqueness and work with it.*

Whether aged five or fifteen, children who help decorate their rooms always enter that room knowing it is special, and in turn, feel special about themselves. A child's room can either nurture or stifle a growing mind, spirit, and body. As a parent or guardian, it's important to take the time out to learn about your child's individual needs and desires. Then, equipped with your child's ideas, your own practical concerns, and an endless supply of products on the market, you can begin decorating your child's room, keeping in mind *safety, durability, function, aesthetics, and stimulation.*

Bringing
Love home:
family
harmony
centers

———

239

The Kitchen That Nurtures Around the Clock

People are realizing that although decorating trends come and go, it is the closeness, the safety, the memories, and the aromas of our kitchens that linger in our hearts and minds.

In some homes, the primary, even only purpose of the kitchen is to store and prepare meals, and the primary purpose of the eating area (in that space or in the dining room) is to partake in meals. But more and more families are using the kitchen as the central activity center of the home, all day. Both the sociological and psychological meaning and purpose of the American kitchen has been experiencing a reverse metamorphosis. For a good portion of the past two decades, for example, many professionals designed kitchens with the ultimate goal of projecting an efficient, sterile-looking effect. This usually meant using a lot of pure white and shiny chrome, incorporating a perfectly symmetrical layout of appliances, and placing a glossy laminated table to provide a bird's-eye view of the latest electric orange juicer or convection oven.

Unfortunately, over time, such kitchens turned out to be more reflective of the heart of the high-tech world rather than of the heart of the family's physical and emotional essence. In the 1980s, the priority for affluent Americans was to outfit their kitchens with everything from cavernous refrigerators to expresso machines to advanced bread-making systems. But now, with salary and benefit cuts affecting almost everyone, along with an increase in crime, street violence, and other uncertainties, people are changing their priorities. The family home,

DESIGNING
A HOME FOR
YOUR HEART
FROM THE
OUTSIDE IN

240

especially the kitchen, is where many families now turn for safety and nurturing.

Indeed, the kitchen is once again becoming the haven portrayed in old Westerns—the spot where families gathered in the evening to communicate, relax, and feed themselves. That doesn't mean we don't like the conveniences of technology, but there is now less pressure to make technology the focal point of the kitchen. Also, an increased awareness of environmental safety has influenced the ways we cook, clean, and eat. When one is designing a kitchen, thousands of details need to be considered, from layout decisions such as which way to align the sink and what type of storage areas are needed beneath the sink, to whether the client needs a hideaway toaster or food processor to conserve shelf space or whether the client prefers an open shelving unit. The practical must always be considered with the creative.

In reality, the kitchen is the ideal spot of the home for promoting family harmony. It can become a haven as soothing as any other sacred space in the home—if it is designed with care and love.

In the morning, the kitchen can give your family the emotional jump start they need to enter the outside world in a positive, prepared state, or it can act as a negative catalyst that causes them to leave the home physically or emotionally unsettled.

How can you begin to make certain your kitchen or eating area is as nurturing as it is beautiful? As soothing as it is functional?

First of all, you can add a special seating or reading area in the kitchen space where everyone can meet or relax throughout the day. Many people have made their kitchen an extension of the living room, going so far as to add a wing chair and small table in a corner.

The kitchen is often the place where children plop down their books after school, work on special homework projects, and snack throughout the day. Often, the kitchen is the meeting place for friends of the entire family, or the spot to steal a few moments to read the paper, or catch up on a novel. If this is the case with your family, then there are certain things you can do to encourage this type of activity, while also maintaining some level of order. Consider adding storage shelves in the kitchen just for their belongings. (But also establish rules that this all needs to be cleared away prior to mealtime to avoid last minute shuffling of objects.)

You can also encourage your family members to help you prepare meals—even by doing minor tasks such as setting the table or chopping onions. By fostering an environment where meal preparation is truly a family affair, you can positively impact the quality of family harmony during mealtimes, and all the time!

THE ENVIRONMENTALLY
EFFICIENT
KITCHEN

BRINGING

LOVE HOME:

FAMILY

HARMONY

CENTERS

———

241

Kitchens, more than almost any other room in your home, need to function as efficiently as possible. If they don't, then the primary homemaker wastes valuable time looking for things, being frustrated because she or he cannot reach things, or watching helplessly as the tools needed to prepare meals fall into disrepair. When this happens, enjoyment that could be derived from preparing foods for the family is diminished greatly.

On the other hand, a well-designed kitchen, an efficient, organized, ergonomic kitchen, can make cooking and feeding your family a pleasant activity—not a drudge task that you want to get over as quickly as possible.

To me, an efficient kitchen is one that is equipped and ready to go when I am ready to prepare meals. Efficiency stems from knowing your cooking and eating habits, and then placing objects and tools in ways that support those habits. Further, the food preparation site should be as free from excess objects as possible. By planning your kitchen design this way, you can attain a level of efficiency that also promotes ease, grace, and harmony.

If you agree with this premise, then you'll lean toward the needs of the person who does most of the cooking. If you are that person, then think carefully about the types of daily activities you do during your meal preparation. We use the same ingredients, the same pans, the same utensils. We most often cut and dice in the same location as well. Therefore, you'll want to make lists of your most used items, and make these priorities when you are choosing cabinetry or counter styles, or laying out the design of your kitchen storage areas. (See sidebar on the following page for more suggestions.)

If you feel that counter space is most important, for example, then design and purchase with that need in mind. Whether you're creating a six course dinner for a large family celebration or a fast meal between work and a Boy Scout meeting, you'll need ample space to cut and chop in a comfortable physical position. Since you are normally standing for long periods of time in the kitchen, the actual height of the counter is also important. If you cannot afford a custom designed counter, then perhaps you can purchase a less expensive counter on wheels, suited to your height.

If you use a lot of spices, you can start a small window herb garden to allow yourself access to the freshest condiments. If you are forever fumbling for a needed kitchen utensil, then consider dispensing with formal heavy cabinetry and line the wall with open shelves holding your kitchen necessities.

𝒟ESIGNING
A HOME FOR
YOUR HEART
FROM THE
OUTSIDE IN
____

242

In the kitchen you'll want to make an active effort to reduce exposure to contaminents, to design safe storage areas, and to choose major appliances with care.
Some homeowners pay more attention to promoting a health-conscious envi-

The kitchen is the room where you must face the most spills, messes,
and stains, and this can quickly add up to disharmony. There are many
things you can do to make these instances less frequent, and give yourself more time to enjoy the food preparation process itself:

- When storing kitchen accessories, keep them in places that are conve-
  nient. The items you use most should be at hand's, or at least arm's,
  length. Everyday glasses, coffee mugs, and plates can be kept together.
- Think: "Similar can stay together." For example, all baking utensils, all
  mixing bowls, all cleaners, should be near each other.
- Avoid extras: Do you really need four can openers? If you have extras
  you can't bear to part with then place one in the kitchen and store
  the others.
- Cannisters of dry goods such as flour and sugar, along with spice
  racks, are wonderful organizers—if they are accessible. Wall spice
  racks and counter type racks should be near the stove or the area you
  mix your foods before placing them in the oven.
- Some people prefer storing and organizing spices in alphabetical order, but I have found that the spices I use on a regular basis, those that
  I like the best, are better placed near my cooking area and the rest rel-
  egated to the cabinets or drawers.
- If you know that you or yours are particularly messy, then you should
  select fabrics and countertop materials that are easy to clean, such as
  laminated or smooth surfaces that don't hold (and hide) dirt. With fabric patterns, such as those for tablecloths and chair upholstery, strive for
  washable fabrics and busier patterns in medium to dark colors.

ronment than others. Certainly, in this day and age, the more we can all do toward the causes of environmental safety and protection, the better.

$\mathcal{B}$RINGING
LOVE HOME:
FAMILY
HARMONY
CENTERS

243

I worked with one couple, Lin and Bob, who'd finally achieved their dream of purchasing and renovating a large, early Victorian style home in the southern New Jersey pinelands. They were enthusiastic and meticulous planners who spent months and months choosing historically accurate colors, wall coverings, and furniture. Reproduction utensils and pans filled their eating area. Lin and Bob were also meticulous in their environmental planning. Before I arrived to help them design their space, they had already researched many products. In their kitchen, they were willing to take whatever steps were necessary to avoid hazards. We chose a cooking range, for example, that was a reproduction of an old black iron stove, but they had an electric one custom-made as most gas ranges emit dangerous contaminants such as carbon monoxide and nitrogen dioxide. (Gas escapes every time you light your burners, and more escapes if there are minor leaks.) When cooking, they tried to use as much slow cooking as possible since the higher and more forceful the heat (especially on the stove) the larger the amount of noxious fumes that escape into the airways. They replaced the cabinets that came with the house because they were made of particleboard, which over time, is a source of formaldehyde gas. The entire room, and home, was well ventilated.

Even if you cannot take all of the steps that Lin and Bob took, you should strive to do all you can to make your home as safe as possible.

$\mathcal{T}$HE CORE OF THE EATING AREA: THE TABLE

Another way to create a comfortable, nurturing feeling in the kitchen is by mindful selection and placement of the core of your eating area, the place where your family gathers—*the table.*

By now you probably have a good idea as to the type of table you want in your kitchen or dining room. You may have already decided on a pine table or one with a glass top, for example. Perhaps a built-in dinette is needed because of limited space, or an expandable table for twenty because you frequently entertain. But before you make the final decision and purchase that perfect table, I feel it important to place one more thought into your mind: Your table and chairs should not only be chosen with the goal of comfortably accommodating plates and utensils, nor only because the color blends in with the dining room

DESIGNING
A HOME FOR
YOUR HEART
FROM THE
OUTSIDE IN

244

floor, *the style of table and chairs themselves (along with their placement) should actively foster communication and a level of order.*

You can make your eating center achieve your goals for that space, regardless of whether your family dines in the kitchen itself, or in an adjunct dining room. The shape and style of the table you purchase does not have to adhere to any strict guidelines from a magazine, but it should reflect the dining atmosphere you prefer, along with the physical space requirements of your family.

When it comes to size, select a table that is large enough to comfortably seat your entire family (and ideally, a few guests), but not so large that people are constantly groping and reaching for items on the table. If you feel there is a need for more communication during meal times, then select a round table (compact yet comfortable). To enhance this atmosphere, use highlight colors that promote creative thinking and mental activity. In addition, the type of chairs you select is also important, especially if family meals are the major social events of the day, or you entertain frequently. To ensure that this is a comfortable time, choose chairs with higher or sturdier backs and soft, comfortable upholstery that encourages lingering at the table.

On the other hand, if you feel your family's present dinner time is a chaotic disjointed event, then select a longer rectangular table that unconsciously fosters structure. The seating arrangement can also help establish a less chaotic, more relaxed atmosphere. In some families, for example, bad table manners and children's inappropriate actions are distracting, and can often ruin a meal for everyone else. No one likes to admit that their family is anything less than idyllic, but this must be addressed if you want to be honest about your needs. You may consider the old tradition of authority figures at the head of the rectangular table. This can establish a conservative boundary of sorts around unruly offspring. When things calm down, you can ease up on this arrangement if you so desire.

Lighting is another important consideration in the kitchen, and really in every room of your home. Lighting can perform magic when you are attempting to create a certain mood. Some people prefer an open airy feeling at lunchtime, but when entertaining guests they like either a romantic or soft intimate mood.

I know of one couple who liked to entertain their guests in an environment that made guests feel they were in an exotic restaurant. The couple not only decorated the dining/kitchen space in a sleek Oriental style (highly lacquered surfaces in blacks, whites, purples, and reds) but placed designer lamps throughout the room and pin dot halogen recessed lighting in the center of the table to make the overall effect of the meal a truly dramatic occasion.

In a very basic sense, keep in mind that well-positioned lamps and fixtures not only create drama, but they should also be chosen with the consideration that most diners like to see their foods while eating. You can always use candle-light for additional light.

BRINGING
LOVE HOME:
FAMILY
HARMONY
CENTERS
———
245

LIVING ROOMS: THE FAMILY GATHERING • SPACE

As with every other room in your home, the objects you select for your living room, and how you position them, all depends upon your family's desires, interests, habits, and needs. And just like the kitchen, both the living room and recreation room are natural gathering places for the family. But unlike the kitchen, which can be specifically designed around the family's cooking and eating habits, the living room most often has no specific purpose—other than to function as a place to relax.

You will want to determine how much space is required to comfortably accommodate each activity. For example, if your living room is used primarily for watching television or listening to music, then the objects associated with that activity would take priority in terms of space. If your family prefers to use the living room as a reading center, then bookshelves and good reading lamps will be a major investment. However, if you use your living room only when you are entertaining guests (and encourage family activity to take place in a separate recreation room) then your furniture and accessories will need to reflect that lifestyle.

Whatever your family's profile, when it comes to living rooms and recreation centers there is a universal need for one, or several, places to sit down.

We spend a great amount of time sitting (and reclining) in our homes, especially in the living room. It naturally follows that objects we use in that space should be as comfortable as possible. Although some items are purchased purely for aesthetic reasons, such as a museum quality antique chair, the vast majority of family seating serves the dual purpose of allowing us to relax in a sensory sense (it feels good), while also satisfying our aesthetic taste.

Sofas and chairs can run into large amounts of money. But considering the vast amount of time spent in these objects, most people are willing to make the investment in quality furniture. To make certain that you get the most for your investment, you should seek quality in *form, texture,* and *construction.* Do not rely

DESIGNING
A HOME FOR
YOUR HEART
FROM THE
OUTSIDE IN

246

totally on how a piece looks in a show window! It may look beautiful but feel terrible when you actually use it! You should strive to select merchandise that is durable and comfortable.

The quality of the materials and the construction techniques used in seating furniture have much to do with the comfort you seek. But how do you know if an object is quality? Once again, you can safely rely on your sensory-testing to find out for yourself.

Here are a few guidelines:

- CHOOSING WOOD FRAMES: With sofas, love seats, and all types of chairs, you begin seeking out quality by assessing the object from the inside out. This means paying close attention to the frame, springs, foam, decking, padding, and covers. You want the frame to be very stable. It gives the object its shape and endurance. In general, solid woods like mahogany and walnut offer a solid and equally durable frame. Alternatively, and somewhat less expensive, are plywood polymers and some soft metals. If the piece is going to be used a lot, or needs to withstand the use of a lot of company, you may consider white ash, white oak, or American elm. Soft woods like pine are attractive but wear down quickly.

- SPRINGS AND WEBBING: Springs or webbing attach to the frame to provide an elastic quality. There are two common types, coil and sinuous (sagless) springs. In days gone by, the preferred mode of stuffing was hair and feathers, but in the mid-1800s the "8-way tie" was born. This is a desirable alternative in any seating piece. If it is a coil spring, you will have a firm, uniform seat. But if you want a very high quality object, then look for upholstered combinations of spring and webbing covered with flexible fabrics or soft cushioning materials.

- CUSHIONS: Whether loose or attached, most cushions are made of polyurethane foam. Others contain down or synthetic fabrics. High-density foams offer added support and comfort. Cushions can be wrapped or capped with a polyester low density foam or other soft material for added surface plushness. The wrapping gives the cushion a softly rounded look. Most important, it helps prevent the fabric from rubbing against the dense foam core and fills cushion corners.

  You should read the labels with cushions in particular. Visually, cushions should be smooth and uniform in length. Lumpy cushions will ruin an otherwise beautiful piece and in the long run may cause discomfort. You may also want to know if the cushions can be reversed. This will make them last even longer!

Bringing
love home:
family
harmony
centers
———
247

With seating furniture, it is vital that you actually sit on the piece before you buy it. Does it wobble or can it comfortably hold your weight? Is this the type of chair and sofa that you feel you can spend a good deal of time in? If you like to recline, then make certain the chair reclines easily and doesn't squeak. If you like a nested feel, and also spend a good amount of time reading, then consider a wing chair. When selecting furniture, everyone's body finds comfort in different ways. The length of one's torso is a factor in comfort, as is the pitch in seating. In choosing living room furniture, your senses, along with your knowledge of materials, and knowledge of your family's needs, will help you make the best decision.

Living rooms, when designed thoughtfully and lovingly, attract people (and objects) like a magnet! It is not unusual for many people to be sharing that space at once, nor is it unusual to spend a great deal of time in family centers. Therefore, along with aesthetics and space planning, you should make safety a priority in your design plan.

Cross ventilation between windows and doors is very important! David Rousseau, author of *Your Home, Your Health and Well Being,* suggests that, if possible, you have a large opening window or door located on the side of the room oriented toward the desired wind direction; a similar opening on the opposite side is highly desirable. Ideally, a mechanical air filtration or cooling system should be installed to keep the air free from contaminents. If family members are prone to allergies, you may need to forego the wool carpeting for a hypo-allergenic nylon-poly blend. The same advice would apply to the types of cushion fillings that you use, since down fillings are hard on allergy-prone individuals. Even seemingly minor accessories such as afghans should be chosen with sensitivity in mind.

Read the labels before you use products to clean your living room. Many products can cause serious respiratory problems if used incorrectly. Disinfectants, polymer resins used in floor waxes, even certain window cleaners, carry toxic contaminents that can get inside your skin. Actually, the most basic products often work best, without the risk. Try baking soda, borax, and vinegar for fighting stains, and beeswax instead of canned furniture polish.

DESIGNING
A HOME FOR
YOUR HEART
FROM THE
OUTSIDE IN

248

VENTURING OUT: SHOPPING FOR OBJECTS

Although seating furniture will no doubt be one of your major investments, you will also be purchasing many other things for your home. When it comes to the topic of furniture styles and decor for the family room, you have countless options. You should continue your research process, your visits to showrooms, your reading of catalogs, to learn what is available to you.

When you go on a shopping trip, allow yourself to be led into unexpected places, to view this experience as a shopping adventure. An excursion, a sensual sensory experience. See things, feel things, try out new things.

And if you do allow yourself free reign, don't be surprised if along the way, you find yourself drawn to a completely different furniture style or motif than you set out to find. This happens sometimes no matter how much someone plans ahead.

You set out to a showroom to price an American country wood bedroom set and get all excited over the pastel Santa Fe styles along the way. This happens when you allow your instincts to take over, and it also happens when you have the patience to explore, to give yourself the time to choose—to make sure what you think you want for yourself is what you really want.

Finally, you will be ready to venture out into the marketplace. It is important that you enter the marketplace with a basic technical knowledge of what is available to you. You should be aware of the types of fabrics that are most durable, for example, or how the period of a furniture style promotes a certain mood, or the various types of lighting that will help illuminate your work space. Such knowledge promotes confidence, and thereby allows you, as the consumer, to select what is best suited to your home.

But it is even more important to venture out with an awareness of the home decorator's most powerful, natural tool: *an open mind and heart that relies on sixth sense.* Therefore, I am going to ask you, once again, to focus on your sixth sense, your sensory emotional awareness which transcends the traditional knowledge that most people use while shopping.

There is a misconception, especially relating to furniture, that the primary (or only) purpose of objects is that they be functional. They should be practical, they should serve a specific, recognizable purpose. A chair is needed to seat people. A table is needed for a family to place dishes on while they eat their meals.

BRINGING
LOVE HOME:
FAMILY
HARMONY
CENTERS
———
249

A curtain rod is there purely for the purpose of hanging a drapery. That objects should serve a practical purpose is true, but an equally important function of furniture and decorating accents is *to please the user.*

After you bring an object home and place it into your space, you can derive continual pleasure from looking at and living with that object, from using it, and from sharing it with others. Quite frankly, if an object doesn't please you, it will begin to take up extra energy in your home, and make you eventually regret your decision to buy it in the first place.

The reason furniture and other objects can affect you like this is twofold. First of all, objects have their own energy, and you respond to this energy in either a negative or positive way. Second, there is a definite relationship between furniture and its user that cannot be discarded in lieu of pure function.

One of the most accurate and insightful commentaries on this phenomenon was offered by Stanley Abercrombie in his book, *A Philosophy of Interior Design.* In his chapter on furniture, Abercrombie noted: "Pieces of furniture relate not only to one another and to general design concepts, they relate very intimately to those who live with them. In Thomas Mann's short story, 'Tristan,' a character frequently 'carried away by an aesthetic fit' at the sight of beauty, confides that there are times when he simply 'must have' the static control of Empire furniture around him in order to attain any sense of well being."

Later in the book, the author recalls the words of designer Mario Praz to accentuate this point, "The play of memory gets out to objects, relieving them of their utility or market value. They are then free to speak to us . . . although the house as a mirror to the soul, place elect for our sense of intimacy, is a modern discovery close to us in time, by now it is part of our sensibility. The pull, the fascination places and things have for us, lies in the flood of memories they summon up."

Most home designers tend to be *true to the interior space.*

What I do is to be true to the *people living in that space.*

As the designer of your own home, you too should strive to be true to the individuals in your space. If you think along these terms, then you have unlimited options, styles, and colors to work with. If you are sharing your space, you can learn to think in terms of "us"—the people sharing your space as walking, living, moving sculptures in that space. And you need to look at how each individual relates to specific shapes and textures.

For instance, in choosing a couch, or any large piece of furniture, it is not only desirable that it fit into the room like a piece of a puzzle, but also that it fits

𝒟ESIGNING

A HOME FOR

YOUR HEART

FROM THE

OUTSIDE IN

———

250

the size (and preferences) of the person or persons who will be using that piece of furniture most.

Some people like pieces hard, other people like them soft with lots of down. Actually down is a luxurious material and long lasting as well. Foam can get very hard. When it comes to the size that would be best for each person, I have found that tall people (especially those near or over six feet) like a long couch; they don't want their feet dangling over the edge. I also know couples who spend a lot of their free time on the couch, and in this case, a couch roomy enough for two is as important as the color.

The examples go on and on, but my point is that all of these things should influence your buying choices. Thinking about these things will make a major difference in how you will ultimately feel in your interior space—for your bodies, for your lives, for your family, for your guests.

So, we see that this connection between object and user is very real, and has been affirmed for a long time. You should keep this in mind during your quest to find a perfect piece for your home. That means that your shopping trips should be comprised of more than going to a particular store because there is a sale going on, or because you need a dresser for the bedroom and you happen onto a department store that carries one in a nice color. Before you place your money on the counter, you should also make sure you really love it, and that you will be very happy living with that object, day in and day out, for a substantial length of time. To achieve this, you need to use your sensory-emotional responses to tune into that object, and then give yourself time to ponder your options.

If you stroll through the stores with your mind and heart open, you will soon begin to notice that furniture (particularly used furniture) has an energy of its own, and this energy has a definite positive or negative effect on you. Some objects leave you feeling wonderful, others make you feel empty, still others incite no response at all. Several of my clients have stated that the furniture actually seems to call out to them, as if it were whispering, "Take me home. I belong to you."

This energy, or calling, often manifests itself at unexpected times, in unexpected places. You may be wandering through a showroom or flea market and suddenly a particular piece of furniture seems to call out to you. It draws you nearer, and before you know it you are thinking, "I must have it."

This stage of the game is tricky, however, because when an object calls out to you, and your emotions click into gear, you must still step back from yourself and decide if you really need that piece. Would it really work in your home? Can you afford it? If not, is it worth it to you to plunge ahead and get it anyway?

Simply because an object seems perfect, it does not necessarily follow that you should buy it. It may be that for whatever reason you have an affinity for the piece, but do not need it at this place and time in your life. This can be a confusing dilemma, which is why I always suggest that people make up floor plans, "I love" lists, "I need" lists, and inventories, before they go shopping.

Bringing
love home:
family
harmony
centers

251

Learning Restraint

When I first moved to New York City and I had just begun decorating my new apartment, it seemed that in every street, every little byway, everywhere I looked, *there were things I wanted.* In the expanse of Manhattan and other large cities, there is much inspiration and temptation in close proximity, simply because unique items, specialty shops, and antique stores abound. One day, after I had spent much more than my day's budget, I forced myself to leave the shopping area repeating the words: "There is always plenty to buy in New York. There are more beautiful things to find every day. I do not need them all at once." Fortunately, I counseled myself before I spent every dime I had in reserve, and I advise you to think through your own needs before you repeat my almost folly.

I have also developed something I call the "garage sale parking test." Stopping at garage sales and roadway street markets is an exhilarating experience because one never knows what old treasures will be there. But it is also common to overindulge in impulse buying at such events. I tell clients that if they spot a fabulous, but high-ticketed object, they should go back into the car and *sit for ten minutes.* Think about whether it truly is what you want and need. Is it a gem or is it a whim? After the ten minutes are up, if you still have the same strong feeling, then go ahead and make that purchase.

Combining Your Senses to Make Mindful Choices

Even if you heed my advice and give yourself time to ponder your options, you still might find yourself uncertain about whether or not you should buy an object. In cases like this (actually, in any case where a lot of money or space is

DESIGNING

A HOME FOR

YOUR HEART

FROM THE

OUTSIDE IN

———

252

involved), you should further explore the object itself using your perceptive and tangible senses. Whenever possible, you should study, test out, or otherwise examine an object before you take it home with you.

Aristotle said, "The soul never thinks without an image." Jung advocated the symbol as the psychological mechanism that transforms energy: the images of a mythology to manifestation. In Angeles Arrien's book, *Signs of Life: The Five Universal Shapes and How to Use Them,* she conducted a cross-cultural study and found that different shapes have a universality to them. The circle is about wholeness and unity; the cross about relationships, resolution, and duality; the spiral is growth, change, and evolution within ourselves; the triangle is goals, dreams, and visions; and the square is stability, solidity, security, the process of constructing a foundation, and completion. She refers to an archetypal process of choosing among the five universal shapes.

Your preferences or dislike of any of these shapes is a revealing barometer of your internal world. In furniture, there is a different quality about round pieces versus more squared off or triangular shaped pieces or patterns in carpeting, fabrics, or wallpaper.

The first step is usually to tune into your visual response. Do you like the way it looks? Do you like the color? The external shape? Then, you could move onto your other senses. Your hearing can detect structural flaws such as "grinding sounds" that shouldn't be there in a well-oiled and maintained dresser, for instance. Your senses of touch and smell are also invaluable in making purchasing decisions. *Common sense* should be utilized as well.

IN THE MOOD

There are many types of furniture styles. The style or period of furniture that you place in a room has much impact on the overall visual effect and mood created by that room. In deciding which style is best for a particular room, you can go back to your notes and see what type of feeling or mood you wanted to portray in that space. The pieces you select should be a comfortable size in the sense that they fit into the room like pieces of a puzzle. They shouldn't overwhelm or look lost in the space—they should be chosen by scale. On the other hand, some people choose to use furniture out of scale in order to make a statement or create an effect. Placing giant stuffed animals in a child's room can be whimsical; placing oversized, stuffed sofas in a living room can be cozy. But generally, certain period furniture is so commanding that even small pieces seem to rule a space.

Whatever your choice of furniture style, or however you choose to actually place them in a given room, remember that you are not merely looking for good quality, you are looking for what is right and best for you and your family on many different levels.

Keeping your mind open for possibilities is a very important part of the buying phase of home design.

I have found that most people have more than ample ability to purchase good quality furniture. My concern is that people will get caught up in the traditional way of shopping and thereby miss the many alternative, interesting possibilities that lie waiting for them out there. Most people will automatically dash to the nearest Ethan Allen showroom or Ikea store and buy furniture there, without really looking elsewhere. And although these types of stores may indeed have what they need, certainly they will get good quality pieces, there *are* other places to look—for the furniture, and for ideas.

There is a British publication called *World of Interiors,* for example, that has a unique approach to home design not normally seen in American home magazines. There are also many specialty stores and catalogs that offer unusual storage solutions and dual purpose furniture that are quite exciting. There is even a book called *Catalogue of Catalogs* that lists thousands of such publications, covering every conceivable element of American lifestyles including sources for home design and remodeling. Along with unusual catalogs, there are countless specialty shops in small towns, large towns, and rural towns. You need only take the time to look!

There is also the option of custom-made furniture. I have found that most people are afraid of that con-

BRINGING
LOVE HOME:
FAMILY
HARMONY
CENTERS

253

FURNITURE STYLES

EUROPEAN: Euro-styled furniture is rather formal and dramatic in appeal. If you have a shared space that is also used for entertaining, you may consider this line of objects. European furniture comes in many types of designs, but if you want a sleek look, you may consider researching this style further.

ITALIAN RENAISSANCE: This style, first introduced between 1443 and 1564, is quite ornate. It usually incorporates carvings of the human body, of trees, and of flowers. Seating pieces are formal looking, with heavily upholstered bracings. Italian Renaissance objects are not usually the best choices for comfort, but they do add a dramatic touch to a room. In addition, many of the reproductions are indeed comfortable. If your heart is set on this style, you should seek out manufacturers specializing in comfortable Renaissance.

ORIENTAL OR CHINESE: These styles are sparse and clean looking. They sometimes have Parsons legs, or legs with open fretwork and lattice work. Shiny, highly polished woods and deep red lacquers are popular. This style varies in terms of comfort.

LOUIS XV: Debuting between 1715 and 1774, this style offers objects with sinuous curves and contours. It is delicate and refined, and incorporates a lot of ornamentation. Rock and shell motifs, known as Rococo, are predominant, along with short, flaring chair arms. Reproduction pieces have toned down some of the ornamentation, so now Louis XV furniture can be used harmoniously in less formal settings.

(continued)

DESIGNING

A HOME FOR

YOUR HEART

FROM THE

OUTSIDE IN

———

254

cept. They tend to assume that custom or tailor-made automatically means ultra-expensive. The immediate reaction is: I can't buy that. It is too expensive. Only wealthy people can afford the luxury of something made personally for them. That is not always the case, however. If you don't like what you see in a store, you can often have it custom-made for you at reasonable cost.

Sometimes the difference in cost between a ready-made sofa and a custom-made sofa is relatively minor while the difference in quality is major. Certainly, the difference in comfort will be substantial when something is made just for you and your body. Or, in terms of function, the cost of a granite counter-top in the kitchen, as opposed to a plain old Formica top, is really immaterial when looking at the quality.

It is very satisfying to have something made specially for you, to have something in your home that no one else in the world has!

LOUIS XVI: Beginning in 1775 and continuing through the late 1700s, Louis XVI became popular. This style gives one the feeling of being back in ancient Rome or Greece. It is more balanced than its predecessors and features straight lines, long sofas, straight fluted legs, and carvings. Reproduction carvings are of more classic motifs such as urns, leafs, and acorns. It also features tight backs and seats.

AMERICAN COLONIAL: Also known as Early American, this style is influenced by simple country styles featuring exposed wood trims. Often it includes bun feet, exposed arm posts, and riffled or long skirts. This furniture comes in a variety of woods that can be combined with many other styles, and is always a good choice for an entertainment or family room. The mood that colonial style suggests is warm, inviting, and cozy.

ART DECO: This is a French style made popular in the 1920s and seen in many of the song and dance movies of the twenties and thirties. It features a neoclassical tone, disciplined decorations, dramatic lines, and exotic materials and colors. Art Deco is especially wonderful in large spaces.

CONTEMPORARY: Contemporary furniture can mean almost anything! It is your most versatile choice because there are so many sub-styles to choose from. In general, contemporary furniture refers to clean-looking, upholstered furniture that is highly functional. There aren't a lot of decorative ornaments but the choice of patterns is extensive.

THE WORLD BENEATH YOUR FEET

When I think of flooring, I think of *noise*. That doesn't mean noise in the negative sense, either. For example, I just love the sound of my high heels click-clicking across a marble floor in a museum, or the squish of my rain boots sinking into mud. Such noises, and their sensations, truly delight me. The problem is that when I think of these noises in my own home, I'm not as delighted. If I actually walked in my apartment with muddy boots, it would mean a major clean-up afterward, and although the sound of heels across a sleek floor is appealing, it would not be if my upstairs neighbor were the one making it!

BRINGING
LOVE HOME:
FAMILY
HARMONY
CENTERS

255

The point is, before you get carried away to the intricate world of flooring, I urge you to keep in mind one basic fact: Whatever its color or material, *flooring is meant to be walked on.* Actually, a good deal of the time it is trampled on, skidded on, and dropped on as well. This means that durability and ease of cleaning should be primary considerations when choosing flooring. It also means you need to choose a material that is harmonious with the way you and your family make their way across a room, or series of rooms, in your home. If you have a particularly heavy-footed group in your home, then noise (or subduing it) is something to consider.

Just as there are myriad options for selecting furniture and window treatments, there are numerous options when it comes to choosing the best flooring for your home. These options grow daily, as manufacturers try to outdo each other in producing easy-to-clean carpeting, pretty but durable linoleum, impressive copies of Oriental rug designs, or attractive inlays for wood floors.

The best way to approach your decision is to go back to the activity sheets you developed in chapter eight. Which rooms of the home did you target as high-traffic areas? As little-used areas? In places where the family is forever running in and out, such as with a kitchen or mud-room, you may want to keep actual fabric flooring (like carpeting) to a minimum. Use area rugs to add color in the room, and place a simple hand-painted linoleum (a new technique) across the midway. Or, if you are on a strict budget, painting over old floors with high gloss enamels is an economical option that can produce a nice effect.

If you are absolutely set on carpeting, however, you can find one that works in even the heaviest traffic areas. There are fine quality, easily washable, hypoallergenic carpets which are perfect for children's rooms. In covering a low traffic area, such as your bedroom, you have even more alternatives. You will find carpeting in both natural and man-made fabrics that will easily enhance whatever mood or style you choose for that room.

When choosing flooring, the actual *sensation* of how that floor feels below your feet is another factor. There is carpeting that can feel almost like moss outside and rag rugs come out of the drier fluffier than when new. Some people just love to step out of a bathtub or shower onto a thick, warm rug, while others prefer the sleek feel of ceramic floor tiles.

DESIGNING

A HOME FOR

YOUR HEART

FROM THE

OUTSIDE IN

———

256

MIXING STYLES
AND MOODS

Since objects are usually chosen as individual entities, there still remains the challenge of deciding how to mix or match them in one space or room. There can be a great mental and emotional block when it comes to mixing flooring textures, furniture styles, and fabrics. It seems we are taught early on that we should stay with one style lest the result lack sophistication, or look gaudy, or create too many contrasts. In terms of color mixtures and pattern mixtures, this is usually even more standardized. We are told never to mix yellow with purple, black with brown, plaids with polka dots, or stripes with flowers.

My feelings about this topic? *Feel free to mix—have fun mixing!*

Let's say you have a mostly blue home right now, and you find a kilim rug laced with salmon and rust. You can't take your eyes off it, but you were told that to mix orange and that particular shade of blue would be a tasteless decision. Still, you love that rug . . .

You should allow yourself to get it. Find a place for it in your home, and then live with it for a few days. Take a chance, even if you are not certain if it will fit. Most retail rug stores have policies that will let you try a rug out with the option to return. Allow for the possibility that it will fit.

Overall, selecting furniture styles, art objects, colors, shapes, and patterns for our homes comes down to a matter of *choosing things which hold special meaning for us, serve a function in our lives, and appeal to us aesthetically.* The objects you finally decide to purchase for your space can appeal to all your senses. If they do, you will be assured that your redesigned environment celebrates, supports, and satisfies the real you, and the feeling of family harmony you want to create through your home for your heart.

Chapter Fourteen

REPLENISHMENT

*"Home is in my blood, my soul, and my nervous system. Devotion to
home runs deep in me as a vital and sensitive core. It summons me with
a primitive force. A home restores me. It has had special value in my existence
and it will continue even after my death. It holds me like an anchor."*

— BETTE MARTIN

Creation is a cyclical process. As you broaden your horizons and discover more about yourself and your home, you will naturally experience urges to change your surroundings. If you listen to your inner voice, and pay close attention to the energies in your space, your heart and soul will let you know what to change, and when to change it.

DESIGNING
A HOME FOR
YOUR HEART
FROM THE
OUTSIDE IN

258

When this happens, does it mean you'll have to start all over again? Absolutely not. As you will soon learn, you need only heed the seasons for clues about how to replenish your home for your heart. You can then add or remove objects to revitalize dormant corners, or surround yourself with new aromas, scents, music, and greenery. You can finesse surface patterns to reflect your evolving style. You can even perform spiritual housecleaning rituals to make your home seem right again . . . to revitalize and rekindle the esprit and vitality of your home.

The cyclical replenishing process of creation is about sensory details. And, as with every other part of home life design, it is about *possibilities*.

LIVING DETAILS AND SEASONAL BOUNTY

Fresh flowers, potted plants, fruit trees, and herb gardens are all wonderful living accents for any home. Nature's bounty can quickly brighten and bring fresh air into plastic, airless environments, can enhance a humdrum room with color and fragrance, or take an otherwise cold environment and fill it with warmth.

Perhaps the loveliest of living accents are fresh flowers, which are, and always have been, an integral part of every culture, used to symbolize love, beauty, regeneration, and celebrations of every kind. "What a barren world this would be," said author Gail Duff, "without the sweet, natural scents of herbs and flowers. For many centuries, they have enhanced gardens, improved living conditions, relieved depression and aroused passions."

Fresh flowers can gracefully adorn and revitalize any sacred space. In deciding which types of flowers are best, you can simply select your personal favorites from those currently in season, or you can choose flowers because of their cultural symbolism. Both agrimony and white bell flowers are good choices for your meditation area or altar as they represent gratitude, in this case, gratitude to your God. Ivy-leaved geraniums (bridal favor), red double pinks, and forget-me-nots (pure love) are ideal for your bedroom. Choose an arrangement brimming over with sweet basil (good wishes) if you're giving a bon voyage party for friends, or a bouquet of snowdrops (hope) during times of family stress.

I encourage my students and clients to use fresh flowers as much as possible, but flowers can be quite expensive. So, on days when you are feeling blue, or when you seem propelled to revitalize a space that seems stagnant, you can choose just one special flower, such as a calla lily or sunflower, and place this in a special vase. Flowers not only beautify your space, they can be used as a gift to yourself (or your loved ones), as a reward for a hard day's work, or for reaching a milestone in your life.

When using fresh flowers as accents, pay special attention to the memories they conjure up in your heart and mind. When I think of daisies, buttercups, and dandelions, for example, I think of happy times in my childhood, memories of counting petals ("He loves me, he loves me not"), of blowing seeds into the wind to start new buds growing in my midst. What are you reminded of when you see a special type of flower or plant in a floral shop or nursery?

Fresh flowers are only one type of living accent. I enjoy nurturing all manner of greenery, and find gardening relaxing. I feel that growing edible plants and herbs is the perfect way for me to nurture natural foods for my body while adding earthiness and color to my home. I have fifteen window boxes which I fill with vegetables, plants, and flowers, according to season. I grow tomatoes on my fire escape and spices on my windowsill.

You can also take advantage of the seasonal changes, holidays, and all types of special events to rejuvenate rooms, windows, and walls. I love Christmas wreaths and it used to sadden me when the holiday was over. Now, I purchase natural wreaths and change the adornments to match the seasons year-round, something you can do as well. You can purchase a heavy duty grapevine wreath, for example, and then simply change the decorations. Feel free to experiment. Although a specific shade of evergreen and holly-red is traditionally associated with the December holidays, don't be afraid to branch out into other variations, such as magenta, olive green, plum, or teal. Thanksgiving doesn't have to be restricted to pumpkin-orange either. The colors of the fall season are plentiful, and can be called on in many hues to spruce up windows, walls, and table centerpieces. Last year I even started to decorate the dashboard of my car in seasonal themes. Around Valentine's Day, I ride down the highway surrounded by glittering hearts and flowers, or by special cards from my loved ones. During Easter I fill the space with tiny rabbits, grass, eggs, and other whimsical objects. For St. Patrick's day my car is a riot of shamrocks and leprechauns—all placed low enough to allow me to see through the front window, of course! Such whimsical, celebratory touches can affect the mood of everyone around you, as well as guarantee that your home for your heart remains a stimulating, fun, and ever-surprising place to be.

DESIGNING
A HOME FOR
YOUR HEART
FROM THE
OUTSIDE IN

260

THE POWER
OF FRAGRANCE

"To Make a Bath for Melancholy
Take mallows, pellitory of the wall, of each three handfulls;
Camomell flowers, Melilot flowers, of each one handfull;
hollyhocks, two handfulls; Isop; one great handfull; senerick
seed once ounce, and boil them in nine gallons of Water until
they come to three, then put in a quart of new milke and go
into it bloud warm or something warmer."

— ARCANA FAIRFAXIANA, CIRCA SEVENTEENTH CENTURY

"Fragrance is fitness for the mind," said perfumer Geraldine O'Keefe. Indeed, flowers and greenery not only beautify your home or move through the seasons with elegance and style, but their fragrances can be invigorating and healing, cleansing, and balancing. Every day, scientists and physicians are learning more and more about the powerful effects of fragrance on our moods, mind, and bodies. We even have names for this phenomena, *aromatherapy* and *environmental fragrancing.* And because of this renewed awareness of an ancient art, you can now choose from hundreds of potions and scents, in just as many forms, potpourris, scented liners and papers, sachets, pomanders, room sprays, perfumed pillows, sleep pillows, incense, and candles. Blends of dried herbs, flowers, fruits, and vegetables can simmer on your stove while you tend to your daily routine, or create your latest masterpiece. You can use coconut for a festive feeling, frankincense for energy and cleansing, vanilla and tonka bean to enhance the feeling of warmth or comfort. Essential oils extracted from plants can also treat and heal imbalances of body, mind, spirit, and emotions. Oils can be used as massage formulas or in your bath, as well as to scent your drawers and closets, or spruce up dried floral arrangements. The prophet Edgar Cayce recommended lavender oil as a natural relaxant, and cinnamon oil as a digestive aid. And now, even the letters you write can be penned with scented inks, like lemon verbena, a delicate aroma that will waft to the reader's nose the moment he or she opens the envelope.

Which fragrances are right and best for you is an extremely personal decision, and you will probably need to experiment with several scents and combinations of aromas before you make your choice.

PERELANDRA

If you choose to use natural decorating accents in your home, then you should know about a very special place, and resource.

In Virginia lies the land called *Perelandra*. Its owners, Machaelle Small Wright and husband, Clarence, call it a research center, "a deva and nature spirit sanctuary," where nature intelligence is studied as a means to understand and implement an alternative approach to ecology and gardening. They have learned that there is a strong inter-dynamic between ecology, gardening, agriculture, and health and have made this their life's work. They have a staff that studies and grows natural wonders, calling on earth spirits to guide and work with them along the way. At the core of Perelandra is a one-hundred-foot diameter garden, which its owners feel is the best place to see results, as well as learn the impact a particular plant has on the gardener's health and balance.

Wright, who calls her methods "new age ecology," learns about the needs and attributes of nature by communicating with the devas who rule over each component. ("Deva" is the sanskrit word for "body of light.") Each of us can hear a deva's message, but we will translate or actually hear the message differently. Still, the essence of the message will remain intact.

In Wright's book, *Behaving As if the God in All Life Mattered,* we see the message passed along by the lilium auratum deva: "We feel it is high time for man to branch out and include in his horizon the different forms of life which are a part of his world. He has been forcing his own creations and vibrations on the world without taking into consideration that all living things are part of the whole, just as he is, placed there by divine plan and purpose. Each plant, each mineral has its own contribution to make to the whole, just as each soul has . . ."

Every spring, a new Perelandra catalog is issued, offering you products, books, flower essences, and tapes that you can use to learn an unusual and special way of gardening, soil balancing, and healing. Through this resource, Perelandra, you can achieve higher levels of spiritual balance and fulfillment while creating your own piece of the whole, your home for your heart.

MUSICAL VIBRATIONS AS STIMULANTS

We move from the replenishing, living accents that involve your senses of smell and sight, into the realm of hearing and sound—*music.*

Music has the power to trigger positive sensory responses, responses as strong

DESIGNING
A HOME FOR
YOUR HEART
FROM THE
OUTSIDE IN
___
262

as those we experience when we inhale the fragrance of fresh, aromatic flowers, or stare at the sunset through a picture window, or touch our cheek to a soft pillow as we drift off to sleep.

Music can be healing, inspirational, or relaxing, acting as a bridge between the other types of sensory home experiences. It entwines you in an umbrella of sound that complements any room of your home, from the library to the kitchen, the meditation area to the bedroom, or even the bathroom.

Throughout this book, I have encouraged you to explore, and then include, the sounds of nature into your life design plan. I now urge you to incorporate all types of music, natural and man-made, into your home for your heart, *on a regular basis.* Open up your mind to the many ways music can be used!

Most of us think of classical music when we think of being relaxed, but there are other types of calming and inspirational music to consider. There is a wide range of styles available from music stores and mail order specialty catalogs. If you feel you need a break from what you're habitually playing, for instance, then consider a tape or CD of water sounds. This music is designed to capture the rushing sounds of the sea, the cycles of the tides, the sounds of the ocean as it ebbs and flows.

Music featuring Native American flutes and Incan panpipes can also create a profound sense of calm in the listener, as can the music of tropical rain forests, or the polyrhythmic sounds from southeast Asia. There are even beautiful, mesmerizing tapes that can lead you on a journey rooted in a shamanic dream. Gregorian chants, American flutes and thunder melodies are all out there for your enjoyment. You can choose a musical recording for every mood. Some music stores, such as HMV, have a try-out policy—if you don't like a tape or CD you can return it, so you can then experiment much more.

When selecting a musical environment, you may also want to consider specific notes, or chords, that are in harmony with your personal astrology sign. Colors healers believe that each horoscope sign vibrates to a specific musical note. Using the chart below, you can match your sun sign (or rising/ascendant sign) to the

---

ASTROLOGY AND MUSIC

Each horoscope sign vibrates to a certain musical note. Find your sun sign below:

Aries	D-flat
Taurus	E-flat
Scorpio	E
Gemini	F-sharp
Libra	D-natural
Sagittarius	F
Cancer	G-sharp
Capricorn	G-natural
Leo	A-sharp
Aquarius	A-natural
Pisces	B
Virgo	C

appropriate note. Then you can select recordings and music that accentuate that note.

If you accept the fact that music is really a vibration, or a series of vibrations, then you also realize that not all music is readily heard through your conscious awareness. Just as the staff of Perelandra moved beyond the perceptual, tangible reality into deeper invisible forces and vibrations of nature, so can you learn to move deeper into the hidden vibrations or songs of objects, such as gems. Gems can be used as color design body accents as well as stimulants. In *Gems and Stones,* a healing book based on the work of Edgar Cayce, Ken Carley explains the song of gems this way: "Our bodies like the universe are atomic in nature. Outside stimuli such as rocks and gems create an electromagnetic influence which helps affect a man's body. There is a word picture which has helped me understand this. Imagine, if you can, an angel with a harp sending forth a tone which, for our example, is the tone of creation. Now imagine a tuning fork which represents a gem. The elements of the body can be thought of as many tiny tuning forks . . . when the gem tuning fork is near the body (those which are 'in sympathy') respond to the stimulus and increase their vibration."

You can use clusters of gems, or strategically placed gems (on your body or atop an object in your space) to achieve a particular mood, to encourage healing, or simply to become more attuned to your space, or spiritual self. In his readings, Cayce emphasized the power of pearls to stimulate creativity, to sustain an even temperament during times of stress or adversity, and to generally strengthen the constitution. He also recommended azurite, the blue lapis lazuli, and malachite (lapis ligurious), to improve psychic abilities as well as decision-making skills.

In seeking out music for your home, look for both tangible and seemingly intangible vibrations to enhance your environment and benefit those who share your space. Work with your energy and the energy of your home regularly, to clear it out, balance it, and stay in tune with it with all of your senses.

𝒫ATTERNS AND SHAPES

As a designer, I am particularly fascinated by the magic of fabric in terms of texture, pattern, and shapes. One of the most versatile ways for you to rejuvenate or change your space, without changing everything, is through the use of fabric and upholstery. Think about how many objects in your home are covered by some type of material. You can economically bring new life to an old treasure,

DESIGNING

A HOME FOR

YOUR HEART

FROM THE

OUTSIDE IN

———

264

or an entire room, simply by changing the fabric on one or more objects through slipcovers, reupholstering, or just pretty throws, scarves, or soft rugs.

When thinking about material and its patterns, you should be aware that you are dealing with something deeper than a mere description of a fabric's content of cotton, linen, or wool—or even beyond whether a sofa cover is blue, orange, or beige. The patterns and shapes in a fabric have a great influence on the total look of a given space, and on your psychological response to your space.

There is also a strong spiritual and evolutionary connection between you and the type of patterns and shapes you choose to surround yourself with, as we discussed in chapter twelve.

Therefore, in choosing fabric and shapes for your home, you might suddenly find yourself drawn to a geometric pattern rather than your usual circular or floral patterns. Arrien has used mythological and historical research to study these shapes, and sees the square, for example, as a representation of stability and security. Then perhaps, if you want to be more organized and more grounded in your home, you would want to select a square pattern, or even a square piece of furniture or artwork, to help you achieve this sense of organization. With the spiral shape, which according to the author represents growth, change, and evolution coming to the same point, you might choose a spiral pattern to bring this new energy, this newfound enlightenment, into your life and home.

Different patterns also conjure up particular memories and moods, and can be used to make personal statements. Therefore, while shopping for fabrics and materials, make sure you take the time to think about these feelings and what you want to say through the patterns. When you bring the material home, you will want to be satisfied with that choice for as long as possible. You should also remember to use your sense of touch to explore the fabric. Rub it between your fingers. Run it across your bare arms. How does it feel against your skin? Is it cold or warm? Scratchy or soft? Would you feel comfortable sitting against it? Is the texture pleasing to your touch? Is the material durable? Well constructed? All of these elements should be carefully considered. The choices of fabrics, types of woods, and leather can almost feel like an extension of your skin and be very familiar to you.

One of the more remarkable examples of making a statement, and of creating a specific mood through shapes and patterns, can be found in the much-photographed East Hampton home of special effects genius Bran Ferren. If you are walking by the external back walls of this estate, you see a semicircular shaped wall designed in the shape of a face; the eyes light the inside den and the lip-shaped window lights a guest bedroom. At night from the outside, it looks like a Halloween lantern, whimsical, slightly eerie, but certainly unusual. Inside, is a keyhole-shaped doorway which frames a wooden soldier, and in another room a tall circular window is flanked by ten-foot stone giraffes. The overall effect is quite extraordinary. What is most striking about Ferren's house is his willingness to express himself. Although you might not have the resources to design in such an elaborate way, you can certainly incorporate different shapes through artwork, sculpture, wall coverings, and rugs, as well as through your choice of pattern, shapes, and colors covering your furniture.

I urge you to explore both the conscious and subconscious meanings of patterns and shapes in your quest to bring your home design process beyond the scope of simple redecorating and into the realm of personal life design.

SPRING CLEANING AND SPIRITUAL HOUSEWARMING

Along with changing, adding, or altering the smells, sounds, and fabric materials in your home, you can also recirculate special energies to replenish your environment. You can do this by moving objects, and by physically and spiritually cleansing your space.

Every day, objects collect memories that you'll outgrow. When that happens, you should replace those objects with new ones, or put them away in storage until you sense it is time to bring them out again. You will find that heavy furnishings, such as sofas and large tables, that are rooted in the same position for long periods of time, can eventually weigh down your space and begin to control the room. When this happens, simply move the object (even slightly) to change and freshen the energy. You can also change the position of chairs, pictures, posters, small wall mounted cabinets, throw rugs, or even pillows on your bed. Although this may sound deceptively simple, moving objects around can make a major difference in the way a room looks and feels. Just as you used the process of moving furniture and other objects to trigger your creative energies to begin redecorating, so can you use this technique to give new life to surroundings that grow stagnant.

To keep your environment beautiful, energizing, and healthful it is important to maintain your sacred space with cleansing, specifically through the annual spring cleaning ritual. Spring cleaning is a wonderful experience, if you undertake the task with a positive attitude. This is your chance to clean your windows and let the sun shine through, physically and symbolically, to rid your home of stale winter odors and contaminants and start anew . . . to celebrate and cheer on the change of the seasons. Spring cleaning does not have to be restricted to

DESIGNING
A HOME FOR
YOUR HEART
FROM THE
OUTSIDE IN

266

spring, of course. You can clean your home top to bottom twice a year if you wish. When you are finished, throw a party or perform a ritual to celebrate. Use that time to make new wishes and dreams for the upcoming months. Having a "New Year's" cleaning celebration in autumn or summer is the perfect way to revitalize and rejuvenate your home, and your being.

A spiritual ritual could accompany the creation of your "new" home. Whether you have completely redecorated, moved into a new place, changed your lifestyle, or simply given your space a home energy cleaning, you can use a housewarming celebration to make it all come together, and to help you make certain your creation begins on a spiritually sound and energetic note.

You can use the ritual on page 267, one that I have found especially cleansing and freeing, or one of your own design, to place the final touches on the home for your heart you have created.

In responding to your primal urge to embellish, to create, to design a home for your heart, you have worked hard to orchestrate the delicate connection between your inner self and your outer world. I sincerely hope that through your own courage and soul searching, through the vast amounts of design information available, and through the exercises and meditations in this book you will be able to create a living space that consciously pleases your eye, nourishes the unseen, and deeply and powerfully affects the sensitive parts of your being.

I also hope that you now understand the difference between traditional decorating and life design, and can use these tools and awareness to make certain your home is as aesthetically beautiful as it is harmoniously related to the lifestyle you want to be living.

Whether home means providing a safe, nurturing place for the youngest minds and the tiniest feet to pad safely through their space, feeling they are loved . . .

Or whether home means a romantic, sensual nest for you and your mate . . .

Or whether home means a person loving living alone . . .

Or whether home means a haven for friends and family to gather together and feel good about the bounty life has to offer . . .

This is all home in the fullest sense.

Remember, a true home for your heart comes from your heart, and is based on loving yourself, your family, your friends, and your surroundings.

Welcome home!

Spiritual Housewarming

TOOLS NEEDED

Candles and candleholders for each room to be cleaned
Incense—a fragrance that you would like to live with
Smudge stick made of fresh natural grasses
Plate
Broom
Onions—you'll need twice the number of rooms

HOUSEWARMING

Clear your mind and calm yourself. Picture the best use for your space. Listen to your home and begin to feel its energy. Calm your mind and your home and see if you can have all the energies in your home meet and befriend each other. Tell your new home what you are looking forward to about your relationship with it. Listen, and it may tell you about itself! When you feel ready, put a candle in the center of each room and then go through the house and light them all, beginning at the door.

Burn incense in the main rooms, or every room, if you wish. Take the broom and make sweeping motions without having the broom touch the floor. Sweep from the door and throughout every room, stopping to make a six-pointed star with your index finger on each window. If someone is helping you, then you can sweep and he or she can make the stars.

Take the smudge stick and light it. You may have to blow on it to get it burning. Put the plate under it as you walk with it. Beginning again at the door, move the smudge stick through the entire space, along the walls, in corners, in all closets and shelves—even on the stove and refrigerator.

With the broom you swept out all the big chunks of old energy. The stars will protect your new home and bring it abundance. The smudge allows the more deeply embedded energy to be released or healed, setting a new vibration in your home that is suited to you and your family's goals and dreams.

Finally, take as many onions as you have rooms, cut them up into quarters, and put a quarter onion in each corner of the room. Leave them there overnight, and if they don't turn gray or black, throw them away after a day or two. If they do turn black, replace them with new onions until they don't turn black anymore. This removes the last of the stale, old energy. Burn the candles for as long as you can, or for several days, but of course never leave your home without extinguishing all the candles!

Happy revitalized home!

SELECT BIBLIOGRAPHY

BOOKS

Abercrombie, Stanley. *A Philosophy of Interior Design.* New York: Harper & Row, 1990.

Anderson, Mary. *Color Therapy.* New York: Samuel Weiser, Inc., 1979.

Arrien, Angeles. *Signs of Life: The Five Universal Shapes and How to Use Them.* Sonoma, Calif.: Arcus Pub. Co., 1992.

Birren, Faber. *The Symbolism of Color.* New York: Carroll Publishing, 1988.

Bonewits, Isaac. *Real Magic.* New York: Samuel Weiser, Inc., 1989.

Brusatin, Manlio. *A History of Colors.* Shambhala Publications Inc., 1991.

Buckland, Raymond, ed. *Llewellyn's Magickal Almanac.* St. Paul, Minn.: Llewellyn Publishers, 1990.

Cayce, Edgar. *Gems and Stones.* Virginia Beach: A.R.E. Press, 1979.

Day, Christopher. *Places of the Soul.* London: The Aquarian Press, 1990.

Fritz, Robert. *Creating.* New York: Fawcett Columbine, 1991.

————. *The Path of Least Resistance.* New York: Fawcett Columbine, 1989.

Jones, Prudence, and Caitlin Matthews. *Voices from the Circle (The Heritage of Western Paganism).* London: The Aquarian Press, 1990.

Lausdowne, Zachary F. *The Rays and Esoteric Psychology.* New York: Samuel Weiser Inc., 1989.

Lawlor, Anthony. *The Temple in the House.* New York: Jeremy P. Tarcher/Putnam, 1994.

Lehmkul, Dorothy, and Dolores Cotter Lamping. *Organizing for the Creative Person.* New York: Crown Publishing Group, 1993.

Linn, Denise. *Sacred Space.* New York: Ballantine Books, 1996.

Mandino, Og. *The Greatest Salesman in the World.* New York: Bantam Books, 1983.

Moore, Thomas. *Care of the Soul.* New York: HarperCollins, 1992.

Peale, Norman Vincent. *Get Confident Living.* New York: Fawcett, 1985.

Phillips, John A. *Eve: The History of an Idea.* San Francisco: Harper & Row Publishers, 1984.

Rousseau, David, et al. *Your Home, Your Health and Well Being.* Vancouver, B.C.: Cloudburst Press/Hartley & Marks, 1989.

Rybczynski, Witold. *Home.* New York: Penguin Books, 1986.

Santo Pietro, Nancy. *Feng Shui: Harmony by Design.* New York: Berkley Publishing Group, 1996.

Stoner, Carroll, and Laura Green. *Reinventing Home.* New York: Penguin Books, 1991.

Swan, James A. *The Power of Place and Human Environments.* Wheaton, Ill.: Quest Books, 1991.

Torrice, Antonio F., and Ro Logrippo. *In My Room: Designing for and with Children.* New York: Fawcett Books, 1989.

Vaughan, Frances, and Roger Walsh, eds. *A Gift of Peace: Selections for a Course in Miracles.* London: Arkana, 1988.

Van Amringe, Judyth. *Home Art.* New York: Bulfinch Press, 1994.

Wright, Machaelle Small. *Behaving As If the God in All Life Mattered.* Jefferston, Va.: Perelandra Press, 1987.

Wright, Susan. *The Learning Annex Guide to Eliminating Clutter.* New York: Citadel Press, 1991.

ARTICLES

Alsop, Susan Mary. "Unconventional Appeal." *Architectural Digest* (November 1989):280–285.

Bender, Tom. "Putting Heart into Our Homes." *Yoga Journal* (September/October 1986):39–41, 50.

Bernard, Joan Kelly. "The Clutter Crisis." *Home* (May 3, 1992):37.

Bienstock, Russell. "Upholstery Educational Guide." *Furniture World* (January 1992):39–54.

Brown, Patricia Leigh. "Special Effects: The House That Fell to Earth," *The New York Times* (January 4, 1990), sec. C, pp. 1, 6.

Cochran, Tracy. "Inner Design." *Omni* (February 1992).

Guimaraes, Dona. "Rediscovering Thrift, or a New Look at the Old Ways." *The New York Times Magazine* (October 18, 1987):94.

Huff, Mary A. "Home: Castle or Cavern: An Architect Solves Your Decorative Problems." *The Wisdom Child* (March 19–25, 1979).

Lawlor, Anthony. "Om Sweet Om." *Yoga Journal* (September/October 1994): 22–27.

Lawrence, Beverly Hall. "Let There Be Peace." *New York Newsday* (September 17, 1992), pp. 65, 68.

Levin, Ed. "The Subtle Art of Feng Shui." *Design Spirit* (Winter 1991):20–28.

Mann, Nicholas. "Geomancy: Improving the Subtle Qualities of Your Home or Office Environment." *Starlite Times* (January 1991):12.

Miller, Leslie. "Too Many Possessions, Too Little Time." *USA Today* (April 14, 1993), sec. D, pp. 1–2.

FOR THE BEST IN PAPERBACKS, LOOK FOR THE

In every corner of the world, on every subject under the sun, Penguin represents quality and variety—the very best in publishing today.

For complete information about books available from Penguin—including Puffins, Penguin Classics, and Arkana—and how to order them, write to us at the appropriate address below. Please note that for copyright reasons the selection of books varies from country to country.

In the United Kingdom: Please write to *Dept. JC, Penguin Books Ltd, FREEPOST, West Drayton, Middlesex UB7 0BR.*

If you have any difficulty in obtaining a title,.please send your order with the correct money, plus ten percent for postage and packaging, to *P.O. Box No. 11, West Drayton, Middlesex UB7 0BR*

In the United States: Please write to *Consumer Sales, Penguin USA, P.O. Box 999, Dept. 17109, Bergenfield, New Jersey 07621-0120.* VISA and MasterCard holders call 1-800-253-6476 to order all Penguin titles

In Canada: Please write to *Penguin Books Canada Ltd, 10 Alcorn Avenue, Suite 300, Toronto, Ontario M4V 3B2*

In Australia: Please write to *Penguin Books Australia Ltd, P.O. Box 257, Ringwood, Victoria 3134*

In New Zealand: Please write to *Penguin Books (NZ) Ltd, Private Bag 102902, North Shore Mail Centre, Auckland 10*

In India: Please write to *Penguin Books India Pvt Ltd, 706 Eros Apartments, 56 Nehru Place, New Delhi 110 019*

In the Netherlands: Please write to *Penguin Books Netherlands bv, Postbus 3507, NL-1001 AH Amsterdam*

In Germany: Please write to *Penguin Books Deutschland GmbH, Metzlerstrasse 26, 60594 Frankfurt am Main*

In Spain: Please write to *Penguin Books S. A., Bravo Murillo 19, 1° B, 28015 Madrid*

In Italy: Please write to *Penguin Italia s.r.l., Via Felice Casati 20, I-20124 Milano*

In France: Please write to *Penguin France S. A., 17 rue Lejeune, F–31000 Toulouse*

In Japan: Please write to *Penguin Books Japan, Ishikiribashi Building, 2–5–4, Suido, Bunkyo-ku, Tokyo 112*

In Greece: Please write to *Penguin Hellas Ltd, Dimocritou 3, GR–106 71 Athens*

In South Africa: Please write to *Longman Penguin Southern Africa (Pty) Ltd, Private Bag X08, Bertsham 2013*